Reinterpreting the Haitian Revolution and Its Cultural Aftershocks

Edited by

Martin Munro

AND

Elizabeth Walcott-Hackshaw

UNIVERSITY OF THE WEST INDIES PRESS

JAMAICA • BARBADOS • TRINIDAD AND TOBAGO

University of the West Indies Press
1A Aqueduct Flats   Mona
Kingston 7   Jamaica
www.uwipress.com

10 09 08 07 06   5 4 3 2 1

CATALOGUING IN PUBLICATION DATA

Reinterpreting the Haitian Revolution and its cultural aftershocks / edited by Martin Munro,
Elizabeth Walcott-Hackshaw.
p. cm.
Based on papers presented at a conference organized and held at the University of the West Indies,
St Augustine, Trinidad and Tobago, June 2004 . . . Intro.
Includes bibliographical references.
ISBN: 976-640-190-X

1. Haiti – History – Revolution, 1791–1804 – Influence. 2. Haiti – Civilization. 3. Haitian
literature – History and criticism. 4. Haiti – Politics and government. 5. Toussaint Louverture,
1743?–1803. 6. Nationalism – Haiti. I. Munro, Martin. II. Walcott-Hackshaw, Elizabeth.

F1923.R457 2006   973.5

Cover illustration: Édouard Duval Carrié, *Le Général Toussaint enfumé* (General Toussaint
Enshrouded in Smoke). Mixed media in artist frame, 60"x60" (2001). Collection: Famille
Nazon, Cap Haïtien. Courtesy of the artist.

Book and cover design by Robert Kwak.

Printed in the United States of America.

Reinterpreting the Haitian Revolution and Its Cultural Aftershocks

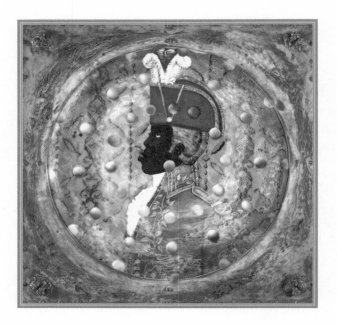

Cover illustration: Édouard Duval Carrié, *Le Général Toussaint enfumé*
(General Toussaint Enshrouded in Smoke).

CONTENTS

Acknowledgements

The editors would like to thank all those at the University of the West Indies, St Augustine, Trinidad and Tobago, who supported the 2004 Haitian bicentenary conference there, especially Dr Ian Robertson. We are particularly grateful to M. Jean Dastugue of the French Embassy in Port of Spain, Trinidad, for his generous support of the conference. Thanks go also to Linda Speth of the University of the West Indies Press for her support and enthusiasm for this project. Special thanks to Shivaun Hearne for her professionalism and attention to detail at the editing stages.

INTRODUCTION

MARTIN MUNRO AND ELIZABETH WALCOTT-HACKSHAW

As we sat to write this introduction in March 2004, the name of Haiti was once more being relayed around the world, this time attached to live images of looting, beatings, murder and chaos. Two hundred years after the Declaration of Independence, Haiti finds itself again in political limbo, its president in exile, its people divided, its society in a new apocalyptic meltdown. In a country where history has formed itself around circular, repetitive movements, deadening cycles of internal political ineptitude and nefarious external interference, there was almost a sense of inevitability, of ineluctable destiny about the events of 2004. As we stand back from the immediacy of the situation and the extraordinarily swift descent into near anarchy, it seems fated that the great bicentenary anniversary should have ushered in once again so many phantoms of Haiti's past. In 2004, Haiti was revisited by its ghosts, by the memories and realities of dictatorship and political violence; and, most strikingly, by the French and American troops once again on Haitian soil, spectres of the first black republic's unfinished history, revenants whose very presence in Haiti is an unavoidable reminder of a nation's failings, of history's swirling, eddying movement.

Suddenly, too, everyone has an opinion on Haiti. Curiously, these opinions are themselves echoes of the past, shaped as they are around long-standing proprietary misinterpretations of just what Haiti "represents": on the one hand "black" nationalists (and certain "white" liberals) see nothing in this latest episode but further evidence of a Western, "white" plot to undermine the Haitian people, who are themselves but naive reincarnations of Toussaint or Dessalines. On the other hand, Europe and the West sit transfixed before television and computer screens, deriving disavowed, vicarious pleasure in seeing some of their deepest fantasies and fears of "black" savagery apparently confirmed, and at a safe distance, too. For if there is a difference between today's Western fascination with Haiti and that of 1804, it is that this time around the West feels little immediate threat, as the ripples of Haiti's current chaos will not extend far from its Caribbean shores, whereas two hundred years ago, the "Haitian Fear" spread with tsunamic intensity across the Caribbean to Guadeloupe, Cuba, Trinidad, Jamaica, Venezuela and Brazil; northwards to the slave-holding societies of the American South, and eastwards to Europe, sending shudders through commodity markets and polarizing emerging debates on "race" and the abolition of slavery. In the Western imagination, Haiti is a place outside of history, a kind of phantasmal time capsule whose most visible signs recall a previous, still unspent exotic imagery of amoral violence and abandon.

Where, then, is the truth of Haiti, its history, its intellectual traditions, its culture? What were, what are the cultural repercussions of Haiti's revolution, in Haiti and elsewhere? What role has culture played in shaping Haiti's history, and conversely, how has Haiti's history determined, inspired, liberated and restricted Haitian culture and thought? In a land that has constantly relived its past, how can we imagine a Haitian future? Can we rethink history and memory, can an understanding of post-independence culture and thought point tentatively to a way out of the traps of the past, without effecting a counterproductive forgetting of the revolution? These are the fundamental questions that inspired us to organize a conference at the University of the West Indies, St Augustine, Trinidad, in June 2004, and around which the chapters in this collection are based. The authors seek to come to terms with and go beyond the debilitating misinterpretations and appropriations that have distorted views of Haitian history and culture, as much on the inside as from overseas.

The opening chapter is, fittingly, by René Depestre, one of Haitian culture's most important figures and a prominent member of the La Ruche group of young intellectuals which was instrumental in bringing down the American-backed president Émile Lescot in 1946, an event that has passed into Haitian historical memory as a second revolutionary moment. Written before his return to Haiti in 2004, Depestre's "Open Letter to the Haitians of 2004" has a poignancy, a sense of an unbridgeable chasm between this long-standing exile and his land of origin. It is perhaps because he had been separated for so long from Haiti that he says he has "no lesson" to offer his compatriots. Any movement towards democratic progress must, he says, draw on the resources of "intelligence, invention and wisdom" of the Haitian people, and must finally transcend the divisions of colour and class that are the legacy of colonialism and which have contributed so much to Haiti's historical decline. Sketching an historical outline of the two hundred years of independence, Depestre emphasizes the as yet unfulfilled emancipatory promise of the revolution and the vicious historical cycle that this initial failing has engendered; in particular, he denounces the Duvalier period (1957–86) as a "return to the terror of the slave plantation". The 1994 reinstatement of Jean-Bertrand Aristide is reinterpreted by Depestre as a great lost chance, a point which promised a decisive breakthrough for Haitian democracy, supported by the military and juridical authority of the United Nations and the United States. Depestre moves towards a call for a "Declaration of Interdependence", that is, for Haiti to emerge from its introverted solitude and to take up its true place in the modern world. In an implicit challenge to Afrocentric interpretations of Haiti's situation, Depestre condemns the belief in a global "white plot" against Haiti, and urges his compatriots to shed racial thinking and to accept their history in all its glory and degradation. This, he suggests, is the only way out of circular history, the only way out of the spiral into which Haiti has thrown itself.

Michael Dash's chapter probes a central problematic of the Haitian condition: its history of revolutionary universalism and its application to the Caribbean. The Haitian War of Independence, as Dash argues, was fought in the name of a universalist ideal that superseded the French state's appropriated Jacobin republicanism. The black Jacobins in St Domingue were ahead of the game, so to speak; they were testing the ideals of the French Enlightenment and attempting a radical application of universal human rights. But these explorations into the notions of freedom beyond race, culture and identity were not meant to be applied to a Caribbean plantation society. In Dash's chapter we see the dynamic movement along a continuum that spans radical universalism and reductive, monolithic views of place and identity. The Haitian Revolution, Dash argues, was both a foundational moment in French universalist thought and a point of origin for postcolonial Caribbean societies, but its enigmatic nature created a "*Haïti chimère*" that continues to elude and resist ideological containment.

Martin Munro's "Petrifying Myths" offers a similar ideological challenge, this time to the critical orthodoxy of the Caribbean region's inherent "historylessness". This notion of a "*non-histoire*" has been systematically theorized and creatively explored by one of the most influential contemporary figures engaged in rewriting Caribbean historical narrative, Édouard Glissant. Munro exposes the limitations of this all-encompassing Glissantian model when it is applied to Haiti's singular historical discourse, which he says has been curiously excluded from the prevailing theories of both Caribbeanness and postcoloniality. In developing his idea of a divergent Haitian historical narrative, Munro draws on the ways in which the memory of the revolution has affected both the individual and the collective imagination to create haunting, heroic and at times "petrifying" myths. Haitian historical discourse is, he argues, atypical in many ways, and implicitly critiques the Glissant-led tendency to see only lack and dispossession in Caribbean history.

Elizabeth Walcott-Hackshaw's piece plays provocatively and tellingly on the notion of the revolutionary in Haitian culture. Basing her chapter on a close reading of Yanick Lahens's novel *Dans la maison du père* (2000), Walcott-Hackshaw challenges the idea that revolution must always uniquely designate dramatic, wide-reaching and violent change in society. As she argues, the change, or revolution, that takes place in this novel occurs on an individual rather than a collective level, as the narrator retraces the transformations, transgressions and rebellions she effects on her return to Haiti. The return in this novel is unheralded, anonymous and mundane: the narrator returns to the privacy of her father's house and to all the histories contained within those walls. History here is a far more complex, polyvalent phenomenon than the officially sanctioned popular version of glorious revolution, heroes and race-based resistance. As Walcott-Hackshaw argues, the novel negotiates the movement between the private and public worlds of the protagonist, and by extension between the personal histories of the interior and the national historical narrative, the outside events that do impact on her life but do not ultimately define it. This novel effectively reverses Haitian literary tradition and dares to prioritize the personal and the quotidian and to displace History to the margins of Haitian experience. As Walcott-Hackshaw argues, Lahens's writing has much in common with Marie Chauvet's earlier "revolutionary" work, in that both expose the individual psychological oppression that is born out of broader political dictatorship. In both cases, the "revolution" is announced not through grandiloquent speeches or acts of violence, but through silences and "the words within". This chapter implicitly suggests that a feminized narrative of Haitian history is long overdue, that these silenced female voices are crucial to a radical rethinking of Haiti's past, present and future.

Similar concerns pervade Mireille Rosello's chapter on Edwidge Danticat's 1998 novel *The Farming of Bones,* a work that Rosello argues expresses Danticat's "unique desire for a certain type of history". As in Lahens's novel, history for Danticat has less to do with the originary, glorious rebellion, less to do with liberation and nationhood, and more to do with the personal experiences of a silenced witness-narrator.

Rosello argues persuasively that Danticat's "historical" novel is significant in that it draws attention to the historicizing process itself, to the way that official and academic histories obscure or, worse, ignore personal testimony. Drawing comparisons between Danticat's approach to history and new historicist practice, Rosello proposes that Danticat's narrator seeks to create a new kind of storytelling, one that is both a testimonial to suffering and an account of the very difficulties of testifying. History, as Danticat sees it, is an "uncomfortable space", a site of ambiguity and paradox, of narratives that crumble under the weight of their own contradictions and unsustainable oppositions. Rosello argues that Danticat's work is about the dialogue between past and present, processes of individual remembering. In interpreting the telling as a "translucent" narrative, Rosello points to the way that Danticat's vision of historical truth is hybrid, in constant flux, and constitutes an indirect, though powerful, challenge to national identities and histories and their tendencies to alienate, polarize and divide around fixed categories of nation, class and colour.

For Georges Fouron, the Haitian Revolution marked a turning point in world history, for it stood as a symbol of black civilization, dignity, regeneration and power. By tracing the evolution of racial ideology through antiquity, early Christianity and the Age of Exploration to a newly independent Haiti, Fouron reveals the way in which the revolution of 1804 both exported and imported constructs of race and culture. However, this ideological exchange, according to Fouron, created a crisis of national identity: Haitians established themselves as the mouthpiece for Africa and the defenders of the rights of Africans everywhere, but constructed their identity along the tenets of French nationalism. The dichotomy of race and culture has both obscured the true meaning of the Haitian Revolution and alienated Haitians from their "true" identity. However Fouron argues that despite these contradictions or perhaps because of them the revolution continues to be a force of inspiration and a site of interrogation.

Carolyn Fluehr-Lobban's chapter complements Fouron's in that she also dissects racial ideology, this time through a close study of the ideas of the pioneering anthropologist Anténor Firmin. Fluehr-Lobban traces the ways in which Firmin's critical view of race in *De l'egalité des races humaines* (1885) challenged and was itself challenged by those who refused to concede defeat in their insistence on the "truth" of biological determinations of race. Several examples are given in which racial scientists of the nineteenth century manipulated data to draw their foregone conclusions of racial difference and ranking. The influence of Firmin can also be seen in the work of

Jean Price-Mars, founder of ethnological studies in Haiti and intellectual descendant of Firmin's anthropology. Both these Haitian scholars, Fluehr-Lobban argues, have been marginalized from the canon of anthropology as a result of the revolutionary tradition of Haiti, their race and the fact that they wrote in French. However, their work in redefining racial ideology and constructing the tenets of pan-Africanism have created a lasting, still-relevant legacy.

In Keith Cartwright's "Re-Creolizing Swing" the focus shifts from the history of racial ideology to the history of ideas and the effects of cultural transmigration. Cartwright explores the creolizing effects of Haitian migration during the time of the revolution, when twenty-five thousand refugees left St Domingue for North America. The chapter focuses on the dynamic cross-cultural exchanges that took place in New Orleans, which offered a unique "housing" or *govi* to St Domingue's migrant *lwas* or "saints" and the manner in which they thrived to inspire early jazz. The Haitian Revolution, writes Cartwright, can be seen as one of the most profoundly creolizing cultural actions of New World experience. Cartwright's chapter effectively argues that any discussion of a creole religion like Haitian vodou or a musical form like jazz cannot look in a single direction for origins; it must keep in mind Glissantian notion of creolization as "confluence" and the profound pluralism that exists in New Orleans's diasporic *govi*.

The investigation into the spread and transmigration of cultural narratives continues in Bridget Brereton's chapter. She traces the manner in which the "Haytian Fear" narrative shaped political discourse in nineteenth-century Trinidad. Through analysis of numerous articles and letters in the Trinidadian press, Brereton illustrates how Haiti became a metaphor and a source of propaganda in contesting discourses of slavery and abolition. The "Haytian Fear" narrative perpetuated alienating narratives in which blacks on the whole and Haitian blacks in particular were portrayed as dangerous and barbaric. The fear of contagion and contamination was always present. Creating a counter-discourse was a battle in itself but competing narratives were constructed to create alternative images of Haiti and the presumed Haitian threat. As a result of the collection of these stories, Brereton's work underlines how the terror and the lessons of "San Domingo" had a special resonance for Trinidadians for decades after 1804.

Charles Forsdick's chapter deals similarly with the transmission of myths of Haiti, and in particular with post-independence representations of Toussaint Louverture. Adapting Edward Said's concept of "travelling theory", Forsdick traces the posthumous itinerary of this enduring figure and considers in particular the translation of Toussaint between a range of different twentieth-century contexts and assesses the ways in which these transfers have reworked the image and memory of the original revolutionary leader. The central focus of the chapter is on an inter-related network of twentieth-century interpretations. As Forsdick demonstrates, Auguste Nemours's hagiography continues a Haitian tradition that transforms Toussaint into a messianic figure, whereas C.L.R. James saw in Toussaint a more contemporary and incendiary figure, with resonance for anticolonial struggle and revolutionary struggle more generally. As this chapter shows, Toussaint was a key figure to Aimé Césaire, is mentioned in one of the most memorable passages of *Cahier d'un retour au pays natal,* and is the figure around which Césaire's 1961 political essay "Toussaint Louverture" turns its meditations on the dilemmas of dependency in the contemporary francophone Caribbean. As Forsdick carefully argues, there is a tangible influence of both James and Césaire in Édouard Glissant's *Monsieur Toussaint,* a play which offers a "prophetic vision of the past", a vision of a creolized Caribbean moving beyond the transatlantic axes of neocolonial depend-ency. The diverse textual evidence leads Forsdick to ultimately argue, as does Said himself, that any initially schematic notion of "travelling" ideas and interpreta-tions should be replaced by a more uneven understanding of the processes of transmission – an understanding that moves away from a model of progressively declining revolutionary impact in order to develop a more attenuated understand-ing of shifts, slippages and movements in representations of Toussaint.

René Depestre's closing piece effectively validates Forsdick's argument that "the interpretation, mythologization, instrumentalization and exemplification" of Toussaint will continue to evolve. For Depestre's chapter invokes once again the "Great Precursor" and adapts the memory of Toussaint, takes it "travelling" to express his own vision of Haiti, its past, present and future. Written to com-memorate the bicentenary of Toussaint's death in 2003, and initially presented at an official ceremony at the Château de Joux, the site of Toussaint's death, Depestre's short chapter seeks to reinterpret and reshape history with the aim of reaffirming "the solidarity between France and Haiti" and to inspire Haiti to finally fulfil the demo-cratic promise of Toussaint's "lofty ideals of justice and rights". Depestre's Toussaint is, therefore, a kind of bridge between Haiti and France, an unyielding believer in racial equality, a supporter of the liberationist impulses of the French Revolution and, above all, a moderate, forward-thinking politician who recognized the historical import of that period in global history. Depestre's conciliatory chapter implicitly seeks to lay to rest the ghosts of Franco-Haitian history, to move Haitian sensibilities beyond a state of self-destructive victimhood and to project the image and ideals of Toussaint into the globalizing twenty-first century where, he argues, qualities of wisdom, civility and democracy are needed more than ever before.

For all its breadth of vision and diversity of focus, this collection makes no claim to completeness: it is not our aim to have the final word on the cultural and intellectual repercussions of the revolution, but to open up debate and point the way to future research. Our hope is that this collection will provoke new work in the various, interrelated fields they explore. In times of crisis, Haiti, like many other countries, has often sought the palliative reassurance of myth. It is our belief that one of the most effective ways out of this self-perpetuating, self-destructive cycle lies in developing a truer understanding of Haitian history and culture, in rescuing the revolutionary legacy from the traps of myth. Much work remains to be done: we hope that you, as scholars, artists, writers and readers, will in your own ways accept the challenge.

Chapter 1

Open Letter to the Haitians of 2004

René Depestre

> *Neither laugh, nor cry; one must understand.*
>
> – Spinoza

My name is René Depestre. I am a Franco-Haitian writer, little known in his native land. One time only did it fall to me to take a direct part in Haiti's civic affairs. In that year of 1946, the review *La Ruche* promised new light, new hope for a democratic renewal in a land where the rights of man and of citizenship had long lain comatose. After the failure of my generation's struggle, in order to survive in a multiplicity of "elsewheres", I had to add on, adopt other roots before finding in France, as an old man, a place to settle finally.

Haiti is afflicted by a state of existential stasis, one that exists in a context of cruel inhumanity. My country of origin is a cry for help. For all that, I have no lesson to offer Haiti. Retired in the south-west of France, I do not seek to dictate from so far away the conduct of destitute women and men in the Caribbean. Humility, respect and the understanding of others inspire me as I look towards Haiti's suffering.

The SOS with which I am obsessed is not that which nations at bay habitually send to the International Monetary Fund or to the World Bank. Nor is it the alarm that sounds at the doors of the White House or the United Nations. A third of an island in the Americas, tortured by all the desolation of the world, echoes, reflects its suffering into the very consciousness of its sister humanities across the planet.

On the bicentenary of their victory over slavery and colonization, the Haitian people cannot avoid the questions that surround their terribly damaging drama. Two centuries after the independence of St Domingue's slaves – a major event in the political and cultural history of civilizations – Haiti is stuck, trapped beneath the threshold of absolute misery. Its days and its labours are mired in civil violence, political instability, all sorts of criminal activity; garbage is piled high in the street, hardships are endlessly accumulated in every household. In world opinion, the "Haitian question" is often described as an "empty parenthesis" or as an "endless tragedy of decolonization": many millions of people are cornered, trapped for life in the impossibility of ever being themselves.

In this catastrophic situation, one must not look to the International Monetary Fund or the World Bank, to the United Nations or to the powerful members of the G8, to react in place of and instead of the citizens of Haiti. It falls first and foremost to the Haitian people, *in an unprecedented burst of vital energy,* to invent the collective, sustainable strategy, capable of holding at bay the influential centres of international aid. The first acts of mutual aid and of lifesaving must emerge from, in the words of Aimé Césaire, "the great reserves of faith, those great stores of strength where people, in their times of need, find the courage to come to terms with themselves and to take control of the future".

Our unprecedented new movement along the road towards democratic progress has no chance of success unless it is based on the mobilization of the Haitian people's resources of intelligence, invention and wisdom. Fusing all shades of opinion, belief and hope, Haiti must radically recast its symbolic heritage of resistance to adversity. The country came onto the international scene in 1804 under the monumental mask of an impregnable fortress. Embodied in the stones of the Laferrière Citadel, a myth of extreme violence some years later came to symbolize in the eyes of the world the hope of redemption of the former slaves of the American plantations. The myth was entirely justified, even necessary, from 1791 to 1804, during the period of violent rupture with the terror of the colonial regime. A contemporary of the French Revolution's Jacobin model, it was to fulfil to great effect its revolutionary, emancipatory role. Thereafter structured as black Haitian Jacobinism, our founding myth was to condition the historical conduct of our nation-state for two hundred years. In contrast to the French Revolution's ideology whereby the Rights of Man, the Civil Code, democratic civility and individual freedom became republican values, our Jacobin négritude became enmeshed in *the worst excesses of meaningless political violence.* In Haiti, as History's great cogwheel turned, it brought back recurrently the colonial structures of terror to the institutions and mentalities of Haitian national society. Two centuries later, we still have not managed to free ourselves from a regressive and mystifying ideology whose religious function (an early form of "fundamentalism"?) holds our destiny trapped in the deleterious logic of violence!

With the Duvaliers (father and son, 1957–86), what we saw was purely and simply a return to the terror of the slave plantation. The symbolic representations of state Tonton Macoutism deformed and distorted sickeningly the interior truths and nationalist foundations of the Haitian people. The murderous rituals of the Papadocracy reproduced indefinitely the nihilism of the creole and African-born slaves that for thirteen years was called upon to unlock the doors of lawful society and democratic modernity for Haitians.

At the beginning of the 1980s, after three decades of this "Third World fascism", the rumour went around that the most deprived (and as a result the most discredited?) third of an island in the world had, thanks to the destructive impulses of the Haitian people, plumbed the depths of opprobrium and destitution. It was predicted at the time that the post-Duvalier period would quickly see Haiti drown. It was impossible to imagine Haiti rising from its ruins, after the merciless logic of self-destruction to which Papa Doc had submitted it.

But these predictions did not take into account the enlightened side of the history of Haitian identity. After having studied this positive aspect of Haitianity in Haiti, a French observer recalled to me once that the Haitian, black or mulatto, poor or rich, manual worker or intellectual, mystic or atheist, when his being is not a poisonous cactus in the garden of Baron Samedi, manages with grace to harbour, in his convictions and his conduct, "a treasure greater than the diamond mines of Kimberley or the oil wells of the Middle East".

The metaphor of my friend and traveller evoked also the "unique spirituality" which is still able to redirect Haiti's life along the straight road towards the ideal of justice and freedom that is at the origin of its national adventure. After the debacle of Jean-Claude Duvalier in 1986, did we not see a highly charismatic man make popular, fruitful use of this spiritual store? Jean-Bertrand Aristide's *mouvement Lavalasse* succeeded in establishing the first democratically elected political set-up in Haitian history. Many signs of civic maturity were thereafter to prevail over the populist attempts to derail the movement. Free elections took place in the debris of thirty years of barbarism. The conditions seemed right for a true "demacoutization" of Haiti's institutions and mentalities. Such was the early strength of this process of democratization that the military putschists of 1991, after having interrupted it brutally in a coup d'état, failed to block the return to power of the democratically elected president. Three years after going into forced exile in the United States, Jean-Bertrand Aristide was reinstated as president of Haiti.

There is good cause to question rigorously the exceptional circumstances that marked the 1994 reinstatement. For my part, I see it as a historical moment that the entire political class, leaving aside all ideological divisions, should never have allowed to go up in smoke. That year, Haiti came very close to a decisive reversal of its tragic history. In effect, for the first time in its history, the country came out of its diplomatic isolation, the kind of quarantine that the "civilized" nations together imposed on St Domingue's "black revolution". The dramatic tête-à-tête between a small, poor and "black" state and the "white" imperial superstate unexpectedly gave way to a multinational approach to the Haitian question. Our chaos ceased to be presented as a trivial affair in a colonial backwater between "a little black republic in the Caribbean" and the North American imperial giant.

An open debate placed the Haitian question under the scrutiny of the member states of the United Nations. In this democratic forum, our misfortune was on full display; it was also shown and examined from every angle in the world media. Haiti suddenly benefited from the understanding, indeed at times the sympathy, of world public opinion. There was a strong prospect of a whole range of political, cultural, moral and material benefits: Haiti was to be afforded a financial aid package estimated to be worth several hundred million dollars.

To reinstate Mr Aristide to his democratically elected role, it was necessary to throw out by force the criminal junta of General Raoul Cédras. The United Nations gave Bill Clinton and the United States a mandate for military intervention in Haiti. Was this the spectre of the American occupation of 1915–34 returning to haunt Haiti? In reality, this was quite the opposite of a new colonial expedition; the American intervention of 1994 was one of the first beneficial applications of the right to intervene for humanitarian reasons, a right which is still often heard in the mumblings of international relations discourse. A decision of the Security Council brought United Nations assistance to a people in danger. Within the legal framework of the United Nations, one reinforced by the regional juridical system of the Organization of American States, the Clinton administration was invested with the task of helping Aristide, Haiti's legitimate president, to rule democratically in the post-Cédras period. Mr Aristide promised to do all he could, together with the Lavalas movement, to assemble the living strength of the nation in the service of the democratic and legal state that Haiti has been searching for since the first glorious, uncertain steps of 1804.

This took place in the post–cold war period, at the very moment when there was a widely felt need for a new world social contract to correct and redress the many destabilizing effects of globalization. In the post-communist period, the establishment of a worldwide civil society would allow the world community to take up the globalized challenges of the market economy. The fundamentals of democratic civility, projected intelligently across the world, would offer new hope and expectation, first to those nations experiencing the gravest postcolonial crises, such as Haiti. The double military and juridical authority of the United States and the United Nations would create – in close cooperation with the democratic breakthrough in Haiti – the conditions of a pluralist governance capable of resolving the apparently irresolvable legal, civil and development problems. In contrast to the kind of external tutelage envisioned in the United Nations Charter, Haiti would serve as a pilot project in the framework of a supervisory regime; a set-up more in line with the age of interdependent national sovereignties, which globalization is bringing irresistibly to the order of the day of the history of societies and civilizations.

Instead of seizing patriotically, as one, the chance offered by the United Nations, with the military and political backing of the United States, the Haitian people let themselves fall apart into seven million interpretations of their tragedy. Entirely absorbed by our traditional cacophonies, we were to miss the historical rendezvous of 1994. Ten years later, instead of taking the leap forward, away from all the Haitian madness, here we are still stuck in a rut made of our own suicidal incomprehension of ourselves!

Without the blessed union of the Haitian people to help carry out their mission, the United Nations, the Organization of American States and the United States were unable to establish direct, intelligent, clear and imaginative contact with the particularities and complexities of the situation. We succeeded in turning our multinational UN supervisors, who came into our chaos as friends or as allies, into dumbfounded, discouraged and helpless witnesses to our self-destructive gesticulations. The glaring proof of this catastrophic bungling is there to see: ten years after 1994, Haiti's special financial aid does not always leave the coffers of the International Monetary Fund and the World Bank.

We were taken back once more to our endless antagonisms between "blacks" and "mulattos", reduced once more to our incorrigible frustrations as "tropical Jacobins"; have mercy on us! The solitude of 2004 has come to remind us that we have sown in the desert the meanings and values of the 1804 Declaration of Independence.

To come out of our solitude on 1 January 2004, in the "black sun" of our suffering, we need, as of now, all the bravery of the world to find the words and the truth of the Declaration of *Interdependence* that we will need to share in the future with all the other nations of the planet.

Two centuries after independence, this is where we are. The first black people in the Americas to rise up against colonial oppression is today an abandoned child who rakes around in the public refuse dump of history, fighting with superstitions, fears and insecurities of every kind. In such a situation, in order to move beyond the religious control of our consciences, to face up to our own moral tensions on the bicentenary, we need to invert the national idea that has made us believe in political violence as the only route to maturity, both for the individual and for the nation. We have urgent need of new civic and spiritual values. The man who was once called "the prophet of the shanty towns", President Jean-Bertrand Aristide – I imagine him today, faced with the tragedy of his people, as a wounded being in his "evangelical radiance". That is why my letter is also addressed to him. I sincerely hope that he is still capable of ensuring that the steps towards self-control that I have just mentioned are part of the commemoration of 2004.

At the beginning of the twenty-first century, it would be a collective suicide to rely on an umpteenth civil conflict, on yet another military coup d'état, on our doubly secular experience of massacres and bloodbaths; in short on the idea of revolution à la Haitian, "to want, to achieve something impossible! Against destiny, against History, against Nature!" The command pronounced in Césaire's theatre rang long ago in the ears of Toussaint Louverture, Dessalines, Pétion and Christophe who, even in their most dreadful misadventures, are forever the fathers of our identity. Two hundred years after them, destiny, nature, history, that is, the globalization that we are subject to, demands of Haiti – its rulers, its elites, its churches, its trade unions, its societies, its prosperous citizens, its most wretched outcasts of town and country – that they be *reborn* at all costs, as adult women and men, courageously determined to break free for once and for all from the chaos of the old cycle of hatred and revenge that slavery left for us as a common, toxic heritage. The coming together of 2004 offers us all the chance of a process that is at once critical and therapeutic.

The first of our civic duties is to take our human potential in Haiti back to square one, politically and socially, so that the new symbolic deal may build for us, no longer a formidable military machine, but a humanely democratic present and future. The state of our export markets can be described as "zombified", in that we have a "national economy" without oil or cobalt, without uranium or bauxite mines, without coffee or sugar quotas, without exports of banana or cocoa, without even a tourist industry, so wary are the holiday companies of Haiti. Does this mean that our third of an island no longer has any presence in the affairs of the world?

Haiti, without underground reserves of gold or diamonds, can hang on to its ultimate treasure: the Haitian people, whose creative force is shown in their every manual or intellectual piece of work. In effect, the most humble Haitian hands can joyfully, naturally work as happily as life itself! The plastic arts, music, literature, creative craftwork and the carnivalesque imagination have never broken down because of shortages of petrol or electricity. Haitian culture has not suffered the pathological breakdowns that have long troubled the legal justice system. In this regard, Haiti should be thought of as the opposite of "the poorest country in the Western hemisphere". Haitian mothers' tenderness and pain have always shaped our sense of human universalism; that is the oxygen without which globalization will not be able to survive.

Without forgetting the effects of racism and colonialism, let us dare to take on in full view of the world the *Haitian responsibility* for that which has happened in our nation over these two centuries! It is only through so doing that the celebration of 2004 will attract justly the attention and solidarity of the world. It is only thus that we will reverse at once the international ostracism that strangles Haitian credibility, and the discredit which is a kick in the guts for the suffering of sub-Saharan Africa. The slave trade, cargoes of ebony: an Atlantic sea of suffering that we have continued to cross for these two centuries. Is it not the very same nightmare that continues to poison the same, recurring historical adventure?

Let us rail against accepted ideas and wounds: there is no international "white" plot that, at the very sight of Haiti on the map of the Americas, wants to devour it like a Bengal tiger! Let us rail against the sacred obsession with blaming only the "white" colonists of the eighteenth century! Let us rail against the "black" fury of our ethnicisms and tribalisms! Let us decide immediately on the abolition of our second period of slavery: the one which, forgetting our independence, has made us the enraged slaves of our resentments and culpabilities! Let us abolish the perpetual need to fight with ourselves and our colonial past!

Let us accept the great pile of nothingness that we have amassed in our ongoing underdevelopment! Let us refuse the two-hundred-year breakdown in political civility! Let us spread everywhere the good news: far from being lost Haiti has in the best of its people the treasure that acts to demystify the roots of the hatred in their lives, and to place them at one go into the order of justice and love. Let us say what needs to be said: at this time we are all party to an exceptional slow death, a patriotic combination of a truce and a wake, which has been taken on voluntarily in all Haitian homes, as a mark of contemplation, and of saying farewell to two hundred years of hatred and civil war. Let us accept, our lamps lit, the great death throes of the bicentenary! Let us accept the year when we take on a new skin in two ways: Haitian public-spiritedness, burning bright as it faces the tides of the future; and as for globalization, let us share immediately with the world a renewed sense of human, and humane, universality.

René Depestre
Lézignan-Corbières

Translated by Martin Munro

CHAPTER 2

HAÏTI CHIMÈRE

REVOLUTIONARY UNIVERSALISM AND ITS CARIBBEAN CONTEXT

J. MICHAEL DASH

> *Any totalizing theory of history which would underestimate the fearsome lived experiences of the world and their outbursts (their possible dead ends) can constitute a trap.*
>
> – Édouard Glissant, "The Trap That Is History"

> *If some events cannot be accepted as they occur, how can they be assessed later? In other words, can historical narratives convey plots that are unthinkable in the world within which these narratives take place? How does one write a history of the impossible?*
>
> – Michel-Rolph Trouillot, "The Haitian Revolution as a Non-Event"

Aimé Césaire, one of the prominent figures in Caribbean thought, declared in 1969 at the conference of his Parti Progressiste Martiniquais, "we have remained profoundly *quarante-huitards*", thereby indicating that, for him and his party, the founding moment for Martiniquan identity was 1848.[1] In that year, forty-four years after Haitian independence, Victor Schoelcher brought liberty (if not equality and fraternity) to France's Caribbean colonies. In this moment of euphoric gratitude for France's gift of liberty and universal human rights, even Césaire seems to have forgotten that instance in the modern world of one of those unpredictable "lived experiences" that defy historical calculation, that time when revolutionary universalism entered the slave societies of the Caribbean through the revolt in St Domingue that led ultimately to Haitian independence. As C.L.R. James vividly reminds us in *The Black Jacobins*:

> Phases of a revolution are not decided in parliaments, they are only registered there . . . [The slaves] had heard of the revolution and had construed it in their own image: the white slaves in France had risen, and killed their masters, and were now enjoying the fruits of the earth. It was gravely inaccurate in fact, but they had caught the spirit of the thing. Liberty, Equality, Fraternity.[2]

The slaves' capture of "the spirit of the thing" meant that a revolutionary ideal of universal human rights had entered the Caribbean at the end of the eighteenth century, one that would change the region irrevocably. In its appropriation of this universalist discourse, the Caribbean had become one of the explosive borders of enlightened modernity.

If nothing else, the Haitian War of Independence was fought in the name of a universalist ideal that supersedes the French state's appropriated Jacobin republicanism, the distorted version of universal French values which eventually ostracized Haiti and justified France's *mission civilisatrice*. The version of French universalism applied in the Overseas Departments projected the French as trustees of revolutionary universalism and emphasized their generosity in offering universal rights to their grateful subjects. The idea of the French as the guardians of universal values and Victor Schoelcher as their ultimate embodiment led almost inexorably to departmentalization, as the 1946 Bill provided the equality and fraternity which did not immediately follow emancipation in 1848. It is precisely this false universalism that Frantz Fanon, a revolutionary universalist if ever there was one, unmasks when he accuses Sartre of drowning "*l'enthousiasme noir*" in the promise of an empty universalist ideal.[3] To Fanon, even Sartre, whose work inspired the Martiniquan's own concept of a revolutionary consciousness that transcended racial determination, was not immune from France's ethnocentric appropriation of the universal.

Revolutionary universalism in St Domingue, however, was not linked to cultural and historical difference, but made for a radical application of universal human rights. As Susan Buck-Morss has recently put it, "the black Jacobins of Saint Domingue surpassed the metropole in actively realizing the Enlightenment goal of human liberty, seeming to give proof that the French Revolution was not simply a European phenomenon, but world-historical in its implications".[4] If, as she goes on to say, 1804 was the "trial by fire for the ideals of the French Enlightenment", then the Haitian Revolution can be seen as an emancipatory project within a globalized colonial world where ideas were now circulating freely and could take root in the most unexpected places. The liberatory possibilities of the Enlightenment were not meant to be applied in Caribbean plantation society. Global interaction in a modernizing world meant, however, that the periphery could now become the site of a concrete, radical application of ideas from the centre, that a local European revolution could be "world-historical in its implications".

The Haitian Revolution was therefore both a foundational moment in French universalist thought and a point of origin for postcolonial Caribbean societies, one that privileged global interaction and transcended ethnocentric models of nation, race and identity. To this extent, Trouillot is right to label it "the most radical political revolution of that age"[5] as it symbolized the possibility of understanding human rights beyond race, territory and gender, and moreover laid bare the unpredictable nature of globalizing modernity and the ways in which it made the colonial system totally untenable. As Eugene Genovese puts it, "the revolutionary ideology that emerged in the 1790s fed both sides of the Atlantic. It Africanized France in ways that helped send the colonialist Girondists to a well-deserved fate; it Europeanized Saint Domingue in ways that pointed to the rise of a modern black state."[6] And yet, despite this conception of the Haitian Revolution as a nodal point in a global inter-active history, we continue to see it as unique or exceptional, a moment in a simple, heroic foundational narrative for Caribbean anticolonial resistance. The Caribbean imaginary continues to feed on dreams of apocalyptic beginnings that make the cosmopolitan, universalist contours of the Caribbean past ideologically inaccessible.

For this reason one needs to revisit the Haitian thought of the already post-colonial nineteenth century to see how a revolutionary universalism was applied to the defetishization of colonial categories of race and nation. The idea of Haiti's singularity or uniqueness was invariably underplayed by her early thinkers and often recognized in the nineteenth century as a direct or indirect product of a discourse that sought to ostracize the revolution. In his dismantling of the idea of Haitian exceptionalism, Michel-Rolph Trouillot reminds us that

> Before the twentieth century, Haitian writers rarely if ever promoted singularity in their studies of Haitian reality. In fact, quite the opposite, especially for the early part of the nineteenth century. Indeed, Haitian intellectuals rightly saw the theories of Haitian exceptionalism that were spreading in Europe and North America as implicitly – and often explicitly – racist . . . these writers did not think that Haiti escaped the paradigms of their times.[7]

In this way, Trouillot compellingly reminds us that the Caribbean's first revolutionary modern state comes into being with neither the rhetoric of difference nor the championing of originality. Indeed, the model for liberation that pervaded early Haitian intellectualism, according to Trouillot, foregrounded the universal and the transnational as the most revolutionary means of making modernity fulfil its emancipatory ideals.

Without doubt, the most important champion of Haiti's modernist internationalism in the nineteenth century was Anténor Firmin. No other intellectual seemed as able to follow through on the revolutionary universalism of Haiti's War of Independence. Firmin arguably wished to harness the utopian, emancipatory possibilities that had been released in 1804 by the unpredictable global interconnectedness of modern European expansion. His monumental *De l'égalité des races humaines* (1885) was written as a response to a theory of biological difference and racial perfectibility that had been put forward by Joseph-Arthur de Gobineau. Arguing against Gobineau's narrowly deterministic and rigid racial hierarchies, Firmin invoked a non-essentializing universalism, and rejected the belief that cultural difference can be explained by any innate, genetic qualities. Firmin was acutely aware of the implications of an essentialist theory of racial difference in Haiti and the extent to which Haiti's survival depended on a militant internationalist, anticolonial politics. As he puts it in his conclusion, "human beings everywhere are endowed with the same qualities and defects, without distinctions based on color or anatomical shape . . . It is a fact that an invisible chain links all members of humanity in a common circle."[8]

Firmin's radical universalism leads him to be profoundly sceptical regarding the question of grounded difference and nationalist identity politics in Haiti. In one of his more startling assertions he praises the nineteenth-century Haitian poet Paul Lochard because it would be impossible to discern "the strong dose of African blood that flows in his veins" and approvingly comments that "there is nothing, absolutely nothing to distinguish him from a French poet of the purest French stock".[9] Firmin argues that it is easy enough for the Haitian poet to perform his blackness for a foreign market, as "easy success" could be found "among foreign readers by pandering to their love of the exotic, imitating in his verse the sound of the *bamboula* and evoking the charms of the frisky Creole woman".[10] What Firmin therefore finds reactionary is the nostalgia for fixed and unchanging racial and national stereotypes. Acutely aware as he was of the world-historical nature of the Haitian experiment, Firmin felt that a new hybridizing modernity was rendering the idea of absolute racial difference obsolete. The acceleration and proliferation of cultural and racial intermixing was the fate of the modern Haitian state. Certainly, one of the more overlooked areas of *De l'égalité des races humaines* is his defence of hybridization and creolization against Gobineau's charge that interracial mixing led only to degeneration.

In his last work, *The Letters from St Thomas* (1910), Firmin was no longer writing back to Gobineau and contesting a theory of racial determinism that he saw as a mere mask for continuing colonial oppression. He was now directing his attention to the politics of territorial self-sufficiency and the rhetoric of grounded difference that had become prevalent in Haitian political practice. Exile in St Thomas takes Firmin temporarily away from the violent factional politics that were pushing Haiti toward chaos and the very landscape offers a kind of liberation to the exile's imagination, allowing him to "discover, from almost every side, a vast majestic horizon, awakening the idea of the infinite, which is like a liberation for the human soul".[11] The tiny island's topography and its arid isolation seem to offer here the possibility of transcending the specific and the relative for broad internationalist vistas. The main objective of these letters is therefore not surprisingly to persuade his fellow Haitians to transcend exclusionary notions of identity and boldly enter a modernizing global space. In making the difficult case for increasing foreign investment in Haiti, and against an intensifying xenophobic reflex, Firmin chides his compatriots:

> Ought we to forget, with the interweaving of interests that create modern civilization, no people desirous of progress and social wellbeing should shut itself off behind a wall of China. Do you think that the Haitian people . . . can reasonably do without both the material and intellectual capital that the advanced foreigner would alone be able to provide for the development of this land of Haiti of which we are rightly proud but whose admirable fertility is not sufficient to procure happiness for us?[12]

In these letters Firmin is the first Haitian intellectual to make the case for national survival by resiting Haiti hemispherically, in terms of a regional "Antillean Confederation". Such prescience was as unpalatable at the time to Haitian nationalists as to US policymakers, who viewed Firmin's activities with suspicion. Firmin's dream of Haiti as a privileged site in which to contest an identity politics based on race and nation would be thwarted as, within five years of his death, the United States occupied Haiti in the name of the West's civilizing mission.

Firmin's efforts to conceive of and apply a more supple and hybridizing universalism, in the face of the totalizing Eurocentric racial theorizing of Gobineau and later of the imperialist remapping of the Caribbean by the United States, may have failed as politics, but they left behind a crucial legacy for Haitian thought that may well be its distinguishing feature. One only has to look at the impact of two, not unrelated within Haiti, systems of universalist thought in the twentieth century – Marxism and surrealism – to see how the defetishization of race and place had found ready application in the post-1934, post-occupation period. The militant cosmopolitanism of the period that followed the American occupation has been invariably clouded by the reductive nationalist mystifications of the Indigenist and Africanist movements of the thirties and forties. Both of these anti-American ideologies championed race and nation and dismissed earlier writers and intellectuals as insufficiently Haitian because of their cultural alienation or "*bovarysme collectif*". Nevertheless, the prominent role of Marxist thought and surrealist poetics in Haiti at this time indicates the extent to which the most creative expressions of a defensive nationalism became once more contextualized in a global modernity.

The foremost figure in the early nationalist politics of the occupation period, Jacques Roumain, offers a clear example of how militant internationalism was used to demystify many of the monolithic notions of race and territory that prevailed in the struggle to free Haiti of an American military presence. Roumain's posthumously published novel, *Masters of the Dew,* has invariably been hailed as the masterpiece of Haitian Indigenism. It might, however, be more useful to see it as an imaginative site where the contradictions of revolutionary internationalism and cultural nationalism are played out. On one hand, the author clearly intended to project the Haitian peasant condition as part of a global mass movement against US imperialism. It is not hard to see the main protagonist, Manuel, as a figure who has been ideo-logically internationalized by his cane-cutting experience in Cuba, nor to be aware that Roumain wished to see in the *coumbite* a modern-day "Bois Caïman" ceremony where the transfer from sacred to secular is made and masses mobilized using an ancient rite. No doubt, in Roumain's imagination the French Revolution's impact on plantation slavery in St Domingue could find a parallel in the twentieth century in the Russian Revolution's impact on communities of uprooted, migrant workers in the northern Caribbean.

Yet, the transposition of the message of liberty, equality, fraternity to the peasant locale in the novel is irreconcilable with the novel's genesis as a work of nationalist fiction grounded in a legitimating, pastoral setting in an effort to consolidate the fragmented Haitian nation. *Masters of the Dew* after all has its genesis in the thir-ties and in Roumain's fascination with Charlemagne Péralte and the caco resistance movement. Manuel's mother in the novel is a transposition of the figure of Péralte's mother, first evoked in a meeting with the author in 1930,[13] and the very title of the novel, *Gouverneurs de la rosée*, had been given to a short story dealing with a band of caco guerillas published many years earlier.[14] Unfortunately, international worker solidarity founders on the rhetoric of blood and territory. *Masters of the Dew* is a foundational romance very much in the Latin American mode, which ultimately centres on the fertility of the monogamous, heterosexual coupling of the main protagonists. Excess, eroticism and random violence in peasant life give way to a fantasy of the world rebuilt on the healthy ideal of reciprocated, purposeful union of the two modern-day descendants of the same patriarch, General Johannes Longeannis.

It seems an irony that the reputation of a writer who so often attacked the practice of literature in Haiti should depend almost exclusively on a posthumously published novel. Roumain was at least as important as a man of scientific documentation and ethnographic detail, as indeed his most important fiction attests. In this regard, it is far more useful to analyse how his practice of modernist transnationalism engaged with Haiti's traditional culture in the brief period after his return from exile in 1941. It is important to see how Roumain at this time positions his cultural activism vis-à-vis the Catholic Church's persecution of the vodou religion, Marxist materialism and the mystifications of Haitian *noirisme*.

Roumain's main interest lay in social transformation, and to this end he denounced the Catholic Church's attack on vodou principally because the Church did not seek to change the religious mentality of the peasantry but simply replaced one superstitious world view with another. Roumain was painfully aware that the world of the Haitian peasant was in a state of flux, as dislocation and migration had followed American imperialist adventures in the northern Caribbean at the beginning of the twentieth century. Increasingly, because of US investments in plantations in Cuba and the Dominican Republic, the peasantry was being used as cheap migrant labour and its future was now inextricably bound up with the vagaries of global capitalism. Consequently, his founding of the Bureau d'Ethnologie in 1941 was an attempt to preserve something of a world that was under threat both locally from Catholic conservatives and globally from US imperialist interests. Interestingly, his work with the Bureau focused as much on pre-Columbian ethnology as on producing scientific monographs of the vodou religion. As director of the Bureau, Roumain was surrounded by various kinds of cultural nationalists: there were the *noiristes* of the Griot movement, obsessed with non-Western authenticity; the ethnographers and their preoccupation with ethnographic salvage in a world in which fragile cultures were under threat; and the state which was interested at the time in suppressing peasant culture as a basis for restoring it in a sanitized, stylized form for nationalist cultural reconstruction. Importantly, Roumain did not align himself with any of these cultural nationalist factions, but sought to conceptualize modern Haitian subjectivity and culture in a situation where the Haitian subject risked ending up stateless and rootless.

Roumain's short-lived involvement with the Bureau d'Ethnologie was arguably an attempt to put Haitian culture beyond the reach of nationalist mystification and to suggest that its accelerated plunge into a global arena since the US occupation would lead to unpredictable, hybridizing possibilities in the future. Roumain's premature death in 1944 cut short his quest to conceptualize Haitian culture in the context of a modern geopolitics. This task was left perhaps to Jacques-Stephen Alexis, whose essay on the Marvellous Realism of Haitians can be seen as both an attempt to reflect on Roumain's sense of Haiti's cultural predicament in terms of surrealist ideas and as a refutation of Alejo Carpentier's interpretation of the Haitian Revolution exclusively in terms of an Afrocentric grounding in religious ritual.[15] Roumain was as dismissive of surrealism as the next Haitian generation was receptive to its ideas, in particular as expressed through Pierre Mabille, the surrealist ethnographer who had come to Haiti in the 1940s as a war refugee.[16] Mabille's view of Haitian culture as inscrutable and resistant to ideological containment is crucial to Alexis's formulation of the Haitian imaginary as irreducible and dynamic.

The "marvellous" is then reread by Alexis as a transgressive, unpredictable force that makes Haitian culture a process of "accelerated fusion" and unpredictable, convulsive metamorphosis. The whole thrust of Alexis's theorizing was aimed at liberating Haiti from a static alterity by invoking its inter-American context and the universalist legacy of its revolutionary past. Soon after his treatise on the concept of the marvellous, Alexis published "La belle amour humaine 1957",[17] an essay which echoed the militant universalism of Anténor Firmin and which reached beyond race and nation for a broad activist internationalism. In an almost fated replay of Firmin's tragic end in exile, Alexis found himself pitted against the monolithic racial mystification of Duvalierism in Haiti, and he was murdered in 1961.

The strength of the post-Duvalierist literary imagination today lies in its resistance to a reductive, monolithic view of place and ethnicity, and in this sense it echoes the engaged universalism of the nineteenth century. Haiti's singularity is not the main subject, for instance, of Edwidge Danticat's stories of the lives of migrants and wanderers who express their creolized modern identities in the borderlands of the Dominican frontier and Brooklyn.

Similarly, Dany Laferrière's fictional cycle, "An American Autobiography", constantly places Haiti within a larger geopolitical system. The very first in this series of ten novels, *An Aroma of Coffee,* is sited in Petit Goave, which is anything but a forsaken, seaside country town. Petit Goave in the summer of 1963, at the high point of Duvalierist repression, is made out to be as connected to a global arena as was the Bois Caïman in 1791. The novel is set on the narrator's grandmother's verandah, which opens to the street, which in turn opens to the sea. This verandah, familiar yet open to chance encounter and the marvels of street theatre, is a threshold that reverses concepts of interiority and exteriority, spaces of origin and points of return. As opposed to Duvalierism with its doctrine of national singularity and racial authenticity, Laferrière's Petit Goave is a disruptive threshold that transcends borders and frontiers, where bread bags come from Chicago and a sudden tropical deluge makes "the earth smell like the earth".[18]

Laurent Dubois has recently observed, "There is redemption to be found in searching for the Haitian Revolution, for in its story lie lessons about the racial orders that continue to haunt us and about ways to confront them."[19] Unfortunately, despite the existence of C.L.R. James's *The Black Jacobins,* Haiti's symbolic presence in the Caribbean literary imagination has never been understood in terms of radical universalism. Rather it is the discourse of mysterious singularity and heroic uniqueness that has prevailed. There are those like Aimé Césaire, Alejo Carpentier and Kamau Brathwaite who evoke a Haiti of upright négritude, those who fatalistically view Haiti in terms of the sigh of history and the fated failure of the antics of megalomaniac generals, or worse yet those who succumb to the Naipaulean nightmare of black savagery. The choice is between reductionist triumphalism and reductionist scepticism when it comes to Haiti. It is rare to find Haiti invoked as an unreadable, disruptive space such as Wilson Harris suggests when he speculates in *Tradition, the Writer and Society* that Toussaint was "groping towards an alternative to conventional statehood, a conception of wider possibilities that still remains unfulfilled today in the Caribbean".[20] The redemptive conception of "wider possibilities" reaches back to the universalist radicalism born of the Haitian Revolution's challenge to colonialist discourse.

It is precisely such a view of Haiti as a post-originary space of transnational contact that Glissant reconstructs in his play *Monsieur Toussaint,* where the Haitian

Revolution is relocated to and replayed in the Jura mountains by chimerical characters, and where the prison in Fort du Joux becomes an incalculable border for a constitutively homeless, transatlantic Caribbean space. *Monsieur Toussaint* in Glissant's own words aspires to a "prophetic" or future-oriented rereading of the Haitian past, that is, to a dislocated revolutionary Haitian space that allows the Caribbean the possibility of transcending the pieties of anticolonial and postcolonial thought.[21] In an almost direct response to Césaire's cult of Victor Schoelcher, Glissant reminds Martinique of the importance of conceiving of Toussaint as a Caribbean and Martiniquan hero when he asks the question:

> Is Toussaint Louverture another's hero, and Schoelcher our "true" one? That Martiniquan intellectuals are still debating such issues reveals, in a disturbing way, the intensity of the disorientation inflicted on them . . . Other people's heroes are not ours; our heroes, of necessity, are primarily those of other people.[22]

If, as Fanon states in the opening of *Black Skin, White Masks,* revolutionary activity for the Caribbean is either always too early or too late, the Haitian slaves seem to have turned their ploughshares into swords just on time, thereby permitting the rest of the region to live vicariously its dreams of heroic resistance. Haiti has therefore become an overdetermined island space, oversaturated with meanings that our psychic needs project onto its enigmatic surface. The truth may lie elsewhere. The Haitian Revolution should be retrieved for what it was, as radically disruptive, always on the outside, always opaque, and yet it is also our only insight into the play of relational forces that constantly destabilize our temptation to believe in grounded difference. The year 1804 is not sacred ground but a New World site that first unleashed those secular creolizing forces of a Caribbean modernity. It is the very "unthinkable" nature of the Haitian chimera and its resistance to ideological containment that makes it the only kind of point of origin the Caribbean could ever have.

NOTES

1. Quoted in Auguste Armet, "Césaire et le Parti Progressiste Martiniquais", *La Nouvelle Optique* 1, no. 2 (1971): 69; see also Césaire's "Hommage à Victor Schoelcher", *Tropiques,* nos. 13–14 (1945): 229–35.

2. C.L.R. James, *The Black Jacobins* (New York: Vintage, 1963), 81.

3. Frantz Fanon, *Peau noire, masques blancs* (Paris: Seuil, 1952), 129.

4. Susan Buck-Morss, "Hegel and Haiti", *Critical Inquiry* 26, no. 4 (Summer 2000): 835–36.

5. Ibid., 837.

6. Eugene Genovese, *From Rebellion to Revolution: Afro-American Slave Revolts in the Making of the New World* (New York: Vintage, 1981), 90.

7. Michel-Rolph Trouillot, "The Odd and the Ordinary: Haiti, the Caribbean and the World", *Cimarron* 2, no. 3 (1990): 7–8.

8. Anténor Firmin, *The Equality of the Human Races,* trans. Asselin Charles (New York: Garland, 2000), 450.

9. Anténor Firmin, preface to *Feuilles de chêne,* by Paul Lochard (Paris: Ateliers Haïtiens, 1901).

10. Firmin, *The Equality of the Human Races,* 301.

11. Anténor Firmin, *Lettres de St Thomas* (Port-au-Prince: Fardin, 1986), ii.

12. Ibid., 35.

13. Jacques Roumain, "Port au Prince – Cap Haitien", *Haiti Journal* 3–4 (April 1930).

14. Jacques Roumain, "Gouverneurs de la rosée, récit haitien", *Regards* 25 (August 1938).

15. See my discussion of Alexis's essay in *The Other America, Caribbean Literature in a New World Context* (Charlottesville: University Press of Virginia, 1998), 94–97.

16. See René Depestre, "Pierre Mabille, une aventure de la connaissance", *Le Métier à métisser* (Paris: Stock, 1998), 56–67.

17. Jacques-Stephen Alexis, "La belle amour humaine 1957", *Europe* (January 1971): 20–27.

18. Dany Laferrière, *An Aroma of Coffee,* trans. David Homel (Toronto: Coach House Press, 1993), 41.

19. Laurent Dubois, "In Search of the Haitian Revolution", in *Francophone Postcolonial Studies,* ed. Charles Forsdick and David Murphy (London: Arnold, 2003), 34.

20. Wilson Harris, *Tradition, the Writer and Society* (London: New Beacon, 1967), 45.

21. Édouard Glissant, preface to the first edition, *Monsieur Toussaint* (Paris: Gallimard, 1998), 9.

22. Édouard Glissant, *Caribbean Discourse,* trans. J. Michael Dash (Charlottesville: University Press of Virginia, 1989), 69.

CHAPTER 3

PETRIFYING MYTHS
LACK AND EXCESS IN CARIBBEAN AND HAITIAN HISTORY

MARTIN MUNRO

> *then History hoisted on its highest pyre*
> *the drop of blood of which I speak*
> *where the strange rupture of destiny*
> *came to be reflected as in a deep parage.*
>
> — Aimé Césaire

> *The French Caribbean is the site of a history characterized*
> *by ruptures and that began with a brutal dislocation, the*
> *slave trade. Our historical consciousness could not be depos-*
> *ited gradually and continuously like a sediment, as it were,*
> *as happened with those peoples who have frequently produced*
> *a totalitarian philosophy of history, for instance European*
> *peoples, but came together in the context of shock, contraction,*
> *painful negation, and explosive forces.*
>
> — Édouard Glissant

It has become a critical orthodoxy to talk of Caribbean history in terms of loss, emptiness and lack. Across diverse intellectual movements and inter-island linguistic boundaries, the shared past of transportation, slavery and colonialism has time and again been interpreted as a kind of break with history itself, leaving in its wake only voids and silences. Understandably so, as the writing of Caribbean history was long the univocal discourse of the master, one sub-chapter in the wider European colonial narrative of history which Edward Said describes as the "homogenizing and incorporating world-historical scheme that assimilated non-synchronous developments, histories, cultures, and peoples, to it".[1] Consequently, the Caribbean has been widely interpreted as a "historyless" place, where history is always "an account of events that happened to the population rather than of events that the people made happen".[2]

When an internally situated Caribbean discourse did finally emerge it inevitably was compelled to rewrite and reclaim the region's long, tortured history, to "make it happen" for itself. The great (re)birth of Caribbean sensibility which began in most islands in the mid–twentieth century has been effected largely through works of fiction, theatre, philosophy and poetry, and these texts are documents of the region's troubled historical consciousness. In Caribbean poetry, for instance, images of rupture and splitting have expressed both the violence of New World history and its legacy of spatio-temporal nothingness, as in Aimé Césaire's *Notebook of a Return to the Native Land*: "Islands scars of the water / Islands evidence of wounds / Islands crumbs / Islands unformed." Similarly, individual and collective memory have been characterized by lacks, lacunae and traumatized absences – Césaire again: "So much blood in my memory! In my memory are lagoons. They are covered with death's-heads . . . My memory is encircled with blood. My memory has a belt of corpses!"[3]

Questions of memory and history have therefore been the primary area of interest for Caribbean authors, and the most prominent literary projects have in their own ways been attempts to disalienate the collective memory, and to restore, create or imagine a more satisfying sense of history. The most influential contemporary figure engaged in rewriting Caribbean historical narrative is Édouard Glissant, who describes the experience of history there as a

> struggle without witnesses, the inability to create even an unconscious chronology,
> a result of the erasing of memory in all of us. For history is not only absence for us,
> it is vertigo. This time that was never ours, we must now possess.[4]

Glissant's suggestion that the history problem leads to a sense of fissured, incomplete memory at once echoes his predecessor Césaire, and also prefigures the later work of the Créolité group – Jean Bernabé, Raphaël Confiant and Patrick Chamoiseau – who write that "Our history (or more precisely our histories) is shipwrecked in colonial history. Collective memory is the first thing on our agenda."[5] The Créolité group has relentlessly sought to rewrite this history, to reclaim time, sharing Glissant's aim to "struggle against a single History for [historical Relation, which] means repossessing both a true sense of one's time and identity". The prevalent conclusion drawn from these related literary, historical and philosophical works has been that the Caribbean subject exists in a state of "nonhistory", which Glissant says is characterized by a "dislocation of the [historical] continuum, and the inability of the collective unconscious to absorb it all".[6]

This kind of historical thinking has become commonplace in Caribbean studies, and moreover in the wider sphere of postcolonial studies, in that many postcolonial authors and intellectuals share the desire to "reappropriate" or "rewrite" history against what Robert Young terms the hegemonic "white mythologies" of history which the West has perpetuated and imposed on other traditions, notably through colonialism. As Young (drawing on Levinas) argues, "History is the realm of violence and war; it constitutes another form by which the other is appropriated into the same. For the other to remain other it must not derive its meaning from History but must instead have a separate time which differs from historical time."[7] This is easier said than done in the Caribbean where colonialism all but annihilated pre-Columbian peoples, and consequently any readily accessible concept of a "separate time". In effect, it is this absence of an alternative to Western time and to Western historiography which leads to the recurring images and notions of lack, emptiness and "nonhistory" in Caribbean thought: in rejecting imposed histories, the Caribbean intellectual, with no "separate time" in which to exist, is suspended, radically inert, silently roaring his or her frustration. Césaire remains the most eloquent communicator of this silenced inertia:

> from the depths of a land of silence
> of charred bones of burned vine shoots of storms of screams held back and muzzled
> of a land of desires inflamed by a restlessness of branches
> of a shipwreck right against (the very black sand having been force fed with a peculiar silence in the quest for prints of bare feet and sea birds).[8]

Césaire's "peculiar silence" is born out of historical trauma, collective repression and the intellectual, moral and philosophical claustrophobia that has long been associated with Caribbean experience. Like Césaire, Glissant and the Créolists, Derek Walcott is sensitive to the destructive effects of the "Muse of History", of the workings of historical memory in the New World, whereby, he argues, "The further the facts, the more history petrifies into myth." History, Walcott says, is "a kind of literature without morality", prone to invention and fictionalizing, and the subjective vision of it "depends on whether we write this fiction through the memory of hero or of victim". Walcott's well-known "Adamic" perspective on Caribbean history, one which "neither explains nor forgives history" and which abandons any desire to find redemption or justification in history, is essentially a response to (and also one way out of) the common problem of the perceived lack of history, the absence of an alternative time, for when he does look back he, like the others, sees in "the seeded entrails of the slave" a "new nothing, a darkness".[9]

The idea of Caribbean "*non-histoire*" or its anglophone equivalent "history-lessness" has become so pervasive that it risks "petrifying into myth" itself, risks obscuring discourses of history which conflict with the critical orthodoxy. As the influence of francophone Caribbean thought, and particularly of Glissant, spreads across the region and the hemisphere, there is a risk that alternative, divergent Caribbean histories will be ignored, silenced and forgotten. And even if Glissant speaks most fundamentally of the particular status of the French islands, the scope of his vision extends far from Martinique, across the region, and is widely interpreted as a broadly Caribbean discourse.

In this chapter, I want to argue against the all-encompassing "*non-histoire*" model, to expose some of its limitations, and to propose that Haiti provides a quite singular historical discourse, one which diverges radically from the Glissantian model, and which has been curiously excluded from the prevailing theories of both Caribbeanness and postcoloniality. Haitian historical discourse is, I argue, atypical in many ways, and implicitly critiques the Glissant-led tendency to see only lack and dispossession in Caribbean history.

The primary factor which differentiates Haiti's historical sensibility from that of the rest of the Caribbean is apparent: the revolution which, let us remind ourselves, was the result of probably the largest and most successful slave uprising in human history, one which defeated the armies of the three main colonial powers, France, Britain and Spain, and which instituted the "first black republic" in the New World. In his recent re-evaluation of the revolution, the historian David P. Geggus cuts across time and place to suggest some of the revolution's manifold repercussions:

> From the Mississippi Valley to the streets of Rio and the council chambers of the European capitals, the Haitian Revolution had a multifarious impact. The fifteen-year struggle for racial equality, slave emancipation, and colonial inde-pendence alarmed and excited public opinion on both sides of the Atlantic. It shaped great power politics, generated migration movements, and opened new economic frontiers. It stimulated slave resistance and new expansions

of slavery, while embittering the debates developing about race and abolition. The revolution also inspired one of William Wordsworth's greatest
sonnets, Victor Hugo's first novel, works by Heinrich von Kleist, Alphonse
de Lamartine, and John Greenleaf Whittier, and in the twentieth century,
the new literary genre of marvelous realism. It made an imprint, too, on the
philosophy of Georg Wilhelm Hegel.[10]

Never before had the events on such a tiny "speck of land" been felt so acutely
and so deeply in the centres of colonial power. The basis of my argument here is that
the epic scale and the heroic register of the revolution have had a cathartic effect
on Haitian historical sensibility, that the proto-Fanonian violence of the revolution
has purged Haitian history, at least in part, of the memory of the Middle Passage,
the plantation and the sense of deadening emptiness which permeates historical
thinking in the wider Caribbean.[11] This is not to say that pre-revolution history can
be neatly discounted or forgotten, but that the revolution was a new cataclysmic
moment in Haitian history which for many has become the predominant historical
reference point, an inescapable memory, even a spectral presence for generations of
Haitian intellectuals. Nor is it to say that history is any less troubling for Haitians
than for other Caribbean peoples; it is deeply troubling, but in different ways, and
for different reasons. The rest of this chapter will develop and justify my argument
in two central ways: first, by tracing the evolving, often paradoxical and troubled
interaction between history and literature in Haiti from the revolution to 1946,
and second, by analysing the historical "haunting" of selected Haitian novels of the
post-1946 period.

Two Revolutions and an Occupation:
Haitian Historical Consciousness, 1804–1946

As is the case in the rest of the Caribbean, what we know as Haitian historical consciousness has largely been created through literature: poems, stories and, later, novels.
Most critics agree that the period from 1804 to 1915 can be read as a distinct period,
one that marked the beginning of Haitian literature. This was, however, something of
a false start, in that, as Jack Corzani writes: "In spite of its independence, Haiti had
lingered over a fairly sterile contemplation of France and French culture. Far from
leading to any kind of rupture, the young nation's economic and social difficulties
throughout the nineteenth century encouraged the educated bourgeoisie to become

enamoured with French culture."[12] Corzani's critique of the postcolonial mimicry of nineteenth century Haitian literature is echoed by Fleischmann, who characterizes the writing of the period as an "apologetic literature",[13] and by Dash, who argues that it was only pioneering "in the limited sense of being representative of the beginnings of a national and historical consciousness".[14] Despite its formal limitations, therefore, the literature of this early period did nonetheless lay the foundations of a collective "historical consciousness", one which is glossed by the author Justin Devot in his *Cours d'instruction civique,* and which draws on the "glorious memories of an independence gained by the liberatory effort of human personality". The memory of the revolution is, Devot says, "an indivisible heritage that we must conserve as such, by adding to it other glorious memories, so that we may transmit it to our descendants who, in their turn, will keep it intact and enhance its worth for their own descendants".[15] According to Devot, therefore, Haitian history is a unified, "indivisible" discourse, to be transmitted faithfully from generation to generation in apparently unending succession. All that would or should change in this passage is the enhancement of the historical consciousness. The final key characteristic is the temporal linearity of this historical discourse: history exists on a timeline and progresses surely through time in a forward movement. Events in the twentieth century were, however, to expose both the frailties and the dangers of this linear conception of history.

In particular, the American occupation of 1915–34 shook the Haitian elite's view of itself; the neo-colonial moment at once posed a threat to the viability of the "glorious memories" of 1804 and introduced an unforeseen circular or repetitive quality into Haitian history. It could be argued that Haiti has been going around in circles ever since. A case in point is the indigenist movement, which was born out of the sharp contradiction between Haiti's glorious historical consciousness and the indignity of the nation's new subjugation, and which is often seen as a radical break with the previous, heavily francophile notions of Haitianity. In reality, however, the two basic elements of nineteenth-century Haitian historical and cultural sensibility – cloying francophilia and unflinching patriotism – largely survived the indigenist period, metamorphosed, and even re-emerged stronger than ever. In the first issue of *La Revue Indigène,* for example, Normil G. Sylvain writes of the contemporary malaise in Haiti, and argues, "It is not only in the heart but also in the head that our country is ill. The problem is, first, one of intelligence, then of sensibility." Sylvain's solution, remarkably perhaps, inheres in a new realignment with France and French culture, as he proposes: "We will have to attempt a cure of national rebirth here by drawing on the great parallel effort carried out with a rare goodwill in France", for, he says in the New World, "ours is the glorious destiny of maintaining with Canada and the French Antilles the language and traditions of France".[16]

Just as the occupation reinvigorated Haitian francophilia, so it led to a revalourization of the "idea of the homeland", and the consolidation of a rigid patriotism, as Louis Morpeau writes in 1925:

> The occupation brings a benefit: it provokes a revitalization of the idea of the homeland, forces us to rethink our moral, intellectual, and social values, forces us to understand the extent that we have sinned against the nation and the race. It forces us to see how much our Gallo-black heredities, our Afro-Latin affinities, our French culture found itself opposed to the crude North American pragmatism and unrefined neo-Saxonism, which are so disdainful of nuances, ignorant of finesse and convinced that every civilization is first and foremost material.[17]

The memory of revolution, and its corollary – staunch patriotism – therefore survived the economic, social and political decline of the nineteenth century and remained more or less intact throughout the indigenist phase of Haitian writing, which Fleischmann dates from 1915 to 1935, and which is generally, though questionably, seen as the time in which a "truer", that is, a less derivatively francophile Haitian literature finally appeared. Haiti during this period held on to what it knew, turned in on itself and, tragically, started to believe its own myths.

The dominant literary genre during both the early and indigenist phases of Haitian writing was poetry. In a later (1959) piece on post-revolution Haitian writing, the figurehead of indigenism, Jean Price-Mars, himself not averse to lauding French culture and language, argues that Haitian literature has always been "the expression of the state of the people's soul", and that it was in poetry that the memory of revolution has remained strongest: "In the past, our poets sang, exalted, glorified the herosim of our ancestors who transformed the group of slaves from whom we are descended into a nation."[18] This is significant in that Price-Mars makes clear that the memory of the revolution in Haitian literature had been transmitted not through any kind of balanced, rigorous historiography, but almost exclusively through nostalgic, inflated ideas of "heroism", through the veneration of "our ancestors" and the cult of the "great men".[19]

Given the epic scale of the revolution, and the pressing need to create a post-1804 Haitian historical consciousness, the cult of the hero was an almost inevitable and in some senses positive phenomenon. And yet, it has itself become a dangerous, introverted and petrifying myth, for the very same cult can be linked directly to the post-occupation, post-1946 rise of *noirisme,* the upward political movement of a black middle class which, drawing on indigenist-inspired ideas of racial authenticity, sought to install itself as the rightful ruling elite of Haiti. Seeing themselves as the genuine heirs of Toussaint, Dessalines and Christophe, the *noiristes'* stated mission was to rid Haiti of its light-skinned political elite and to finally fulfil the "promise" of the revolution by establishing a black government. This aim was achieved in August 1946 when, in the wake of the popular overthrow of Élie Lescot (Haiti's second revolution), Dumarsais Estimé, a black schoolteacher of peasant origin, was elected president of the republic. Foremost among the *noiriste* group was, of course, François Duvalier, who, rewriting history, proclaims that "1804 represents an Evolution rather than a Revolution. First, in order to have a Revolution, there must be a change in the mentality . . . . a transfer of power, a renewal of values." Evoking and manipulating the memory of 1804, he presents himself as the mythical inheritor of the revolutionary legacy:

> Liberty! Liberty! Independence! Independence! . . . Magical, sonorous words that create the pride and dignity of the Caribbean black! And, jealous of this liberty and this independence, in my dreams of a strong, unified and prosperous homeland, I am the fierce maroon looking for the pure rays of the radiant sun that will lead the black people of Haiti towards more progress and well-being.[20]

In effect, the rise of Duvalier and of *noiriste* ideology confirms Dash's idea that "in times of national crisis" in Haiti there is a strong tendency towards "ideological mythmaking" and that "in the period that followed the occupation the temptation was to react against the radical insecurity of the past and through ideology make the world intelligible".[21] Haitian history therefore finally petrifies into myth with the Duvaliers and *noiriste* ideology; the long road from 1804 leads ultimately to an historical dead end, and history repeats and defeats itself, becoming, ironically, once more the univocal discourse of the master. Far from being linear or forward-moving, as Justin Devot had envisaged, Haitian historical consciousness now moves in circles, trapped by itself.

THE HAUNTING OF HAITIAN FICTION

This historical circularity permeates the modern Haitian (post-1946) novel, and brings back in cycles unwanted but inescapable spectres of the past. Haitian fiction is therefore haunted by history, haunted not (only) in the glib sense, but (also) in the sense intended by Derrida in his critique of Marx's attempts to "exorcize" his philosophical "spectres". Arguing that Marx's spectres – those of German idealist philosophy – keep reappearing in Marx's writing, Derrida formulates this idea of haunting:

> To haunt does not mean to be present, and it is necessary to introduce haunting into the very construction of a concept. Of every concept, beginning with the concepts of being and time. That is what we would call here a hauntology. Ontology opposes it only in a movement of exorcism. Ontology is a conjuration.[22]

In this section, I will argue that however much modern Haitian fiction tries to exorcize the ghosts of history, it remains "haunted", it cannot "conjure up" a new ontology, as the spectres of the past survive, and reappear unsummoned in its every expression.

In contrast to the early post-revolution heroic poetry, the Haitian novel, the dominant genre in the postwar era, does not celebrate history, but enacts (failed) exorcisms of the nation's history, which now (re)appears as a troubled and troubling phenomeneon. Paradoxically, these exorcisms are not attempted by invoking history, but largely by absenting and silencing the memory of the revolution for, given the cataclysmic historical importance of the revolution, there are remarkably few direct references to it in modern Haitian fiction. And yet, Haitian fiction remains undeniably haunted by the revolution, and this haunting manifests itself in various ways.

In René Depestre's 1979 novel *The Festival of the Greasy Pole* [*Le mât de cocagne*], for instance, the central character, Henri Postel, is a kind of internal exile, cast out politically and socially in the "zombified" (un)reality of a Duvalieresque Haiti. For rather opaque, never fully iterated reasons, Postel enters a greasy pole competition, a fragment of pre-Duvalier cultural memory which has been co-opted by *noiriste* dogma to serve the state's propaganda machine. Despite Postel's enthusiasm for the competition, there is a clear sense of a reduction in, or a degradation of, political possibilities for the Haitian hero. The national history of glorious revolution and anticolonial struggle haunts Postel, in that he feels impelled to preserve or rekindle the revolutionary spirit, yet his only outlet for resistance lies in the greasy pole competition. He is aware of the parochial nature of his actions, of their insignificance on history's wider scale: "Win or lose, of course, there won't be any emergency meeting of the U.N. Security Council to consider your case. No chapter entitled 'The Crisis of Tête-Bœuf' in any history book."[23]

Haitian history frames his actions and limits them, in that its spectral presence constantly reminds him of the scale of its achievements, sets an unrepeatable precedent, and yet its legacy compels him to continue. There is deep irony in the fact that he lives on "*avenue Dessalines*"; it is as if history is inescapable for him, as if he is forever compelled to situate himself politically, morally and even physically, in relation to this history. This situation is clearly far from the one described by Glissant of a Caribbean "nonhistory", of history as an absence, and of the collective memory as a void. Post-revolution Haitian history in this sense transmits to each generation not absence and emptiness, but a haunting legacy of unrepeatable victories and incomparable heroism; in short, almost an *excess* of history. The collective imagination, like that of Postel, is constructed around the contrasting, richly coloured images of the past and the deglorified images and realities of the present. The retention of a synchronic conception of past events casts a heavy, impossible shadow over the diachronic degeneration of Haitian history.

In *Le Métier à métisser*, Depestre talks about this double aspect of Haitian history and historical memory, saying, "we have an extremely complex history that has many lessons for the whole Caribbean" and then, qualifying his statement, remarking that "at the moment, this 'historical memory' has lost its way". Crucially, Depestre draws a clear distinction between Glissantian and Haitian historical discourse, and emphasizes the importance of the Duvalier era in undermining Haitian historical memory: "There is today, far removed from Glissant's vigorous *Caribbean discourse*, a *Haitian discourse* that repeats deliriously episodes of 'black jacobinism', after the thirty years of 'totalitarian negritude' that Papa Doc and his band of 'tontons-macoutes' brutally inflicted on the Haitian people." The consequences of this "deliriously" repeating history are, first, "a disfiguration of the historical memory", and, second, a situation whereby the Haitian people are "prisoners of this double-edged memory".[24] *The Festival of the Greasy Pole* enacts this situation of historical imprisonment and, in Postel, evokes a character caught in Haiti's haunting double-edged history.

The most significant effects of Haitian fiction's historical haunting are felt in relation to time. As Derrida has it, ghosts are untimely ("*intempestifs*") and "exist" outside of time: "It is a proper characteristic of the specter, if there is any, that no one can be sure if by returning it testifies to a living past or to a living future, for the *revenant* may already mark the promised return of the specter of living being.

Once again, untimeliness and disadjustment of the contemporary."[25] Incidences of such spectrally induced "disadjustments of the contemporary" are commonplace in modern Haitian fiction. In Jacques-Stephen Alexis's novels, for instance, history appears as cyclical and repetitive, so that the sense of the present is always touched by the returning spectres of the past. There is a memorable scene in his 1957 novel *Les arbres musiciens* where American bulldozers are clearing the Haitian land and, seen through the eyes of the character Gonaïbo, the event appears as a repetition of the Columbian encounter:

> These apparitions acted like conquerors or masters. A feeling of his whole self being ripped apart ran through his entire body . . . Five centuries ago, the lookouts of Anacaona the Great must have felt the same when, in an apocalyptic surging, Ojeda's cavalry came into sight, violating the borders of the cacique.[26]

Perhaps nowhere in modern Haitian fiction is this historical haunting, this temporal disadjustment felt as acutely as it is in the work of Émile Ollivier, in which, as one critic observes, "the past renews itself, reproduces itself in the present: the parallels drawn by the text evoke double or triple analogies that take us either to the contemporary history that binds Baby Doc's reign to the horrors of 'papadocquisme', or back to the history of the nineteenth century".[27] In Ollivier's fiction, it is not only time but also space, the Haitian land itself, which is haunted by history. The opening lines of his 1991 novel *Passages* evoke this sense of a haunted Haitian hinterland:

> There is the sea, there is the island. On the island side, memory is not new . . . The smallest plot of land can be considered as a magical burial mound where hide the spirits of the dead, the faces of the heroes of the Revolution, mysteries, *loas* and gods of blood. Mountains and hills, rivers and estuaries, springs and lakes, roads and paths, shacks and minds are inhabited by memory. Without it, there is no depth of knowledge.[28]

The land, therefore, is invoked as a place of historical memory, of vodou, and the deepest elements of Haitian tradition. In sharp contrast to Césaire's "islands crumbs/islands unformed", everything, everywhere in the Haitian hinterland – "The smallest plot of land" – is loaded, or perhaps *overloaded,* with significance. Without the land, there is no real self-knowledge, no "depth of knowledge" at all. Although, or perhaps because, the land is historically overloaded, it is also presented as a threatened, precarious space. The village of Port-à-l'Écu seems to epitomize this precariousness. Situated in a mangrove swamp in a remote corner of the north-west Haitian coast, the village and its environs are presented as a distinctly premodern space: "A landscape like those one sees in the Bible."[29] The mangrove swamp's chaotic, shifting entanglement of unrooted roots has of course been used by Maryse Condé (and others) as a model of Caribbean identity. Counter to the preoccupation in Césaire and, to a lesser extent, Glissant, with trees and solid, deep roots, the mangrove offers a model of Caribbean identity as unfixed, opaque and impenetrable. In Ollivier's case, the swamp carries with it connotations of precariousness, a kind of "in-between" space between the rooted, folkloric Haiti of the hinterland and the absolute fluidity of the sea:

> *Tangled up with roots and creepers,* Port-à-l'Écu repeats over and again the same scenery, the same boundaries, over many kilometers, exhaustingly, as far as the eye can see: swampy, sulfurated lands, *a territory of uncertainty where one does not know if it is the sea that is invading the land or the land that is annexing the sea.*[30]

The uncertainty and precariousness of the village's existence is underscored in the narrator's statement that there is no need to look up its name on a map, as it exists no more and "is to be found nowhere".[31] The disappearance of the village suggests its provisional, temporary nature; almost thrown upon the shore, without ever becoming truly part of the hinterland, it is itself an indeterminate place of *passage,* an interim stop somewhere between two other places. It is somewhere to arrive at and to leave from, not somewhere to remain permanently. Despite its instability and transitory nature, the village is also something of a prison as it offers no "hope of escape".[32] In interview, Ollivier elaborates on his vision of Haiti as a closed, restricted space: "[Haitian] space is insular. Thus, paradoxically, although you're living on an island, one could have the impression that the island opens up to the sea, but I do not think that this is true in Haiti. For me, the island has often been lived and seen as a closed space."[33]

If Haitian space is historically haunted in Ollivier's work, so time is repetitive and circular, and history is lived as a constant return to indeterminacy and deracination, in that it keeps returning the Haitian people to their point of arrival, to boats, ships and the Middle Passage. There is therefore a direct correspondence between the sense of a repeated *spatial* return to the place of arrival (the littoral), and the idea of a similar temporal, historical circularity. In interview, Ollivier makes this link explicit: "As we are in what we might call an eternal return, it seemed to me that Haiti existed in a circular time . . . . the history of this country, from independence to today, . . . has been an endless series of banditry, corruption, and chaos."[34]

In this sense, Ollivier echoes Depestre's formulation in *Hadriana dans tous mes rêves* that "in our country, for sure, history repeats itself more than it does anywhere else".[35] Similarly, and in an implicit challenge to the "nonhistory" model of Caribbean history, Antonio Benítez-Rojo identifies repetitive, cyclical history as an all-pervasive trope in the cultural productions (or "performances") of the Caribbean's "repeating island". Benítez-Rojo celebrates the instability inherent to the Caribbean as an intensely creative force; repetitive time and history are seen as products of the plantation:

> the big bang of the Caribbean universe, whose slow explosion throughout modern history threw out billions and billions of cultural fragments in all directions – fragments of diverse kinds that, in their endless voyage, come together in an instant to form a dance step, a linguistic trope, the line of a poem, and afterward repel each other to re-form and pull apart once more, and so on.[36]

In contrast to Benítez-Rojo's lyrical celebrations, however, Ollivier's novel offers a far more muted vision of repetitive history in the Caribbean. In *Passages,* history is not so much an "explosion" with its connotations of outward movement, new shapes and forms, as an *implosion,* a violent collapse inwards, whose aftermath leaves only stagnation and disillusionment.[37]

Although Ollivier's sombre, muted style contrasts sharply with Dany Laferrière's ludic, parodic approach to writing Haiti, there are similarities in both authors' visions of a nation haunted by its unending past. In Laferrière's *Down Among the Dead Men* [*Pays sans chapeau*], in particular, history is indirectly, though unequivocally, critiqued as a deadening force in contemporary Haiti. In Laferrière's under-played but insistent intertextual references to Jacques Roumain's *Masters of the Dew* [*Gouverneurs de la rosée*], the character Manu can be read as a reincarna-tion of Manuel, Roumain's hero and martyr. In Laferrière's text, Manu is a self-proclaimed "man of the people" – he says, "They're me. I'm them" – who has sacrificed himself to working for the greater good in Carrefour, one of Port-au-Prince's poorest districts.[38] Yet, Laferrière's Manu is a pathetic charac-ter, and the full pathos of his situation is gradually laid bare in the course of the novel: he is a "man of the people" who has followed futile small-scale com-munity projects, a patriot who has sacrificed his life to resisting the Duvaliers, and yet who lives, and dies, in a roofless shack in one of Port-au-Prince's shanty towns. In choosing a Manuel-like epic route of self-conscious martyrdom in

Duvalier's Haiti, Manu finally comes to a dead end, and is an unwitting victim of the historically inherited cult of the hero.

Haitian historical sensibility, as is now clear, is entangled with the epic struggles of revolution, and these are the implicit inspiration of Manuel's quest in *Gouverneurs de la rosée*. As Haiti's post-revolution history plays out, however, the epic and the myth have become ever more untenable. The degraded present – modern-day Port-au-Prince is described as "one of the worst human jungles on earth" – not only implicitly demythifies Haiti's glorious past, but is also in many ways a *product* of mythical thinking.[39] For myth ignores history, and lends a delusory sense of constancy which can have the effect of obscuring a changing reality. In Roland Barthes's analysis, myth is an essentially conservative, reactionary force in society:

> In passing from history to nature, myth makes a saving; it abolishes the complexity of human action, gives it an elemental simplicity: it suppresses all dialectic, or anything which takes us beyond the immediately visible; it organizes a world without contradictions because without depth, a world displayed in the obvious. Myth creates a happy clarity: things give the appearance of meaning something in their own right.[40]

Down Among the Dead Men seems to play out the consequences of just such an over-reliance on myth: Manu's adherence to the Haitian myth of self-sacrifice "suppresses all dialectic", and the novel's play of mirrors between Manu and the Duvalier dictators leads to a final resemblance among the three figures. Moreover, Haitian intellectual history shows that the thinking of Duvalier and Roumain (and, by extension, Manuel and Manu) shares common roots, as both were important figures in the indigenist movement. Despite the ideological discord between on the one hand Duvalier and the Griots' racial essentialism, and on the other Roumain's Marxism, they all shared, cultivated and promoted a fundamental myth – the indigenist belief in an essential Haitian self – and this offered a delusory comfort in the face of political and historical disempowerment. In *Down Among the Dead Men,* Manu is the modern-day perpetuator of indigenist-inherited myths, only now, as Haiti's decline continues, these myths have become ragged remnants of the past and offer no real comfort. In Laferrière's indirect critique of Haitian political and cultural history, Roumain and Duvalier are two sides of one coin, or as the character Philippe says of Manu, they are involved in a complex "mirror effect" where apparent ideological differences at times dissolve into sameness and convergent identities.

In essence, Laferrière echoes Laennec Hurbon's argument that there is a close resemblance between the radical intellectual and the despot in Haiti for, as Hurbon says: "In each intellectual as in each political leader, one can see the emergence of nothing but the phantom of Duvalier."[41]

ENDING SILENCES

Literature and history in Haiti have for two centuries fed off each other: history has become poetry and fiction, and poetry and fiction have become history. In this sense, Haiti stands apart from the other Caribbean islands, particularly the other francophone islands, whose true literary/historical awakening arguably began only in the mid-twentieth century with Césaire's *Cahier d'un retour au pays natal*. And yet Haiti is strangely absent from discourses of both Caribbeanness and postcoloniality; rare are the references to the first black republic in the New World in the wider theoretical discourses. Haiti is a kind of theoretical and historical blind spot, there but unseen, speaking but unheard. The disjuncture between the critically accepted Glissantian version of Caribbean nonhistory and the excessive, haunting history in Haiti that this chapter has outlined testifies to the discreet, convenient silencing of Haitian experience. For Haitian experience is in many ways unsettling and poses some awkward, perhaps unanswerable questions. How can, for instance, Haiti, its authors, its peoples, ever come to terms with the majesty, the tragedy, the excess, the drama, the blood, the (self-inflicted) violence, the passion, the absurdity, the narcissism of its History? How can the grand historical memory ever nourish a present or a future Haiti, famished yet bloated on History? Will the phantoms ever be exorcized, will the haunting ever end, will time ever escape itself, will space ever be cleared of the debris of the past? And finally, does anyone really care?

More than two hundred years after Haitian independence, it is time to revise the pervasive idea that the Caribbean exists irrevocably in a "nonhistory". The example of Haiti shows, if it shows anything, that history has indeed happened here, that history has been made to happen here by Caribbean peoples, and that, despite everything, a "sedimented", if disturbed and cloudy, real history exists. It is time to move out of the shadows and the silences, the dank domains of myth, and into the true acceptance of Haitian and Caribbean history. History has been made here, glorious or otherwise, and Caribbean peoples have long been agents in creating this history. The movement into acceptance and agency carries with it responsibilities, chiefly the responsibility to eschew the myths, nationalisms and racisms that have provided delusory comfort to, and supplemented the perceived void in historical consciousness. This leap towards acceptance and agency is imperative at this bittersweet moment in Haitian and Caribbean history, for in taking responsibility for history, individuals and peoples simultaneously transform themselves into the guardians of the present and the enactors and enunciators of the future.

NOTES

1. Edward Said, *Orientalism* (London: Routledge, 1978), 8.

2. Jeannie Suk, *Postcolonial Paradoxes in French Caribbean Writing: Césaire, Glissant, Condé* (Oxford: Clarendon Press, 2001), 72.

3. Aimé Césaire, *Césaire: The Collected Poetry,* trans. Clayton Eshleman and Annette Smith (Berkeley and Los Angeles: University of California Press, 1983), 75, 59.

4. Édouard Glissant, *Caribbean Discourse,* trans. J. Michael Dash (Charlottesville: University Press of Virginia, 1999 [1989]), 161.

5. Jean Bernabé, Patrick Chamoiseau and Raphaël Confiant, *Éloge de la créolité,* bilingual ed. (Paris: Gallimard, 1993 [1989]), 98.

6. Glissant, *Caribbean Discourse,* 93, 62.

7. Robert Young, *White Mythologies: Writing History and the West* (reprint, London and New York: Routledge, 1992 [1990]), 15.

8. Césaire, *Collected Poetry,* 281.

9. Derek Walcott, *What the Twilight Says* (London: Faber and Faber, 1998), 37, 39. René Ménil similarly argues, "The mystery of our impossible history lies not in the absurdity of our past but in the incoherence and inconsistency of our present social consciousness. The prerequisite to any history of Martinique is the study of our consciousness as it exists today." *Antilles déjà jadis précédé de Tracées* (Paris: Jean Michel Place, 1999), 47.

10. David P. Geggus, ed., *The Impact of the Haitian Revolution in the Atlantic World* (Columbia: University of South Carolina Press, 2001), 247.

11. See Fanon's view of anticolonial violence as a purgative force: "This violent praxis is totalizing, as everybody makes him or herself a link in the big chain, in the great violent organism that rises up as a reaction to the initial violence of the colonizer. . . . On the individual level, violence purifies. It removes from the colonized his inferiority complex, his contemplative or hopeless attitudes. It makes the colonized intrepid, rehabilitates him in his own eyes." *Les damnés de la terre* (Paris: Maspero, 1968), 51.

12. Jack Corzani, *La littérature des Antilles-Guyane françaises,* vol. 3 (Fort-de-France: Désormeaux, 1978), 150.

13. Ulrich Fleischmann, *Écrivain et société en Haïti* (Fonds St-Jacques, Sainte-Marie, Martinique: Centre de recherches caraïbes, University of Montreal, 1976), 9.

14. J. Michael Dash, *Literature and Ideology in Haiti, 1915–1961* (Totowa: Barnes and Noble, 1981), 4. Dash qualifies this critique of nineteenth-century Haitian thought in a more recent essay where he argues that Anténor Firmin was a precursor of contemporary ideas of inter-American cross-culturality. "Nineteenth-Century Haiti and the Archipelago of the Americas: Anténor Firmin's *Letters from St Thomas*", *Research in African Literatures* 35, no. 2 (Summer 2004): 44–53.

15. Quoted in Lélia J. Hérisson, *Manuel de littérature haïtienne* (Port-au-Prince: Département de l'Éducation Nationale, 1955), 179.

16. Normil G. Sylvain, "Un rêve de Georges Sylvain", *Revue Indigène* 1, no. 1 (July 1927): 4, 5.

17. Quoted in Naomi M. Garret, *The Renaissance of Haitian Poetry* (Paris: Présence Africaine, 1963), 61.

18. Jean Price-Mars, *De Saint-Domingue à Haïti: Essai sur la culture, les arts et la littérature* (Paris: Présence Africaine, 1959), 13.

19. Examples of this myth-making poetry are legion in the early period of Haitian writing; for instance, the poem "Toussaint Louverture" by Tertulien Guilbaud, written "Upon seeing the French flotilla" in 1902, evokes the memory of Toussaint in its righteous defiance of France, and presents the "Grand Précurseur" in almost superhuman terms: "Woe betide he who advances on our deep gorges! / In my vast plans, I have as an accomplice . . . God / And I feel boiling in my veins on fire / This creative power that gives rise to worlds" (quoted in Hérisson, *Manuel de littérature haïtienne,* 278).

20. François Duvalier, *Bréviaire d'une révolution* (Port-au-Prince: Henri Deschamps, 1967), 19, 20.

21. Dash, *Literature and Ideology,* 112.

22. Jacques Derrida, *Specters of Marx,* trans. Peggy Kamuf (London and New York: Routledge, 1994), 161. I am drawing here on Michael Syrotinski's article "Ghost Writing: Sony Labou Tansi's Spectographic Subject", *Paragraph* 24, no. 3 (November 2001): 92–104.

23. René Depestre, *The Festival of the Greasy Pole,* trans. Carrol F. Coates (1979; reprint, Charlottesville: University Press of Virginia, CARAF Books, 1990), 27.

24. René Depestre, *Le métier à métisser* (Paris: Stock, 1998), 177.

25. Derrida, *Specters of Marx,* 99.

26. Jacques-Stephen Alexis, *Les arbres musiciens* (Paris: Gallimard, 1957), 83.

27. Max Dominique, "L'Écriture baroque d'Ollivier et la crise des idéologies", *Chemins critiques* 1, no. 3 (December 1989): 196.

28. Émile Ollivier, *Passages* (1991; reprint, Montreal: Le Serpent à Plumes, 1994), 13.

29. Ibid., 15.

30. Ibid., 13–14, emphasis added.

31. Ibid., 14.

32. Ibid., 13.

33. Fernando Lambert, "Émile Ollivier, écrivain d'Haïti du Québec", *Notre Librairie* 133 (January–April 1998): 155.

34. Ibid.

35. René Depestre, *Hadriana dans tous mes rêves* (1988; reprint, Paris: Gallimard, 1990), 100.

36. Antonio Benítez-Rojo, "Three Words toward Creolization", trans. James Maraniss, in *Caribbean Creolization: Reflections on the Cultural Dynamics of Language, Literature and Identity,* ed. Kathleen M. Balutansky and Marie-Agnès Sourieau (Gainesville, Fla.: University Press of Florida; Barbados, Jamaica, and Trinidad and Tobago: The Press, University of the West Indies, 1998), 55.

37. This circular vision of Haitian history recurs throughout Ollivier's work. In his analysis of Ollivier's 1983 novel *Mère-solitude,* Max Dominique identifies "This cyclical conception of history [that] says nothing other than the unending return of the same [. . .] no change is possible, no way out of the circular labyrinth." See Dominique, "L'Écriture baroque d'Ollivier et la crise des idéologies", 196.

38. Dany Laferrière, *Down Among the Dead Men,* trans. David Homel (Vancouver: Douglas and McIntyre, 1997), 174.

39. Ibid., 101.

40. Roland Barthes, *Mythologies* (Paris: Seuil, 1957), 217.

41. Quoted in J. Michael Dash, *The Other America: Caribbean Literature in a New World Context* (Charlottesville: University Press of Virginia, 1998), 113. In this respect, Laferrière also echoes the earlier work of Marie Chauvet, who, as Dash says, "has put her finger on the disturbing reality that in every intellectual and writer there lurks the monster of all Haitian intellectuals, François Duvalier". Ibid.

CHAPTER 4

LAHENS'S REVOLUTION, OR THE WORDS WITHIN

ELIZABETH WALCOTT-HACKSHAW

> . . . *much of Haitian's women literature should be read as a literature of revolution.*
>
> – Myriam J.A. Chancy

> *Naturally the artist is an enemy of the state. He cannot play politics, succumb to slogans and other simplifications, worship heroes, ally himself with any party, suck on some politician's program like a sweet. He is also an enemy of every ordinary revolution . . . The artist's revolutionary activity is of a different kind. He is concerned with consciousness, and he makes his changes there.*
>
> – William H. Gass

If we understand the term "revolution" to mean a dramatic and wide-reaching change that creates a new social order, then Haitian writer Yanick Lahens's first novel, *Dans la maison du père,* cannot be considered as literature of revolution.[1] Nor can it be easily classified as literature of resistance, which typically privileges the political rather than the social or the personal as having the power to change the world. The dramatic change that takes place in this novel occurs on an individual rather than a collective level; the reader retraces the transformations, transgressions and revolt of the protagonist, Alice Bienaimé, on her return to her native land. Unlike the famous Césairian return in *Cahier d'un retour au pays natal,* metaphorically located on the exterior, at early dawn, to suggest the all-encompassing potential for collective change and renewal, Lahens's protagonist returns to the interior private space of her father's house and to all the histories contained within those walls.[2]

Dans la maison du père explores the negotiation between the private and public worlds of the protagonist, as well as the Haitian writer's liminality, positioned between interior and exterior exile, oscillating between "*l'ancrage et la fuite*".[3] In contrast to the stress on the collective and the political in Roumain's and Alexis's fiction, Lahens privileges and explores the possibilities of individual speech in the Haitian novel where the "I" does not always contain the "we" of collective protest, and yet does not exclude it. In the tradition of Marie Chauvet,[4] Lahens's writing exposes the problems of psychological and political oppression; yet, it is often through the silences of what is not articulated, through the words within, that her work acquires a unique voice. Writing for Lahens is space where paradoxes, contractions and histories can be explored:

> J'écris parce que j'ai une histoire qui me colle à la peau, et que je voudrais aller jusqu'au bout des paradoxes de l'histoire dans laquelle j'ai été jetée en tant que femme et en tant qu'Haïtienne. L'écriture, c'est un lieu provisoire de résolution de ces questions.[5]

This chapter will explore the manner in which Yanick Lahens's *Dans la maison du père,* a work set against a backdrop of repression, resistance and liberation, can be read as a literature of revolution, redefined and articulated through the perspective of a Haitian, a woman and a writer.

Representations and the Writer's "I"

In *Dans la maison du père* the narrative moves between individual and collective experience, between the exterior "official" history and its repercussions in the private sphere of the father's house; this I/we problematic is a common preoccupation amongst Caribbean women writers.

For example, at the end of *Breath, Eyes, Memory,* the author Edwidge Danticat writes a letter to her protagonist Sophie.[6] The letter engages her readers in a debate on individual and collective representation. By drawing on and transgressing the textual borders of the epistolary tradition, the letter serves to defend the writer's position from the accusations of collective representation. Danticat's strategy of addressing the letter to her character effectively maintains Sophie's individuality by emphasizing her personal experience and at the same time acknowledges the potential for collective representation. Danticat places Sophie in both intra- and paratextual positions; a Sophie exists within the novel but Danticat's letter also places her outside the novel's textual perimeters. And yet Danticat's letter cautions against over-identification with the representation of Sophie:

> your body is now being asked to represent a larger space than your flesh. You are being asked to represent every girl child, every woman from this land that you and I love so much. Tired of protesting, I feel I must explain. Of course, not all Haitian mothers are like your mother. Not all Haitian daughters are tested as you have been.
>
> I have always taken for granted that this story which is yours, and only yours, would always be read as such . . . And so I write this to you now, Sophie, as I write it to myself, praying that the singularity of your experiences be allowed to exist, along with your own peculiarities, inconsistencies, your own voice.[7]

In bringing to the fore questions of representation and voicing of the female "I", Danticat echoes the concerns of Lahens and indicates some of the contradictions inherent to these narratives. Marie-Denise Shelton acknowledges these contradictions, linking the use of the first-person narrative to the problematic of feminine exclusion and dispossession. As Shelton notes: "Generally, the narrative in the first person by a female character presents itself as a frustrated enunciation which affirms and denies, creates, and dissolves the female sense of self."[8] Guadeloupean writers like Simone Schwarz-Bart and Maryse Condé have used the "*je*" to respond to the lack of representation on both individual and collective levels and to create a space for the female voice. Condé argues that the Caribbean writer seldom uses the "I" and even when this is done the "I" always means "we". The use of this personal "I" according to Condé gives the female protagonist a voice within a predominantly male discourse.[9] The contradictions that exist in the use of this "I" become evident when Schwarz-Bart's "*je*" *intime* is revisited. In *Pluie et vent sur Télumée Miracle,* Schwarz-Bart's "*je*" narrates the story of three generations of Lougandor women who have surmounted the many trials they have encountered in their lives. Schwarz-Bart's narrative focuses on the daily lives and adventures of these extraordinary women. In her essay "Memory, Voice and Metaphor in Schwarz-Bart", Kitzie McKinney emphasizes Télumée's centrality: "Instead of being the marginal 'Other' in this text, Télumée is at its center, and her voice controls the narrative from beginning to end."[10] Ronnie Scharfman also sees in *Pluie et vent* a work which "generously allows us to identify with the plenitude of its experience, to incorporate it and assimilate the (positive, nurturing female) bonding mirrored in the act of reading".[11]

The contradictions occur in what the "*je*" comes to represent. Schwarz-Bart's Télumée, like Danticat's Sophie, mythifies into symbols of female strength and survival. Although both narratives use the "I" to insist on the personal and the singularity of their narrators, in both cases the "I" becomes a representation of the collective, so much so that Danticat must write a letter contradicting such a collective claim. The reader finds in these personal writings of the "I"/narratrice individual locations of identification as well as all-encompassing definitions of female strength. The necessary contradiction that lies in this collective representation points to a universalizing definition that in the end undermines the sought-after individuality of the personal "*je*".[12]

This chapter will show the way in which the negotiation of the "I" in the narrative reflects both presence and absence, voicing and silencing, and does not always assume a non-fragmented, centred "I" that can be easily articulated or even distinguished from the "we". Lahens explores what Derrida might call a "disorder of identity", where contradictory forces coexist and the "I" can no longer be seen as an entity. There are no mythical female figures in *Dans la maison du père*, no generations of Caco or Lougandor women who symbolize the collective potential to overcome and surpass their oppressive conditions. Lahens's strength lies in her representation of contradictory forces that combine quiet submission and failure with silent rebellions and personal revolution.

Again, comparisons can be made with Marie Chauvet who in *Amour, colère et folie* (1968) dared to say openly what some thought to be scandalous at the time in a first-person narrative. Chauvet's use of the "I" in the novel does not deny Haiti's sociopolitical history but her treatment of this subject, as Lahens argues, rejects reductive ideological frames located in an all-consuming use of the "we":

> all the writers of the Third World, Haitian writers included, fell into the trap of always wanting to affirm that they were writers, and to demonstrate that they were men. They pursued this to such an extent that both individual speech and the desire to break new ground were strangled from the start. Nor did historical and political difficulties help in any way. The Third World writer was compelled to respond immediately to a social and political imperative. It was as if, in a way, the writer had to go through négritude and social realism as a mode of affirmation. He was thus trapped in a position that prevented the exploration of other directions.

I think that the women writers said, "It is true that all this exists, but would it not be possible to speak of ourselves, of who we are, of our families, or our relationships with our children, of the life in our neighborhoods."

Why is it that a Third World writer cannot, before saying "I am black or I am a Marxist", say simply "I am" and write? In saying so, they would not necessarily be neglecting social concerns, politics, or history. Marie Chauvet understood this, and she traced a new path with *Amour, colère et folie.*[13]

Lessons from Inside and Outside

In Lahens's "L'Exil: entre l'ancrage et la fuite, l'écrivain haïtien", the exile problematic is explored through interrogations of the individual and the collective. The essay describes dual states of interior and exterior exile experienced by Haitian writers. The writers that remain in Haiti experience a "syndrome of inner exile" in which the "I" is exiled from the self. This inner exile is first the result of a history of political persecution where subversive voices are silenced and where writers have never been afforded the right to practise freedom of expression. As Dash suggests, "The ideal of free expression has never really been tolerated by the vast majority of political regimes in Haiti, and writers have often found themselves persecuted by the state, which invariably has seen their ideas as a threat to its existence."[14]

This repression has caused many writers to flee Haiti; and those that remain never forget their tenuous position. Another way in which the writer experiences exile in his own country stems from the writer's personal need to create a necessary distance between the subject matter and the writer's "I"/eye; this self-imposed marginalization creates a state of "inner exile" for the writer. "This otherness," says Lahens, "lives within ourselves in general and with any artist in particular."[15] The writers who remain in Haiti face exterior marginalization through political oppression as well as an interior exile. By drawing on the Baudelarian image of the mocked, exiled poet in "L'Albatros", "exilé sur la terre au milieu des huées", Lahens explains the writer's plight. Although Lahens does not state this explicitly, the poet in Baudelaire's work is also the *flaneur* who observes and maintains that necessary distance that precedes creation.

The possibilities of fictional imagination allow Lahens, the novelist, to explore her prism of exile. *Dans la maison du père,* like her essay, considers the locations of exile, inside and outside, textually and territorially. The novel, told in the first person, recounts the life of the narrator, Alice Bienaimé, as a young girl growing up in a middle-class Haitian household in the 1930s and 1940s. The return to Haiti and, more importantly, to her father's house gives her the opportunity to retrace important historical markers in both her personal history and her country's. The American occupation (1915–34), the 1937 massacre in the Dominican Republic, the Anti-Superstitious Campaign, the 1946 revolution and the first Duvalierist exactions are all part of the novel's historical landscape. The reader is also taken into the culture of the bourgeoisie and that of the servants who inhabit the *arrière-cour.*

Lahens's portraits of these differing, yet merging, cultures are at times abstract, at other times more clearly delineated. Her treatment is always subtle, often leaving spaces, silences and gaps that only the reader can complete. But these exterior landscapes all relate to Alice's own familial culture within her father's house.

The location of the narrator at the beginning of the novel is one of the best examples of Lahens's play on the inside/outside positioning of her protagonist along the perimeters of her father's house. Alice must play both Baudelarian roles of the exile and the observer, a duality that must also be read in the context of her role as observer/participant. From the beginning, then, Lahens forces Alice to engage in a creative act of writing her own personal history, where she must be both subject and object. To emphasize this, the first chapter is structured differently from the others; the reader is led into a house by the narrator, a scene is described and only at the end are the characters identified.

In the house one man is reading on the verandah; another, in a white *costume d'alpaga,* is smoking and rocking gently in a *dodine.* The house is filled with "*un air de ragtime à la mode*", and a woman and narrator dance in the salon until the narrator moves into the garden where she is overcome by another rhythm, another force which soon overtakes her more measured movements.

> J'ôte mes chaussures, mes chaussettes blanches et j'essaie de retrouver les mesures d'une autre musique, celles d'autres gestes scandés par un tambour et entrevus quelques semaines auparavant. . . . Au bout d'un moment je ne danse plus, c'est la danse qui me traverse et fait battre mon sang.[16]

The man in the white suit stares at her and without taking his eyes off of her puts out his cigarette, gets up, walks quickly towards her, brutally grabs her by the shoulders, shouts at her to stop "*cette danse maudite*" and slaps her. The lady in the house looks on from a distance, petrified; she says nothing but eventually goes to comfort the narrator who is crying in the garden, the man who is reading never moves, the old lady looks on from a distance.

We learn at the end of the chapter that the man in the white suit is the narrator's father, the young lady is her mother, the other young man is her uncle, the older lady is the family's servant, Man Bo, and she, the narrator is "Alice Bienaimé, couchée sur l'herbe dans ma robe bleue, je viens d'entrer dans ma treizième année " (p. 13). This technique of deliberate anonymity works on many levels; it forces the narrator to establish a necessary distance from her subjects to recall the events as objectively as possible; but it also gives a lesson in the impossibility of achieving such objective historical recollection. The movement between the impersonal *il/elle/une femme/un jeune homme* and the narrator's eye/"I" seemingly allows for distance between narrator and the event; yet the first-person narrator's ability to survey the entire scene combines the objective and the subjective, the omniscient and the personal. Alice's desire to understand her present through the reconstruction of a past can only rely on the "fitful muse" of memory.[17]

There are many lessons and events that will shape Alice's thoughts and behaviour but this image takes a central place in her life; as she says, "Je suis née de cette image." It destabilizes the relationship that she has with her once idolized, heroic father and allows her to see the impotence of her mother's place in the family. Lahens also uses this scene to indicate several thematic concerns: the question of oppression, of silencing and the possibility of acts of liberation. It is literally the centre of Alice's life, "Elle est le mitan de ma vie", one that she will revisit at both the beginning and at the end of her story before she finally re-enters her father's house.

The house itself on the surface symbolizes patriarchal domination on both the private and public level; the men make the decisions, the women listen, comply and show little resistance (until Alice herself breaks the mould). But Lahens also shows the fragility of this domination, particularly when the father's motivations are informed by fear, oppression and his own submission to external forces beyond his control. His authoritarianism often stems from a desire to protect his family, and Alice in particular, from the possibility of external punishment. Lahens uses the house as a stage where many of Haiti's external political and historical dramas are re-enacted. It is also a place that houses all the contradictory forces that this Haitian family experiences. There is the continual battle to defeat colonial systems of thought that perpetuate prejudice, self-hatred and submission which have been passed on from one generation to the next: "mon grand-père se mit en tête d'avoir les mêmes préjugés que les bourgeois des Gonaïves, interdisant par exemple à mon père de fréquenter les premiers Arabes immigrés dans l'île" (p. 65). The men in the household grapple with the conquered/conqueror dilemma, precariously balancing fear with revolutionary desires. Anténor was once very much like his brother Héraclès in his younger days: "Dans sa jeunesse, mon père avait été comme son jeune frère Héraclès, au centre d'un tourbillon de courants invisibles. Mais ces courants étaient purement intellectuels . . . lisait les historiens haïtiens comme Louis Joseph Janvier ou les philosophes comme Kant ou Auguste Comte" (p. 119). But political and social oppression made Anténor more conservative as he states: "J'ai appris à n'être ni bleu, ni rouge, ni vert. J'ai renoncé à tous les ismes du monde" (p. 118).

By strategically locating two brothers on opposing sides of several political positions Lahens exploits these polemics. The two brothers celebrate the end of the American occupation even though they enter the celebration from opposing sides of the ideological stage. Anténor, with his francophile leanings, and Héraclès, champion of the Indigenous cause, unite (if only momentarily) in their joy at seeing the Americans leave Haiti.[18] Anténor tells Alice: "Les Américains vont quitter le sol haïtien. Notre drapeau flottera à nouveau seul. Regarde et souviens-toi. Ce que tu verras demain, tu pourras le raconter à tes petits-enfants" (p. 18). But the brothers' reconciliation, like the country's unification, is short lived and the old battles return. Anténor's patriotism is often compromised by the reverence he holds for a classical education. He takes pride in Alice's desire to do ballet but does not want her to receive any instruction in vodou dances for several reasons; he is afraid that Alice will be caught by the authorities in their pursuit of an Anti-Superstitious campaign[19] but there is also Anténor's own belief that the *danse* itself is *"maudite"*. His younger brother Héraclès on the other hand, who sees himself as the revolutionary, defies the authorities by taking Alice to learn about the vodou religion and its dances. A clear distinction is also made between the two brothers in their desire to educate Alice; her father tells her stories about the Greeks and Romans whilst

> Oncle Héraclès avait, quant à lui, une prédilection pour les révoltes des nègres dans le monde et aimait retracer l'épopée de l'indépendance en évoquant Dessalines, Toussaint, Christophe . . . mon père faisait le tour des constellations – la ceinture d'Orion . . . la Grande Ourse . . . – tandis qu'oncle Héraclès évoquait des lieux aux sonorités magiques – Tegucigalpa, Ouagadougou, Taj-Mahal, Mandochourie, Guadalajara. (p. 81)

Their historical and political discussions reflect similar philosophical divisions. Anténor's hope for his country's future, consistently undermined by psychological and political oppression, has destroyed any possible illusion of liberty. In another conversation he asks Héraclès to tell him one period in history when Haiti experienced "happiness". Héraclès cannot cite a time but still accuses his brother of being an old cynic. Anténor's response reflects his own sense of disillusionment and impotence, feelings that Héraclès himself will face at the end of the novel:

> Vous n'avez rien compris, mon petit Héraclès. La liberté est une illusion. Ilusion toute moderne d'ailleurs. Une nouvelle idée de quelques Blancs qui s'ennuient en Occident. Les histoires de nègres resteront toujours des histoires de nègres. (p. 110)

His words echo the notion that the *nègres* who perform this "*danse maudite*" are themselves a *race maudite*. Through the brother's fractious relationship Lahens shows the effects of these grand historical and political dramas on the life of a middle-class Haitian family and the way in which the exterior necessarily invades the interior.

WRITING SILENCES AND REVOLUTIONS

The presence of these male voices shows the silence, absence and exclusion of the female voice. The women in the novel, Alice's mother, Man Bo, Man Dia and Alice herself, never participate in these discussions. Lahens effectively uses their exclusion from these ideological debates to explore the manner in which repression and submission become part of their daily lives. Anténor's and Héraclès's questions on the collective destiny of the Haitian people form a direct contrast to the more personal stories told by Man Dia or Man Bo, or the ones that are never told by Alice's mother. It is through the silences in particular that Lahens explores their exclusion. Silence is used to expose the physical and psychological locations of repression of the women in the novel. In the case of Alice's mother, her silence reveals the inhibitions of a woman trapped in a bourgeois *comme il faut* sensibility:

> Loin des tâches conjugales et domestiques, ma mère perdait pour quelques instants le fil de cette femme qu'elle se devait de paraître, souriait avec un air espiègle comme une adolescente qui fait une fugue, comme si ce n'était plus de son âge. Une fois la danse achevée, elle chassait d'un revers de la main toutes ces pensées turbulentes et confuses et se remettait de nouveau à sa place, celle d'une femme du milieu, de la moyenne. (p. 28)

Lahens does not only use silences to show women's voicelessness amongst the men in the house but also to show the absence of communication between mother and daughter. Alice's mother tells her very little about her *féminité* apart from, "les cheveux sont la plus belle parure d'une femme. Ce furent, je crois, les seuls mots que nous échangeâmes sur la féminité". Throughout the novel, Lahens maintains the unspoken quality between mother and daughter; the mother remains protective, submissive, rooted in a bourgeois mentality, teaching her daughter how to keep secrets and silences. And yet, despite the restrictions in their relationship and the ones that the mother imposes on herself, she hopes that her daughter's life will be different from hers: "Je voudrais pour Alice tant de choses à la fois que je ne sais comment m'y prendre" (p. 43).

Lahens's treatment of the relationship between Man Bo and Alice differs from that of mother and daughter. Although Alice's *oncle* Héraclès introduces her to vodou dances, it is in the *arrière-cour,* Man Bo's territory, where Alice learns about the practice of Haitian vodou beliefs. It is also where she sees Catholic saints and *Vodou lwas* sharing the same space even though Man Bo "réservait les lwas pour ses demandes les plus secrètes et Dieu pour les causes publiques" (p. 35). Inside Alice's house there is an attempt to keep the two religions apart; in Man Bo's world they both form part of a single belief system. Man Bo and her sister Man Dia are very similar to an earlier Lahens figure, Tante Résia, from her first collection of short stories, *Tante Résia et les dieux.*[20] According to Ginette Adamson, Tante Résia represents in the short story "le patrimoine culturel puisque'elle sait préserver les coutumes, des ancêtres et la religion vaudou tout en pratiquant le catholicisme"[21] The difference between the two portraits lies in the way Tante Résia holds a privileged position in her community as "pivot de l'économie du pays et pilier aussi de la famille car les pères sont souvent irresponsables ou absents".[22] Man Bo and Man Dia never wield Tante Résia's matriarchal influence. Their tales of *mambos, hougans* or ancestral homelands, like their voices, are never heard in the main house, their powers are restricted to the *arriere-cour.* Lahens's portrait of these women is also complex; in spite of the pride they exhibit in their African heritage they too participate in the perpetuation of prejudices and gendered demarcations. Man Bo tells Alice of the importance of a straight nose that will help her "épouser un beau jeune homme et pourquoi pas un Blanc?" (p. 35). She also reinforces what Alice has already experienced at her school, that is, the benefits of "le lait à ajouter au café noir de la peau" and the difference between good hair and bad hair, "les cheveux mauvais parce que trop crépus". Man Bo also draws a clear division between men and women: "Les femmes devaient marcher, parler et rire d'une certaine façon, les hommes d'une autre" (p. 35). In fact Man Bo articulates what Alice's mother will only intimate. And yet it is her stories about the olden days, "*nan tan lontan*", that awaken Alice's imagination; their influence on Alice moves beyond the location of the *arrière-cour*. Alice becomes the agent of transition and change, negotiating the spaces of the house and the *arrière-cour*, recognizing that her Haitianness comes from both places.

In her work *Framing Silence*, Myriam Chancy examines marginalization, silencing and revolution in Haitian women's literature based on the experience of negotiating her own *Haïtiennitée*:

> I have survived annihilation, both cultural and personal, by clinging to the ves-
> tiges of creole that lie dormant in my mind and by preserving a sense of self in
> an area of my consciousness that seems untranslatable. Where I once thought
> of myself as having no identity, or as having one filled with holes, with what in
> French are referred to as *lacunes,* I have come to understand myself as operating
> out of a *culture-lacune.*[23]

The word "*lacune*" in Chancy's work, which usually connotes a negative absence in French, is transformed when linked to "*culture*" which suggests a positive presence. Her study is an attempt "to reveal the presence of a subsumed, secret, or silenced aspect of Haitian's women's history and/or culture".[24] Alice Bienaimé's revolt can be viewed through the lens of Chancy's *culture-lacune* particularly in the way that it incorporates notions of silencing, absence/presence and revolution. Man Bo and Alice's mother inform Alice's notion of the Haitian women but her own *oncle* Héraclès has also taught Alice how to use silences in her life. If the women teach Alice how to remain silent within the house, her uncle teaches her how to keep silent about her activities on the exterior. He makes her promise to keep her attendance at the vodou ceremonies a secret. Lahens allows her protagonist the most complex use of silences in the novel. They become a form of protection, an acknowledgement of powerless submission, a means of defiance and finally a form of revolt. At school, to combat the self-hatred of her teachers, "Les demoiselles Védin", she uses silence as a refuge and a fortress. Like Alice, they too are of African descent, but they pay more attention to the fairer skinned girls in the class. Alice knows that in their presence she is barely visible, even absent: "Le silence fut très tôt mon premier refuge, ma première retraite farouche et mon seul étendard. J'aimais m'y camper comme dans une forteresse, certaine d'être protégée par cette absence, cette mort momentanée des mots" (p. 40). But the most important lesson she learns from her teachers, apart from the insults, geography, grammar and whippings, is how little these lessons had to do with her "*terre natale*". The most profound lesson comes from what was not said to her, from the *lacunes* in their teachings of history:

> sous cette avalanche de mots, je compris très tôt que se cachait une autre histoire, la vraie, celle des vainqueurs et des vaincus, des conquérants et des défaits de tous les camps, celle où l'amour et la haine, le bien et le mal avaient souvent le même visage. J'y fis enfin l'apprentissage d'une deuxième société en dehors de celle de ma famille et j'y forgeai surtout mon caractère. (p. 43)

CHOREOGRAPHING REVOLUTIONS

The imposed silences in Alice's life encourage her to seek an alternative mode of expression in dance. It makes her go beyond the barriers imposed by her father, mother, Man Bo and her teachers, and transcend the many cultural stages she inhabits. It takes her into the world of ballet, vodou and modern dance, even beyond Haitian borders to New York. She affirms in dance both presence and absence, articulating in her movements spaces where she has been absent or silent. Dance becomes a creative, liberating act that brings together seemingly contradictory forces of ballet and vodou, of the classical and the traditional, of the exterior and the interior. Through dance Alice transcends the contradictions of all the ideological wars fought both inside and outside her father's house. Alice's dance also contains her history and a cultural memory. Joseph Roach's *Cities of the Dead* points to these patterns of genealogies in dance that contain and retain the cultural memory. According to Roach:

> Performance genealogies draw on the idea of expressive movements as mnemonic reserves, including patterned movements made and remembered by bodies, residual movements retained implicitly in images or words (or in the silences between them), and imaginary movements dreamed in minds, not prior to language but constitutive of it, a psychic rehearsal for physical actions drawn from a repertoire that culture provides.[25]

The description of Alice's dance seems to draw on these "mnemonic reserves" since her body appears to have an inherent self-knowledge of patterned movements. Alice realizes that just as she enters the dance, the dance also enters her and another force prevails: "Au bout d'un moment je ne danse plus, c'est la danse qui me traverse et fait battre mon sang" (p. 12).

In the novel, dance represents both loss and rebirth. Alice loses her innocence after she receives that first slap from her father. The slap is meant to silence her expression of liberation, defiance, her Africanness, her Haitianness and her emerging sexuality. And yet this act of violence does not force her to comply but instead further pushes her to pursue her creative expression. Lahens uses dance to respond to the silencing in cultural, social and historical dramas that occur both within the house and on the exterior. Dance becomes the metaphor of transition and transformation for Alice; it revolutionizes her consciousness, causing both an exile and a return. It is the articulation and manifestation of her resistance and revolt.

According to Clarisse Zimra, Yanick Lahens defines good literature as the strong commitment to style and a simplicity of form yoked to the ability to render human experience honestly, in all its fragilities and surprises. Not surprisingly, then, Lahens eschews formalist experiments for form's sake, on the one hand; and on the other, the heavy-handed ideological lessons of social realism and its distant cousin, Indigenism.[26] It is also not surprising, then, that she holds admiration for writers like Jan J. Dominique and Marie Chauvet. Lahens praises Dominique's treatment of the "contradictions of life in Haiti", in Dominique's first novel, *Mémoire d'une amnésique* (1985), particularly for a child growing up under the Duvalier regime. Lahens also admires the way "the political moves through the novel but does not overwhelm it". For Lahens both Chauvet and Dominique reveal certain realities that are absent in the works of the male Caribbean writers:

> I would say that our women plunge more directly into what makes up the day-to-day fabric of our relationships. They bring to light this historical and cultural dimension that is usually kept hidden. Such things can be seen clearly in Chauvet's work, in Dominique's as well: and, because of it, they achieve a much stronger denunciation. As for our men, however talented they may be, they are still hiding behind great theoretical screens, lofty philosophical positions.[27]

Lahens's first novel reflects her critical appreciation of writers like Chauvet and Dominique. She is also not the kind of writer who will take "the short cut of a political agenda in order to explain everything".[28] *Dans la maison du père,* through its silences and *lacunes,* insists on the inability to find all the answers in "isms". Form and function are closely linked to Lahens's own ideological concerns and her creative response to them. Having lived through the dictatorship years and the post-1986 Haiti, political concerns inform her creative and theoretical writings. Lahens's two short story collections *Tante Résia et les dieux* (1994) and

La petite corruption (1999), show the effects of political repression on Haitians. Similarly, *Dans la maison du père* moves through decades of political repression and persecutions in Haiti; the historical events and atrocities are marked but Lahens's treatment is never "heavy-handed" in showing the links between the collective psyche and the Bienaimé household. She focuses on the manner in which the historical dramas are played out on the private stage and as such is able to explore the interior dramas of her protagonist.

Lahens does not write extensively about the effects of the American occupation but the reaction to the Americans' departure suggests the oppressive weight of their presence on Haitians. However for Lahens neither adherence to francophile ideas (Anténor) nor the valourization of *Indigénisme* (Héraclès) offers a response to years of oppression from the American occupation or successive political regimes. In the novel, the play between interior and exterior is continually explored to reveal the complexity of the relationship, to expose the questions, to exploit the possibilities of the creative process and to find a balance between public and private worlds. As Lahens states:

> On résout des questions dans l'écriture; elles sont liées à la langue, à la sociologie, à l'histoire, à la mémoire. Il faut seulement trouver les mots pour le dire: l'écriture doit être un espace ludique, une halte provisoire, le bonheur d'avoir trouvé les mots qui disent – après la douleur – ce que l'on cherche à dire. Quand j'écris, je ne cherche pas à retrouver des scènes d'ordre visuel; je veux trouver l'équilibre entre l'univers privé et l'univers public.[29]

Just as Alice, through dance, negotiates and performs on several stages, so too does Lahens, in her writings, bridge divisions between inside and outside, recognizing that permanent negotiation between herself and her environment, between the "I" and the "we".

Before Alice leaves for New York she comes to recognize that a profound transformation has taken place; where once her father sought to protect (and control) her, she now feels "*la plus forte*". This transfer of power on the psychological level also manifests itself on the physical; at the end of the novel with her father's passing Alice will now reinhabit her father's house with her daughter. Through Alice's experiences Lahens reconstructs and delineates a memory of revolution. The revolution is quiet, personal, on an individual rather than a collective level, expressed through the metaphor of dance. Alice's dance performs acts of resistance against political oppression, it destabilizes the household, exposes reductive polemical debates, transforms a consciousness and liberates. In the end, her dance, like the novel *Dans la maison du père*, becomes performances of the imagination that articulate revolution.

Notes

1. Yanick Lahens, *Dans la maison du père* (Paris: Éditions du Seuil, 2000).

2. Michael Dash recognizes Aimé Césaire as the first Caribbean writer to consciously examine the notion of the subject as a disembodied self, seeking incarnation. For Césaire the subject was not privileged but simply the site where the collective experience found articulation. See J. Michael Dash, introduction to *Caribbean Discourse*, by Édouard Glissant, trans. J. Michael Dash (University Press of Virginia, 1999), xiii–xiv.

3. The phrase is taken from Yanick Lahens's essay "L'Exil: entre l'ancrage et la fuite, l'écrivain haïtien" (Port-au-Prince: Éditions L'Harmattan, 1994). In the essay she looks at both internal and external exile faced by the Haitian writer. This chapter will draw on Lahens's construct of exile to show how it is used in her novel, *Dans la maison du père*.

4. Lahens herself has written extensively on the work of Haitian writer Marie Chauvet, whom Lahens believes opened the way for the modern novel in Haiti. See Clarisse Zimra, "Haitian Literature after Duvalier: An Interview with Yanick Lahens", *Callaloo* 16, no. 1 (1993): 77–93.

5. Lahens, quoted in Anne Marty, *Haïti en littérature* (Paris: Maison Neuve and Larose, 2000).

6. Edwidge Danticat, *Breath, Eyes, Memory* (New York: Vintage, 1994).

7. Ibid., 236.

8. Marie-Denise Shelton, *Caribbean Women Writers*, ed. Selwyn R. Cudjoe (Wellesley, Mass.: Calaloux, 1990).

9. See *Callaloo* 15, no. 2 (1992): 442. In this interview Lahens discusses Condé's contribution to the study of the Caribbean writer's use of the "I". See also Simone Schwarz-Bart, *Pluie et vent sur Télumée-Miracle* (Paris: Éditions du Seuil, 1972); and Maryse Condé, *La parole des femmes, essai sur des romancières des Antilles de langue française* (Paris: Éditions L'Harmattan, 1979).

10. Kitzie McKinney, "Memory, Voice, and Metaphor in the Works of Simone Schwarz-Bart", in *Postcolonial Subjects*, ed. Mary Jean Green, et al. (Minneapolis: University of Minnesota Press, 1996), 22–39.

11. Ibid., 27, quoting Ronnie Scharfman.

12. Édouard Glissant sees a clear link between individual activism and collective destiny. For Glissant the writer's "I" cannot speak for the collective from a position of elevated, exteriorized omniscience. Particularly in the case of Martinique's political and cultural context, the writer's location within the collective reflects the state of dispossession and dependency. And Glissant, like Fanon in *Peau noire, masques blancs*, exposes

the central problematic of the dissociated Martiniquan self. (See Dash, introduction to *Caribbean Discourse,* xxiii.)

13. Yanick Lahens, "Exile: Between Writing and Place", trans. Mohamed B. Taleb-Khyar, *Callaloo* 15, no. 2 (1992): 442.

14. J. Michael Dash, *Culture and Customs of Haiti* (Westport, Conn.: Greenwood Press, 2001).

15. Zimra, "Haitian Literature after Duvalier", 80.

16. Yanick Lahens, *Dans la maison du père,* 12. Subsequent references to this work appear parenthetically in this chapter.

17. In his essay "The Muse of History", Derek Walcott compares the writing of history to that of writing fiction. He states, "the method by which we are taught the past, the progress from motive to event, is the same by which we read narrative fiction". For Walcott, both narratives are selective, "subject to invention", and draw on a fitful muse: "History is fiction, subject to a fitful muse, memory." See Derek Walcott, "The Muse of History" (1974; reprint in *What the Twilight Says* [London: Faber and Faber, 1998], 36–64).

18. This unification of the brothers was typical of the time. As Dash states, "the United States in the nineteen years of the occupation managed to do what no Haitian president had been able to do: unite the elite across the color divide". See Dash, *Culture and Customs of Haiti,* 15.

19. The Anti-Superstitious Campaign – In the early 1940s the conflict between the defenders of Catholicism and of vodou became particularly bitter because of the Catholic Church's campaign against vodou, which was conducted with the support of mulatto president, Élie Lescot. Lescot declared, soon after his election in 1941, his government's support for Catholicism. This was seen as explicit support for the Catholic Church's campaign to rid Haiti of what was called the cult of Satan. The collapse of the Catholic Church's campaign against vodou in 1942 was seen as an early victory for the pro-vodou nationalist opposition that would dominate Haitian politics after Francois Duvalier became president. See Dash, *Culture and Customs of Haiti,* 54.

20. Yanick Lahens, *Tante Résia et les dieux* (Paris: Éditions L'Harmattan, 1994).

21. Ginette Adamson, "Yanick Lahens romancière: Pour une autre voix/voie haïtienne", in *Elles ecrivent des Antilles* (Haïti, Guadeloupe, Martinique), ed. Susanne Rinne and Joëlle Vitiello (Paris: Éditions L'Harmattan, 1997), 107–17.

22. Ibid., 113.

23. Myriam J.A. Chancy, *Framing Silence: Revolutionary Novels by Haitian Women* (New Brunswick, NJ: Rutgers University Press, 1997).

24. Ibid., 17.

25. Joseph Roach, *Cities of the Dead* (New York: Columbia University Press, 1996).

26. Zimra, "Haitian Literature after Duvalier", 78.

27. Ibid., 86.

28. In her interview in *Callaloo,* Lahens uses this phrase to describe *Terminus Floride* by Russell Banks; she sees his style "as unaffectedly simple . . . so that politics are there but only obliquely". Lahens's treatment of political issues in the novel can be characterized in a similar manner. See *Callaloo* 15, no. 2 (1992): 91.

29. Yanick Lahens, quoted in Marty, *Haïti en littérature,* 205.

Chapter 5

Edwidge Danticat's *The Farming of Bones*
Traumatic Memories and the Translucent Narrator

Mireille Rosello

History and parsley, what an odd combination after all . . . A common herb used in so many recipes, found in so many gardens around the world, in so many humble markets, in the richest and poorest kitchens. Until I read Edwidge Danticat's novel, parsley evoked only ordinariness and home, however home may be described these days. History, on the other hand? How does one begin to describe its power and complexity? How does one get past the majesty of the capital *H*? In *The Farming of Bones,* the bizarre encounter between History and parsley is transformed into a sumptuous poetic elegy for the Haitian victims of the 1937 massacre. The alchemy is obtained through the remarkable combination of the author's mastery of narrative techniques and her unique desire for a certain type of history. In one of the most striking passages in her second novel, Danticat writes:

> The young toughs waved parsley sprigs in front of our faces. "Tell us what it is," one said. "Que diga perejil." At that moment, I did believe that *had I wanted to,* I could have said the word properly, calmly, slowly, the way I often asked "Perejil?" of the old Dominican women and their faithful attending granddaughters at the roadside garden and markets, even though the trill of the *r* and the precision of the *j* was sometimes too burdensome a joining for my tongue. It was the kind of thing that if you were startled in the night, you might forget, but with my senses calm, I believe I could have said it. *But I didn't get my chance.* Yves and I were shoved down onto our knees. Our jaws were pried open and parsley was stuffed into our mouths.[1]

Like Amabelle Désir, I now wonder if, "given a chance", I could or could not say "*perejil*" to save my life. And the "if" is the story's gift. For I share, with all the readers of Danticat's novel, a luxury that the narrator and protagonist did not have, and that the story makes me understand. I am in a position to ask myself, safely, whether or not I *could* pronounce a word in a certain way. I experience this moment from a place where I do not *have* to speak, where I can wonder. I can retreat to the theoretical safety of imaginary hypotheses: I can tell myself that "*if* I wanted to", I would, or not, be able to say "parsley" like the "old Dominican women". I am also reminded that the freedom to make such hypotheses is a position that the speaking subject does not always have, that Amabelle and Yves did not have when they were attacked by "thugs". It made them victims, silent victims.

As readers, we are allowed to inhabit a unique space, where detailed historical knowledge – not (supposedly blissful) ignorance – goes together with the possibility of constructing a safe place from which to remember and honour the memory of the dead and acknowledge the broken lives of those who survived. I wish to argue that this text is about the crafting of a unique positioning, that the narrative helps us, non-witnesses, conceptualize and imagine.

At one level of course, the episode in which characters are forced to pronounce a word that exposes their (supposedly foreign) accent will sound like a familiar unit of narrative plot: Yves and Amabelle are confronted with a typical ordeal that the epigraph of the novel, a quote from Judges (12:4–6), explicitly compares to the biblical Shibboleth. As readers, we may know a lot about such structures of violence and the connections that they force us to make between belonging, identity and language. We may have read Derrida's essay, we may already be aware of the terrible risk that is involved in falling into the hands of people determined to violently police any border. But this passage is more than a variation on the familiar issues raised by a Shibboleth-type situation. Here, the word "*perejil*" was, precisely, never pronounced. The object that it designates, the humble referent that the words "parsley" or "*perejil*" or "*pèsi*" stand for and exclude, is here used as a weapon. Real parsley literally takes the place of words when it is shoved into the victim's body, where language should have been. Parsley can now hurt and disfigure, smother the characters.

On the other hand, once the protagonist has managed to become the narrator of the tale after having survived the ordeal, she can express the thoughts silenced by the presence of parsley in her mouth. I suggest that the safe, yet uncomfortable, place created by the novel resembles the fleeting moment during which Amabelle reflects on what it means to use language in the context of a test. Although the men who attack don't give her "a chance" to even pronounce the word, they cannot stop her from thinking. In the text she does not utter a word, and yet, she does much more in a sense: she develops an argument in which she contests the notion that an accent is fixed forever, like an identity. She suggests that *sometimes* she is able to pronounce the words "properly, calmly, slowly". In the story, she cannot articulate the idea but the novel is that chance to talk *about* parsley, historically, without violence.

In *The Farming of Bones,* History is not about the original moment of glorious rebellion that turned Haiti into the country where "negritude rose for the first time".[2] It is not about liberation and nationhood, not even about the dangers that await the liberator or the ambiguities of any violent movement. Unlike classic plays such as Aimé Césaire's *La Tragédie du roi Christophe,* it does not purport to warn readers that the struggle for freedom is often threatened by the ghosts of mimicry and corruption, and can be retrospectively read as the first act of "the unending tragedy that is Haitian history",[3] or more pessimistically, as part of what Jacqueline Brice-Finch calls a "serial territorial carnage".[4]

If Danticat's novel belongs in a collection of essays whose publication is meant to coincide with the anniversary of the foundational event of the Haitian nation it is, paradoxically, because the novel implicitly refuses to automatically embrace the logic of commemorations. Less paradoxically, its presence is also justified by the author's exploration of a unique figure: a type of witness-narrator whose storytelling techniques are directly inspired by the catastrophe it seeks to memorialize, a figure that I call here the "translucent narrator".

At one level, Danticat's *The Farming of Bones* is a much more obviously "historical" text than her previous *Breath, Eyes and Memory,* a (partially) autobiographical account focusing on recently immigrated Haitian-Americans. In her second novel, the story is set in the island shared by Haiti and the Dominican Republic and goes back in time to the horrifying events of 1937. *The Farming of Bones* is bound to teach any reader something that he or she did not know about what happened on the border between Haiti and the Dominican Republic when its dictator Trujillo orchestrated the massacre of thousands of Haitians who lived on the Dominican side of the northern border. It is not inaccurate to describe Danticat's story as a narration about what historians and witnesses still frequently refer to as "*el corte*" (the cutting) in Spanish or as *kout kouto* (the stabbing) in Creole. At the same time, it may be more relevant to point out that this "historical" novel draws our attention to the historicizing process itself as the subject of the tale. It is marked by its own inscription within a historical moment that has reinvented history as a discourse. Just as Césaire was both inspired by and an inspiration to surrealist thinking,[5] Danticat is a writer whose relationship with History has developed at a moment during which History itself has been reaching new conclusions about its own disciplinary practices and tactics. Not surprisingly, several aspects of this story turn the text into a historical novel about the impossibility of believing in the telling of national history rather than about a specific historical event.

First, *The Farming of Bones* can hardly be included in a list of epic celebrations of great national victories: it tells the story of a non-battle that no side wishes to claim, that no one can interpret as a victory in a war of liberation. The novel does not seek, for example, to name an event and change its historical valence. Unlike historians and novelists who, for example, insisted on using the word "war" when the French insisted on viewing the Algerian conflict as "*événements*", unlike contemporary journalists who must decide to refer to guerrilla warfare as terrorism or as the struggle carried out by freedom fighters, Danticat does not choose between two national logics and her novel refuses to take sides or even to identify two peoples and construct them as enemies. *The Farming of Bones* talks about senseless violence without trying to look for historical causes, to identify warning signs leading to the massacre.

My point is not to oppose professional historians and writers of fiction from a perspective that would simplify the quest for the truth. Just as novelists have become sensitive to the status of history as a discourse, contemporary historians are sophisticated storytellers and literary critics who pay attention to the crafting of written or verbal testimonies, to the ethics of the discipline. Within the novel, the question of official history and of the uses that can be made of people's testimonies is raised several times. Danticat's survivors are both ordinary people and sophisticated witnesses who are afraid that their tales will be re-appropriated and twisted: "You tell the story, and then it's retold as they wish, written in words that you do not understand, in a language that is theirs, and not yours."[6] They seem to know that there is a profound difference between people who let you talk and people who listen. When the government starts collecting testimonies, the process is frustrating, fragmented and incomplete: "Tomorrow, listen faster"[7] recommends one witness, angered by the justice of the peace's decision to stop for the day. Finally, the character of the crazy professor wandering by the river at the end adequately represents ordinary people's suspicion that academic history is mad.

On the other hand, contemporary academic historians share many of Danticat's preoccupations and narrative tactics.[8] Among scholars whose works best exemplify academics' attention to historiography are Lauren Derby and Richard Turits, whose perspective is remarkably similar to Danticat's. Like her, they are interested in the point of the view of the victims of the massacre and they have interviewed what we think of as ordinary people.[9] But if one had to explain the difference between professional histories and fictive testimonials using Danticat's text and their work, the most obvious distinction would be that they are defending a thesis and passionately trying to put an end to what they see as a "misconstruction"[10] and a misrepresentation of the function played by the border between two nations.

Their thesis is that Trujillo did not so much exploit previous anti-Haitian sentiments. Instead, the 1937 massacre was used to persuade both Dominicans and Haitians that anti-Haitianism pre-existed the attack. It was then easier to rationalize the violence as a reaction to a phenomenon that was described as an invasion (the so-called pacific invasion by Haitians). They also argue that the myth of prevalent anti-Haitian hostility among Dominicans was later used as one of the key concepts in the creation of the nation: "tanto en la memoria oficialmente promulgada como en la memoria popular, el antihaitianismo se ha convertido en un elemento incuestionable y aplicable a los Dominicanos de todos los tiempos".[11] Paradoxically then, the border as dividing line was created by the Massacre whereas before the event, the area was constructed as a border zone where a border people came and went, and where individuals interacted. According to the picture meticulously painted by Turits in "A World Destroyed, a Nation Imposed", the "world" of the border was a multifaceted community where religious and ethnic, linguistic and economic differences were perceptible, where frictions and stereotypes also existed, but where the opposition between Haitians and Dominicans could in no way produce the kind of violence that was later unleashed by the state and its soldiers.[12]

The novelist's intention, then, is comparable to those new historicists who try to "find a voice for the victimized" (as Goldblatt puts it)[13] and counteract the effect of official histories. But Danticat, of her own admission, had no intention to "make this a history lesson"[14] and the specific contribution of this novel is elsewhere. For, if *The Farming of Bones* does not defend a strictly speaking historical thesis, it does make a narratological proposal that has everything to do with the practice of historiography. I would also argue that Danticat's text constitutes a decisive literary response to the traditional manner in which print culture transmits the legacy of historical events and celebrates (or criticizes) national heroes. As April Shemak notes in her essay, Amabelle belongs in a long and distinguished list of Caribbean "fictional testimonios": she is "a narrator who serves as an eyewitness to acts of brutal oppression. Often these fictional testimonios represent actual historical events, but challenge existing histories through their representations."[15] But as she also points out, *The Farming of Bones* slightly disrupts the generic convention of the testimonio and therefore comments on its effectiveness: "I argue," Shemak writes, "that because testimonials in the novel are often fragmented and at times silenced, the novel critiques the revolutionary potential of testimonio."[16] I would add that Danticat's first-person narrator is not greatly interested in any "revolutionary" potential but rather in trying to invent a new practice of storytelling, the only type of storytelling that enables her to talk both about what happened to her and about the difficulties of testifying.[17] Amabelle barely survived a massacre, lost her lover Sebastien, and must reconceptualize her own relationship to storytelling and to history before coming to terms with the past. The novel as a whole reflects her desire by offering us an exemplary narrator and a metaphorical trope of historical writing that, if I had to name it, I could call "translucidity". Translucidity is Amabelle's unique talent. It is the privileged mode of this translucent narrator.

A translucent narrator is someone who, like Amabelle, is both in and out of the water, or rather, whose story will vary depending on from where she speaks. Her being inside or outside the current is linked to safety and danger but in very ambiguous ways and, much more crucially, determines what kind of light she exudes, that is, what type of narrative she is able to produce. The reference to "translucence" appears right at the beginning of the novel, long before we find out that this story is about a border, a river and a massacre. Translucence is immediately connected to the idea that Amabelle's tale can only be interpreted and understood by a very specific type of audience: in its very first pages, *The Farming of Bones* suggests that traumatic memories and the past in general speak in ways that modify the account that the subject can generate. The bodies of the witness and of the loving presence that watches over her during her agitated sleep are both affected. In the novel, Sebastien is that person who can perceive a special type of light, the sort of ambivalent radiance that Amabelle's historical narrative becomes to others. The translucent narrative, when heard by the right kind of reader, guarantees Amabelle's existence and survival:

I am afraid I cease to exist when he's not there. I'm like one of those sea stones that sucks its colors inside and loses its translucence once it's taken out into the sun out of the froth of the waves. When he's not there, I'm afraid I know no one and no one knows me.[18]

From then on, the novel slowly teaches the reader about the characteristics of a translucent narrative, mainly by drawing our attention to the omnipresence of the river as a site of both origin and fundamental ambivalence. For Amabelle, the river is a primal scene, the place where a tragic drama unfolded while she was still a little girl. At first we learn that most nights, the narrator has "her" nightmare, "the one I have all the time, of my parents drowning"[19]. The first page of the book is about a traumatic event but it will turn out to be a personal memory rather than a reference to the massacre although the river is already at the centre of the crisis: Amabelle lost both her parents when they drowned, trying to cross into Dajabon, on the Dominican side. They died in that river in front of her when she was a child and she was left alone, by the current, on the Dominican side of what then constituted a relatively porous border. Her parents were not trying to immigrate, just to buy pots from a renowned Haitian pot-maker who lived on the other side. After their death, she becomes an orphan and is *de facto* exiled but she cannot really be described as an immigrant. The river was not a dangerous political border and unlike the heroes of "Children of the Sea" in an earlier collection of short stories, the parents are not boat people whose bodies and fictive testimonies will be swallowed by the ocean.[20]

Amabelle was found by the river by her future employer, Señora Valencia, who had come to that space for a reason that, in retrospect, can be interpreted as the encounter between History as read in books and history as "seen" by the witness's own eyes. She wanted to take a look at the Massacre River that her history books taught her about: "I told Papi I wanted to see the Massacre River where the French buccaneers were killed by the Spaniards in my history lesson."[21] The "lesson" tells a tale of war, draws a border between two people and talks about those who killed and those who were killed. A vague sense that history could, as the saying goes, repeat itself, and that the name of the river is prophetic is tentatively put forward. But I would argue that the meeting with the child of the river immediately cancels the proposal and replaces the history lesson with another type of historical narrative inspired by other visions and ideologies.

The explanation for the name "massacre" appears in history books; it is something that Señora Valencia learned at school. Later, she uses this knowledge as the opportunity for a (field or research) trip, but her apparently intellectual curiosity then leads to the meeting with the border child whom she will bring back to her house as a servant. Like the fabulous characters who live by and in rivers in Caribbean folktales, the little girl who stays by the water where her parents drowned is a child of the river, as if her origin was what others want to see as a dividing line between two nations. Her muse, and her alter ego or model, "the goddess of this story", writes Danticat, "is the Metrès Dlo, the female spirit of the river, to whom Amabelle dedicates and tells the story".[22] She is from the place that, marking the division, can only be the very symbol of ambivalence, of proximity and division, separation and reunion.

> "You were sitting on a big rock, watching the water as if you were waiting for an apparition. Papi paid one of the boys by the riverside to interpret for him while he asked you who you belonged to. And you pointed to your chest and said, yourself. Do you remember?"
> I remembered.[23]

Being from the river frees the little girl from types of belonging that have to do with nationalities and territory but this also comes at a terrible price. This ambivalent positioning makes her a perfect metaphor for what Danticat claims she wants to explore in her texts. She calls "uncomfortable places" those junctures where no simple loyalty to one's own (kind, people, nation) can be articulated. Betrayals, but also unexpected alliances, are always possible within and between Haitians and Dominicans, at the lowest and highest level. In an interview with Renée Shea, she states:

> I think there are uncomfortable spaces in all my stories. That's where people often go to war with you, you know, the folks from your own side. There are always uncomfortable spaces in these types of stories. For example, the fact that Africans sold other Africans to the Europeans during the slave trade is an uncomfortable space, because you have to acknowledge the fact that part of this horrendous story involves also being betrayed by people who are more like you than the people they're selling you to.[24]

The uncomfortable place is where "sides" make no sense, where moving to the other shore provides no relief, and where roots are useless because the community of origin cannot be expected to be of help:

One of the uncomfortable spaces in the story is that there was a contract between the Duvaliers and the sugar interests in the Dominican Republic, and a certain number of people were basically traded to work there . . . our government was complicit in turning our own people over, basically selling them into slavery all over again.[25]

This uncomfortable place is where Amabelle speaks from when she accepts her status as translucent narrator. It is symbolized by the impossibility of being from one place, or in one place exclusively, of being one and one to oneself. Like the changing stone, the translucent narrator is double – or rather ubiquitous – and capable of being in different places at the same time. It has a double existence or rather the complex presence of the translucent stone. It is both opaque and silent if taken out of the water and capable of radiating its inner light if immersed. The translucent stone thus provides Amabelle with a model and a metaphor of desirable ubiquity: this is not the heroic ubiquity of the male warrior[26] but the existence of the witness who must be able to be in different places in order to survive. At times, Amabelle must move away from the dangerous border (step out of the river) but she must also retain her intimate connection with the border people (be immersed) in order to turn the trauma of unspeakable nightmares into the type of poetic historical account that is offered in *The Farming of Bones*.

The very first lines of the novel describe the past as a "nightmare": a memory that comes at night, uninvited, that traumatizes and hurts repetitively, obsessively. Already, our attention is drawn to the way in which the past manifests itself: the novel tells us what happened but its most obvious emphasis is always on the process by which the past and the present talk to each other. *The Farming of Bones* is about how the remembering starts, or stops, of what memory and memories do to the protagonists' bodies and souls. Recollection and the transmission of historical events are not (only) a deliberate and conscious decision that is then written up. The story focuses instead on the infinitely complex process of remembering. The difficulty is to record the nature of this act of looking back, its complexities and the evolution that occurs as Amabelle, the heroine of the story, slowly comes to terms with the best way of surviving as a witness. At first, then, the character is victimized by her own nightmares rather than nurtured by her dreams, she is hurt by her own body that channels the memories in a way that paralyses and destabilizes her: we see her "lurch at [Sebastien] and stumble, trying to rise".[27] But those uncomfortable spaces are also the places where history starts radiating because Amabelle's body emits a sort of light that others can see, recognize and understand thanks to Sebastien who makes her body legible. He explains a phenomenon made of contradictory signals: life and death, light and darkness, fire and ashes: "You are glowing like a Christmas lantern, even with this skin that is the color of driftwood ashes in the rain."[28] He is the benevolent listener who allows the narrator to learn how to talk and to mix desire for him and the desire to tell him about her. He is "just a deep echo".[29]

The structure of the text replicates the character's evolution, her changing relationship to her own dreams and nightmares. As result, the whole novel is characterized by fragmentation and interruption. At the beginning, a very systematic pattern suggests the regular oscillation between two different realms. At first, it is tempting to interpret the two types of writing as a symbolic representation of the difference between night and day, dreams and reality. The font is different, and so are the tone and the atmosphere. The first chapter, in bold face, talks about a recurrent nightmare and of the narrator's relationship to Sebastien, her lover, who helps her cope with the traumatic memories of her parents' drowning. It is immediately interrupted by a linear narrative that takes place in the Dominican Republic, before the massacre. Until we reach chapter 25, we get used to that pendulum: one chapter is told in the present and Sebastien is with her. These passages are characterized by their dreamlike and relatively peaceful atmosphere. The next chapter is then written in the past tense, and the series of events slowly form a story that includes Sebastien's disappearance and Amabelle's failure to ever find him again. In odd-numbered chapters, Sebastien is present, but like a ghost. In even-numbered chapters, Amabelle tells the story of how she first came to be in the Dominican Republic, of how she had to flee and how she lost Sebastien. As the novel unfolds, the even chapters become longer and longer, whereas the interruptions of the nightmares or dreams remain very short, sometimes not even one page long. As the violence escalates, the distinction between nightmares and reality loses its relevance: the story, which has become a nightmarish reality, takes over for several chapters and culminates in chapter 30 where Amabelle recalls how she almost died. Twice the text repeats, "She's not going to live",[30] and the narrator explains that she thought that the doctor referred to her. And when she closes her eyes as if to let the (false) diagnosis take its course, a last "dream" sequence proposes an alternative to Amabelle's fear: her mother, now indistinguishable from "the mother spirit of the rivers",[31] offers a version that will save her daughter's life because it persuades her that she was never abandoned, that she was always loved and that death was never an option: "You were never truly dying, my precious imbecile," she says.[32] This direct intervention of the mother's version of what happened contributes to blur the distinction between what Renée Shea calls "linear narratives and poetic dream sequences":[33] the relationship to the past and what history (including the story of one's dreams) means can be readjusted as Amabelle comes of age as a storyteller and slowly comes to terms with the loss of Sebastien and the possibility of survival and commemoration through a certain type of narrative. While violence turned words into parsley when she was attacked and forced to eat mouthfuls of it, Sebastien's absence is slowly and magically turned into the story of his disappearance:

> Accepting that Sebastien will never return and that she will never share a family with him, she understands that her legacy will be her story of the slaughter of their country's people by the duplicitous dictator Trujillo . . . What remains are the haunting words of love unfulfilled and the story of persecution that will endure, preserving, at least on paper, the yearning of two lovers.[34]

A translucent narrative could thus be defined as a type of historical narrative that provides storyteller and audience with a practice of historical translucidity. The light that is normally associated with truth and clarity is not completely abandoned here: and yet, it is a certain type of light. The story retains a certain amount of opacity, and the lucidity of the immersed stone has nothing to do with Cartesian images of clarity. The poetic image of a translucent stone that is both opaque and radiant only under specific local circumstances elegantly combines the values that we normally associate with lucidity and all the connotations attached to the prefix *trans,* which, recently, has been used to refer to diasporic movements and almost replaced postcolonial thinking: the translucent narrator could be said to have internalized the type of hybridity that historians who examine transnational people and border people can only explain. Amabelle's translucidity comes from the possibility of being part of a system that is in flux, and over which she has little control. She is speaking from a place within a river whose flow can kill, can symbolize division as well as unity, but whose ambivalent water endows the stone with a radiance synonymous with memorial energy.

The stone is embellished but not changed by its stay in the river: this is no discourse on identity; the river flows over and around her, not through her, for example, and the change that occurs does not have to do with her nature (she is not infiltrated by the water; this is not about integration). Rather, the way in which she appears to others is changed: she is now translucent, she radiates, she exudes light and memories. The effectiveness of her testimonial depends on our perception of a certain quality of light.

At the end of the novel, Amabelle goes back to the river and lies down in it, physically adopting the position of the stone at the bottom of the current, where dreams, nightmares, history and storytelling become indistinguishable because the body of the narrator, even though it has become a "marred testament",[35] can both survive and testify.

> The water was warm for October, warm and shallow, so shallow that I could lie on my back in it with my shoulders only half submerged, the current floating over me in a less than gentle caress, the pebbles in the riverbed scouring my back.
>
> I looked to my dreams for softness, for a gentler embrace, for relief from the fear of mudslides and blood bubbling out of the riverbed, where it is said the dead add their tears to the river flow.
>
> The professor returned to look down at me lying there, cradled by the current, paddling like a newborn in a washbasin. He turned and walked away . . . [36]

The water has not miraculously turned into a gentle creek, it continues to be associated with real and imagined dangers, natural and historical catastrophes. The river is about "mudslides and blood" and the current is still an ambiguously uncomfortable zone: it is a caress, but the caress is "less than gentle". In order for the experience to be a soothing and healing moment, Amabelle must accept the discomfort, must combine the river and her dreams, she must let her body experience the "scouring" of the pebbles while her dreams tell the story of drowned victims and finally mix "tears" and "blood" in a way that provides a sort of imaginary rebirth in a metaphorical "washbasin". The transformation of the river into a harmless tub where the baby-like heroine is cleansed would probably read like a relatively simple motif of childish regression were it not for the fact that it can only happen when the "professor" is a witness.

This enigmatic and lonely figure, that the villagers have nicknamed "Professor" reminds us that some types of academic knowledge and historical narratives are discredited except as silent witnesses who eventually "turn and walk away"[37] like the "pwofessè" whose name is "the replacement for 'crazy man' that he had been given".[38] As Danticat puts it in her interview with Renée Shea, that character is "a ghost, a reminder of the past, a different kind of survivor".[39] He is the "guardian of a very painful crossroad" even if he cannot make sense of it.

At the end of the tale, Amabelle has reconstructed her own life as a story that starts near the river and ends in it and her trajectory has taught her how to live in or by the river rather than to cross it safely. Two possible consequences of the massacre now appear equally undesirable: silence but also certain types of narratives. Clearly, the victims' story should be heard but perhaps, like Amabelle's own testimony, they could come from a place where people are not bound to national histories. Even the border is not a utopian space comparable to the other two territories and that would become a third though unrecognized nation. Her challenge is to tell the story from the bottom of the river without having this story be the terrifying nightmare of uncontrollable flow of words that continue to hurt rather than to heal. By deciding to lie down at the bottom of the river, Amabelle embraces the danger of positioning herself in the only place from which she can tell the story translucidly: the bed of the river.

ACKNOWLEDGEMENTS

Thank you to Robin Derby for sharing articles and references and for her precious comments on an earlier version of this chapter. Thank you to Bradley Reichek for his assistance at the editing stage.

NOTES

1. Edwidge Danticat, *The Farming of Bones* (New York: Soho Press, 1998), 193 (emphasis added).

2. Aimé Césaire, *Notebook of a Return to the Native Land,* in *Césaire: The Collected Poetry,* trans. Clayton Eshleman and Annette Smith (Berkeley and Los Angeles: University of California Press, 1983), 32–85.

3. Ethan Casey, "Remembering Haiti", *Callaloo* 18, no. 2 (1995): 524.

4. Jacqueline Brice-Finch, "Edwidge Danticat: Memories of a Maäfa", *MaComère* 4 (2001): 147.

5. Michael Dash, *The Other America: Caribbean Literature in a New World Context* (Charlottesville: University Press of Virginia, 1998).

6. Danticat, *Farming,* 246.

7. Ibid., 233.

8. For a rich survey of the different theses elaborated by historians, see Brice-Finch's "Edwidge Danticat: Memories of a Maäfa". She compares passages from Danticat and historical sources, emphasizing areas of overlap and discrepancy. She also emphasizes the differences between several historical analyses of how Dominicans and Haitians perceived their

own identity before and after the Massacre. See her summaries of Alan Belén Cambeira, "Historical and Cultural Connections: La République d'Haïti and La República Dominicana", *Creole Connection* 5, no. 2 (April–June 1999): 4–6; Michele Wucker, "The River Massacre: The Real and Imagined Borders of Hispaniola", *Creole Connection* 5, no. 2 (April–June 1999): 7–9; and Lauren Derby, "Temwayaj Kout Kouto, 1937: Eyewitnesses to the Genocide", *Creole Connection* 5, no. 3, issue 18 (1999): 5–10.

9. Derby, "Temwayaj Kout Kouto, 1937", 5–9.

10. Richard Lee Turits, "A World Destroyed, a Nation Imposed: The 1937 Haitian Massacre in the Dominican Republic", *Hispanic American Historical Review* 82, no. 3 (2002): 593.

11. Derby and Turits, "Historias de Terror y Los Terrores de la Historia: La Masacre Haitiana de 1937 en La Republica Dominicana", trans. Eugenio Rivas, S. J. and Mario Alberto Torres, *Estudios Sociales* 92 (April-June 1993): 65.

12. See Turits, "A World Destroyed, a Nation Imposed".

13. Patricia Goldblatt, "Finding a Voice for the Victimized", *MultiCultural Review* 9, no. 3: (September 2000): 40–47.

14. Zoë Anglesey, "The Voice of the Storytellers: An Interview with Edwidge Danticat", *MultiCultural Review* 7, no. 3 (September 1998): 36–39, 39.

15. April Shemak, "Re-membering Hispaniola: Edwidge Danticat's *The Farming of Bones*", *Modern Fiction Studies* 48, no. 1 (2002): 84.

16. Ibid., 86.

17. See Supriya Nair, "Diasporic Roots: Imagining a Nation in Earl Lovelace's *Salt*", *South Atlantic Quarterly* 100, no. 1 (2001): 259–85, on the different literary tropes and "tactical choices" (n24) that inspired Caribbean authors who imagine ways of writing the history of Caribbean islands torn by violence and tragedy. The author compares Derek Walcott's *The Antilles: Fragments of Epic Memory* (New York: Farrar, Straus and Giroux, 1993) and Antonio Benítez-Rojo's *The Repeating Island: The Caribbean and the Postmodern Perspective,* trans. James E. Maraniss (Durham, NC: Duke University Press, 1992). Walcott's favorite image is that of a poet "lovingly gluing together the fragments of national and continental cultures. But the glue only accentuates more vividly the 'white scars' of the reassembled vase, so that the whole is never quite a seamless reintegration of its broken parts" (p. 263) whereas Benítez-Rojo has a recurrent vision of Europe and the islands linked by suppurating wounds due to the "aftermath of rape and new birth" (p. 5).

18. Danticat, *Farming,* 2.

19. Ibid., 1.

20. In "Children of the Sea", before the boat sinks, the notebook that tells the story disappears into the sea with the characters. For a text that equates the loss of the story with abortion and suggests a link with other short stories in the collection, see Andrée-Anne Kekeh-Dika, "Entre ville et village: Quelles destinées pour le féminin chez Edwidge Danticat?" in *La Ville plurielle dans la fiction antillaise anglophone: Images de l'interculturel,* ed. Corinne Duboin and Eric Tabuteau (Toulouse, France: Presses Universitaires du Mirail, 2000), 59–67.

21. Danticat, *Farming*, 91.

22. In an interview with Renée Shea, " 'The Hunger to Tell': Edwidge Danticat and *The Farming of Bones*", *MaComère* 2 (1999): 19. See also Shea's introduction and her analysis of the book cover: "a detail from Haitian artist Gerard Valcin's painting entitled 'Lasiren et Metrès Dlo' which is from the collection of American filmmaker Jonathan Demme, and prefigures the setting and center, the Massacre River" (ibid., 12). Danticat's character suggests that the rich layer of popular beliefs that view the water as an enchanted place has a direct influence on the way in which her characters construct and imagine their identity. The novel, however, does not make any specific reference to the local water spirits and unique stories that have developed on the border between Haiti and the Dominican Republic.

23. Danticat, *Farming*, 91.

24. Shea, "The Hunger to Tell", 16.

25. Ibid. "Poor people are sold to work in the cane fields so our own country can be free of them" (Danticat, *Farming*, 178), says Tibon, one of the survivors Amabelle meets after Sebastien's disappearance.

26. Danticat mentions the role of the "Marassa" in connection with the possibility of being in two places at once: "Doubling is a similar idea. I started thinking about this because I had often heard the story of our heroes, like Jean-Jacques Dessalines, who is considered the father of our independence. In the folkloric explanation, he was such a strong individual because he was really two people: one part of him could be at home and the other on the battlefield, or two of him could be on the battlefield at once. The idea is that someone is doubly a person but really one person – as opposed to the twins who are really two people" (Edwidge Danticat, "The Dangerous Job of Edwidge Danticat". Interview by Renée Shea, *Callaloo* 19, no. 2 [1996]: 385). On the role of Marassa in general, see Maya Deren, *Divine Horsemen: The Living Gods of Haiti* (Kingston: Documentext, 1953) and on the link between doubling and political figures see Lauren Derby, "The Dictator's Two Bodies: Hidden Powers of State in the Dominican Republic", *Etnofoor* 12, no. 2 (1999): 92–117.

27. Danticat, *Farming*, 1.

28. Ibid.

29. Ibid., 13.

30. Ibid., 207.

31. Ibid.

32. Ibid., 208.

33. Shea, "The Hunger to Tell", 12.

34. Goldblatt, "Finding a Voice for the Victimized", 44.

35. Danticat, *Farming*, 227.

36. Ibid., 310.

37. Ibid., 309.

38. Ibid., 309–10.

39. Shea, "The Hunger to Tell", 19.

CHAPTER 6

THEORIES OF "RACE" AND THE HAITIAN REVOLUTION

GEORGES FOURON

INTRODUCTION

From the time when it was first applied to *Homo sapiens* in thirteenth century Europe to the present, the concept "race" has acquired a multiplicity of meanings and has played varied roles in human relations. In the ancient world of the Egyptian, Greek and Roman communities, "race" thinking, racial classifications and racial prejudice for the sole purpose of control, domination and social acceptance were unknown concepts.[1] During the medieval period, "race" was made into an abstraction that helped describe national cultures and served to trace the genealogy of Europe's upper classes. Beginning with the sixteenth century, however, it became the main psychophysical medium of justification for slavery in colonial societies controlled by Europe and served as a psychobiological agent used to evaluate intelligence and cultural achievement among the world's various peoples. Finally, by the mid-twentieth century, "race" had become so firmly entrenched in the psyche of people that it was transformed into the shibboleth for social stratification and the main identifier for social hierarchy in modern nation-states.

This chapter is not a treatise on "race", nor does it seek to rationalize or debunk the mythology that has always existed around this disreputable concept. Rather, it seeks to examine the ways in which those individuals who believed and continue to believe in the racial dogmas of their period have and continue to react towards Haiti, its people and the Haitian Revolution. In the same vein, this chapter also seeks to examine the ways in which "black" people and progressive intellectuals around the world, and the Haitians themselves, have responded to the detractors of the Haitian Revolution, whether or not they accepted or rejected "race" as a valid measure of people's potential and intrinsic characteristics.

When it is used and understood as a biological construct with important and significant deterministic qualitative characteristics, "race" has no validity or legitimacy. Yet, this does not mean that the usage of "race" as a biologically deterministic concept has been completely eliminated from the discourse of science, politics and philosophy. For, in spite of the fact that "race" has been demystified, denigrated and discredited, it remains true that it did and continues to assume an alarmingly exaggerated importance in the affairs of the world. Indeed, far from being a benign concept used by people "who should know better", the construction of "race" as a biological concept equipped with immutable and predictable intellectual standards and human characteristics has resulted in the disenfranchisement and even in the death of many million innocent individuals around the world. For these reasons, when I use the word "race" in this chapter, I place it in quotation marks to indicate my scepticism about its validity and authenticity.

NEWLY INDEPENDENT HAITI AND THE HEGEMONIC CONSTRUCTION OF "RACE" AND CULTURE

It was in a charged racial atmosphere that Haiti, a nation of blacks and for blacks, saw the day in 1804. At the time when Haiti became a nation, the new and "rational science" of physical anthropology had already ordered humankind in terms of groups' anatomy, culture and phenotype. Cultural and social anthropologists presented the world as composed of "superior" and "inferior" "races" and established the tenets of each group's potential for self-government. The "primitive groups" were denied the right to be in charge of their destiny; the "advanced groups", however, not only enjoyed the right to be self-governed, they also had a God-given mandate to control and dominate the former groups.

Through this racial taxonomy, "Negroes" were slated among the primitive groups. They were "considered void of genius, destitute of moral sense, and incapable of making progress in civilization and science" and incapable of being self-governed.[2] By relying on "this scientific dogma", "racism" became an important ideological weapon of and a justification for imperialistic and nationalistic politics. At that conjuncture, Haiti's independence, which belied and challenged the racial hierarchical ideology of the period, was seen as an irrational act and an equivocation.

In the racist atmosphere of the nineteenth century, the deprecations launched at the Haitians in the works of certain "respected and learned" European and North American intellectuals found a most voracious audience and a fertile ground upon which to bloom. For, as the ostracism Haiti experienced as a black nation thwarted the promises of the Haitian Revolution, and as internecine conflicts marred Haiti's domestic politics, many European and US intellectuals used the black nation as a negative referent to express their racist ideology. Among other arguments they used to demonstrate blacks' inferiority to whites, they postulated that blacks were not only incapable of culture, progress, self-government and civilization, they were also incapable of sustaining political systems capable of delivering social, political and economic stability to their populations.[3]

To consolidate their attacks on the black "race" in general, European and North American writers fabricated negative and unfounded stereotypes about Haiti and the Haitians. These prevarications were accepted without question and repeated with complacency even, or especially, by the most educated elites of these societies. For example, in 1888, Spencer St John, an Englishman who had spent a great number of years in Haiti as consul-general for Great Britain, wrote in *Hayti or the Black Republic*: "I know what the black man is, and I have no hesitation in declaring that he is incapable of the art of government, and that to entrust him with framing and working the laws of our islands is to condemn them to inevitable ruin."[4] In addition, he accused the Haitians of cannibalism, and incriminated them for being insouciant, extremely superstitious, incapable of managing with credit any official position, extremely cruel and vain, uncultured and devoid of financial morality.

However, it was when Joseph-Arthur de Gobineau published his seminal work, *De l'inegalité des races humaines* [Of the Inequality of the Human Races] between 1853 and 1855 to vilify the "negro race" [*sic*] and Haiti in particular, that the crude and self-serving racial stereotypes the Europeans had used to slander the Africans, in general, and the black nation, in particular, reached their highest level of viciousness. In this work, Gobineau presented "Haiti as an awful example of what happened when European forms of government are imposed on people of different and lower races".[5] He also declared that despite being independent since 1804, the mores and morals of the Haitian people had remained as "depraved, brutal and savage" as they were in Dahomey and among the Fellatahs in Africa.

De Gobineau and those who shared his views often cited Haiti as evidence that the "black race" was at "the foot of the ladder" and that it was "incapable of civilization".[6] To bolster slavery and racial discrimination, they painted the same negative images for public consumption and presented Haiti as the prototype of the "extreme example of blacks lapsing into savagery when restraints (slavery and social exclusion) [are] lifted".[7]

THE HAITIAN REVOLUTION AND THE LEGACY OF THE NINETEENTH-CENTURY REVOLUTIONARY IMPETUSES

The events that led to the creation of Haiti were revolutionary in every sense: for the first time in history, a slave revolt had brought down a well-armed European army to bring to bear an unthinkable and unfathomable reality, the first black independent nation in modern times. For the slaves and the freedmen, the Haitian Revolution was a world event of even greater importance than the American Revolution. For while the English colonies constituted themselves into an independent country without altering the pre-existing social and economic colonial relationships, particularly slavery, the Haitian Revolution, on the other hand, dramatically changed the social equation that had been operating in the French colony for more than two centuries. Moreover, it became an emblem of blacks' achievement and was considered to be the first step in slavery's final demise.

Extremely impressed by the Haitians' exploits, Karl Marx placed the Haitian Revolution at the core of the struggles for world liberation and situated it within the scope of the quests for human freedom. In *The German Ideology*, he declared that "the insurgent Negroes of Haiti and the fugitive Negroes of all the colonies wanted to free not themselves, but 'Man' ".[8] Speaking about the father of the Haitian Revolution, Wendell Phillips, the militant abolitionist, proclaimed that Toussaint Louverture's military abilities and moral character were superior to Napoleon's, Cromwell's and Washington's.[9] Loring Dewey, an abolitionist and emigrationist leader, called Haiti "the sun of hope for all oppressed of Africa . . . in her liberty they shall see liberty, and having seen, they will no longer be restrained from enjoying".[10] Juste Chanlatte, a prominent Haitian writer and political figure, proudly proclaimed the imminent demise of the whole colonial edifice. Impassioned, he prophesied that the newly emerging nineteenth century would witness the liberation of all oppressed "races" throughout the world.[11]

HAITI, THE BANNER BEARER OF BLACK NATIONALISM
AND THE DEFENDER OF THE "RACE"

In Europe as in North America, however, Haiti's independence was not received as a good omen. Instead, when independent Haiti sought international recognition as a free nation, heated debates raged throughout Europe and the Americas on issues related to blacks' humaneness. Rebuffed and even snubbed by the North Americans, the Europeans, and even by the South Americans it had helped in their struggles for independence, Haiti remained an isolated and ostracized nation for most of the nineteenth century. However, free of all outside constraints to establish their own domestic political sovereignty, and having rejected the colonial model in defiance of the white nations' racist ideologies, the Haitians became determined to build a theory and praxis of nationhood that used the valuation of the "black race" as its main underpinning.

To explicate blacks' purported "retardation" vis-à-vis whites, Haitian intellectuals postulated social theories that blamed the nefarious and lasting legacy of slavery and the effects of racial discrimination for their alleged backwardness. Juste Chanlatte declared that while observable physical differences among the "races" were evident and while by all measures blacks lagged behind whites, there existed no rationality in indicting the black "race" for their social retardation vis-à-vis the Europeans. Responding to those who sought to bolster slavery through an indictment of the "black race", Milscent, a Haitian social activist, cited Montesquieu's climatological theory arguing that their blackness only reflected the influences specific climatic conditions had on people who inhabited the tropics and that it was not an indication of innate inferiority.[12] Other Haitian polemicists argued that by defeating the French army on the battlefield, the Haitians had once and for all debunked all myths of racial inequality. They maintained that the whites' racist arguments were not only spurious, but were mere shams and simple rationalizations without any merit and that they deserved no serious consideration. Whites' racism, they declared, endured only because it served, protected and defended the narrow economic interests of the dominant classes.

In the end, despite the hatred the contemporary white populations nurtured in their heart for the blacks, the Haitian Revolution marked a turning point in world history. For it stood as a symbol of black civilization, dignity, regeneration and power. By defeating the French colonizers, Haiti had become a beacon of hope for the slaves, the freedmen and oppressed populations the world over. In this vein, Frederick Douglass, the African-American social activist, rendered homage to Haiti and her revolution in the following terms at the World's Columbian Exposition in Chicago in 1893:

> She [Haiti] has grandly served the cause of universal liberty. We should not forget that the freedom you and I enjoy today; that the freedom that eight hundred thousand colored people enjoy in the British West Indies; the freedom that has come to the colored race the world over is largely due to the brave stand taken by the black sons of Haiti ninety years ago. When they struck for freedom, they built better than they knew. Their swords were not drawn and could not be drawn simply for themselves alone. They were linked and interlinked with their race, and striking for their freedom, they struck for the freedom of every black man in the world.[13]

For a long time, the Haitian Revolution loomed large in the imagination of both blacks and whites. Whites who harboured racist penchants were inevitably loath to see blacks become their social equals. As for the masses of the black slaves who toiled on the plantations and in the shops of the colonial establishments, the Haitian Revolution provided them with the irrefutable proof that "the descendants of Africa never were designed by their creator to sustain any inferiority, or even mediocrity, in the chain of being; but [that] they are as capable of intellectual improvement as the Europeans, or any other nation upon the face of the earth".[14]

THE SLAVES AND THE HAITIAN REVOLUTION

The news that the slaves of St Domingue had led a successful revolt that was underscored by the systematic massacre of the island's white population spread like wildfire on the continent's plantations, from the United States to Jamaica and Cuba, from Barbados to South America. Disseminated and vulgarized by black sailors who regularly visited the North and South American ports, by black refugees who followed their masters into exile and by both the white and black press, these reports engendered panic in and among the slaveholding nations.

The colonizers' fear was heightened further when Haiti sought to spread its revolution to other parts of the continent. Indeed, as their first act of international solidarity with the colonized populations of South America, Haiti sent arms, soldiers and ammunition to South American revolutionaries fighting for their independence from Spain. Also, concrete evidence has been discovered which demonstrates that beyond any doubt various Haitian presidents sent, if not arms, at least encouragement to the leaders of US slave revolt movements. In situations where contacts with Haiti had not been established, rebelling slaves throughout the continent found their inspiration and motivation in the lore that circulated about Haiti and its revolution.

To express their pride in the actions of the Haitian revolutionaries and to demonstrate their identification with them, many slaves defied their masters at great personal risk by choosing to name their children after the heroes of the Haitian independence movement. In the columns of the black newspapers of the period, the deeds of the Haitian heroes were recounted in epic terms and the freed blacks used the Haitians' exploits as proof that blacks could take their future into their own hands to command respect and earn their freedom. Moreover, in the United States and throughout the continent, the establishment of Haiti as an independent nation opened the possibility that free blacks could consider Haiti as a place to seek refuge against slavery and racial discrimination.

Haiti, the Redeemer of Africa and the Framer of a Pan-African Vision

Haitian intellectuals also joined in the racial discourse of the period. In effect, soon after the victory over the French forces, the Haitians established themselves as the mouthpiece for Africa, the defenders of the "race" and the protectors of the rights of Africans wherever they resided. In their eyes, by their sublime act, they had rehabilitated the "black race" [*sic*] and avenged Africa and the Africans. The victory of the Haitian troops over the French was presented by the Haitians as the tangible proof that blacks could set up legitimate governments and that their professionals and intellectuals were as capable and competent as their European counterparts. Haitians were also proud of the fact that they, not the Africans, had successfully offered a formal denial in the belief of the inferiority of the "black race". Beauvais Lespinasse stated in 1882:

> Haiti, the eldest daughter of Africa, envisions her history and her civilization as the first page of the history of the rehabilitation of her race. She must serve as a model for her other sisters in renewing incessantly her claims for the civilization of Africa in the concert of nations whose mission is to transform the world into an extensive brotherhood.[15]

Throughout its history, Haiti has been called the African Mecca, the Judea of the "black race", the place where all individuals who had a drop of African blood in their veins had to go on pilgrimage at least once in their life.[16] Along these lines, Edmond Paul, an influential Haitian intellectual and political figure, wrote:

> Once Negro genius has degenerated, once the black race has been pushed into the background, who would take care of developing its abilities? . . . Are there in the Caribbean blacks whose physiognomy reflects more deeply the sense of their humanity than the blacks of Haiti? . . . Have you forgotten that Haiti alone is destined to resolve the great problem of the aptitude of the black race for civilization?[17]

From the early years of the nineteenth century till the end of the US Civil War, Haiti endured in the minds of both the free and enslaved African-American populations as a mythical African homeland in the Americas. And since the first Haitian leaders had invited the US black populations to migrate to Haiti instead of Africa to find solace and respect, the colonization movement to Africa that had sprung up in many US cities found Haiti a more meaningful destination. When given the choice to either go to Liberia or Sierra Leone, two African outposts that had been established through white benevolence, or go to Haiti, many African Americans chose Haiti. By earning its independence on the battlefield against the better armed and superior European forces, Haiti, which had organized itself into a modern state, had more appeal to the black American populations than Africa, which was seen as a barren land marred with tribal conflicts. In their view, Haiti was the "best and most suitable place of residence which Providence has hitherto offered to emancipated people of color".[18]

In the end, through its revolution, Haiti had redefined African-descended peoples' racial and cultural identity. And when Haiti's independence was finally recognized by France in 1825, albeit at the cost of an onerous debt, and when it finally occupied its rightful place in the concert of the bona fide nation-states, William Watkins, a black abolitionist, exclaimed:

> Of all that has hitherto been done in favor of the descendants of Africa, I recollect nothing so fraught with momentous importance – so pregnant with interests to millions yet unborn – as the recent acknowledgment of Haytien Independence, by one of the European Powers, under whom the African population of that island had long groaned in the most abject bondage. . . . our feelings upon this occasion are unutterable.[19]

As the Haitians restored and affirmed their black identity and as they presented themselves as the representatives and defenders of the "black race", Haiti became, in the eyes of the black populations, a *lieu de mémoire* and a symbol of cultural and racial pride and autonomy.[20] As such, the Haitians endeavoured to defend and preserve Haiti's independence and sovereignty at all cost and against all her enemies.

Haitians, the Imitators of Europe

Yet, while the Haitians were proud of their racial identity, for a long time they were reticent to present their African culture as a validation of their nationhood. Instead of developing a perhaps "truer" national identity built upon their African identity, the Haitians, having acceded to their independence in the racially polarized world of nineteenth century politics, constructed their identity according to the tenets of France's nationalist and cultural discourses. The first Haitian intellectuals turned their backs on the masses, and chose to disaggregate the concepts of racial pride and cultural authenticity in the formulation of their national identity. While they rejected racial hegemony, they nevertheless accepted the cogency of cultural hierarchy. Many Haitians felt that while the European concept of racial superiority had no valid basis, they concluded, nonetheless, that their contemporary African culture could not help them build and define an acceptable identity. In their eyes, Africa and the black "race" needed to be "regenerated". Moreover, having received a European education, the few literate Haitians, who were for the most part mulattos, had tacitly subscribed to the racist cultural theories of the period. They regarded the African continent as a barbarous and uncivilized place and considered the Africans as savage people in need of refinement. Thus, the civilization they felt the Haitians should embrace was not to be African, but European, and most especially French. De Vastey, a prominent statesman and intellectual, declared in 1818:

> Black as we are and yellow by complexion, bowed as we have been for cen-
> turies under the yoke of slavery and ignorance, assimilated to the condition
> of the brute; how resolutely ought we to exert ourselves; how much persever-
> ance, wisdom and virtue are necessary for reanimating our race, to this moment
> enchained in darkness.[21]

Almost one hundred years later, the celebrated Haitian author Dr Léon Audain illus-
trated the poor opinion Haitians have of the Africans in the following passage:

Up to now, Africa has been in the throes of such ignorance that moral life is for all intents and purposes unknown. Brutal strength is the only law they respect. *The weak should beware! Niger nigro lupus!* [The Negro acts as a wolf vis-à-vis another Negro]. Continuous war among individuals for control of vulgar material possessions, continuous wars among the various tribes and the various groups, its plundering, its slavery of one by another . . . The only preoccupations our unfortunate relatives from Africa have are to find food, and to elude either through ruse or force their numerous enemies.[22]

In 1910, Anténor Firmin, the brilliant anthropologist who wrote the seminal book *De l'egalité des races humaines* [*The Equality of the Human Races*] to challenge the period's racist ideologies and to demonstrate that blacks' intellectual and moral capabilities were similar to those of the whites, posed the following question: "Will the Haitian mentality develop along the Latin or Anglo-Saxon model?" He responded to his query in the following terms: "Whatever they say, we can, from this moment on, conclude that the Haitian mentality has nothing to lose, but all to gain, by following the French system, which is called Latin and which is, in reality, Latin."[23]

While Haitians of all hues and social classes have never disowned their blackness and while they have regularly acknowledged their racial affinity with black Africa, they have at the same time tended to value the French language and French culture over Creole, their African-derived language, and African culture. Thus, following the indigenous army's victory over the French troops, the Haitians felt that if their independence were to carry any meaning and validity, they had to place it in the context of their acquired European, but most especially, French culture.

In a country where the overwhelming majority of the population was illiterate in both Haitian Creole and French, Haiti was designated as the "black France"[24] and the Haitians were portrayed as "the defenders of France, French language and culture in the Americas".[25] In 1883, Louis Joseph Janvier declared: "France is the capital of all nations. Haiti is the black France", despite the fact that at that time less than 1 per cent of the population spoke French or was familiar with French culture.[26] Dantès Bellegarde, the illustrious Haitian writer and diplomat, opined in 1923 that Haitians were united to France "through blood and language" and whatever the Americans may do, they would never overtake the place that France occupies in the heart of the Haitians.[27] Conversely, France was considered "great and generous among the nations". France was said to "detest those nations that enjoy torturing and compulsion. . . . She was the one who awoke our fathers and showed them the way to freedom."[28]

This infatuation with France and French culture has led some Haitian intellectuals to completely misrepresent Haiti's internal reality to the outside world. In 1882, for example, Louis Joseph Janvier peremptorily declared: "The French language is the current language [in Haiti], the only one used [in the country], and the peasants understand it."[29] In this context, one's ignorance of French culture and one's inability to manipulate French have always been used by the elite groups as excuses and justifications to deny the majority of the Haitian population a share in the country's wealth and to exclude them from playing an effective role in running the country.

The Haitians' struggle to find a happy medium between their love and admiration for French – therefore European and white – culture and civilization and their pride in their "race" and heritage – therefore African and black – has resulted in the adoption of an alienating and counterproductive cultural bovarism.[30] Even those who defended *noiriste* ideology and spearheaded the Négritude and Indigenist Movements in the early 1920s adopted a reactive rather than a proactive attitude toward defending their African identity.[31]

That African identity was "discovered" only when Yankee domination had become intolerable and when they realized that their purported Latin culture could not protect them from the assaults of the Anglo-Saxon hegemonic forces. Along these lines, Leon Laleau wrote in 1956:

> The [1915] American occupation made us face tyrannical and unexpected problems . . .
>
> This invasion of the Anglo-Saxon civilization tried hard to inflict to our culture – literary to the bone, French to the extreme limit – an incontrovertible challenge . . .
>
> Our Latin education, which in the circumstance appeared deficient to resist that assault, became our shield and we opposed it victoriously to the attempts of the occupation forces . . . However, we soon realized that we had the shield and not the arms.
>
> That was when we remembered our race that the Yankee had precisely qualified as inferior while treating us with contempt. Going back to the farthest past, we rejoined our origins. We began to expose in our introverted Gobinism, a certain pride in being Negroes. Africa was everywhere in our writings and in our poems. And as the breeze pushing the caravels, Africa carried our dreams.[32]

HAITI AND THE CRISIS OF NATIONAL AUTHENTICITY

In general therefore Haitians experience life through a curious predicament. They consider themselves Africans by blood, and are proud of it, yet in certain ways and to varying degrees they comport themselves as Europeans culturally. This embrace of French, thus European, culture has persisted despite the fact that the founders of the Haitian nation had proclaimed in a militant manner and for the entire world to hear that all Haitians, regardless of their phenotype and "race", would be known under the generic term *noir*,[33] black, debunking in the process the normative European biological and cultural determinism.

Yet, despite their fierce nationalism and their expressed hatred for their former white tyrants, the majority of Haitian intellectuals have tended to "whiten" themselves culturally. They comport themselves as the legatees of French civilization in the Americas, plead for their full integration into the framework of European civilization and even seek to contribute to its further development at the detriment of their own progress. By embracing without reserve European culture and civilization and by relegating their indigenous black culture and civilization to the domain of the mundane and the trivial, these intellectuals show a net acceptance of the notion that culturally Europe is superior to Africa.

Those Haitians who identify culturally with France have blamed not France for the horrors of slavery, but the French colons who were described as bad Frenchmen, traitors to France and betrayers of France's noble and benevolent sentiments toward all peoples.[34] In the eyes of these intellectuals, the true French were those who had proclaimed the "rights of men and of the citizen" in 1789 in their recriminations against the French monarchy. For example, as late as 1974, Gouraige stated that for a long time, France neglected to grasp the distinction made in Haiti between the *colon* and the French: one was the "oppressor", the other the ally. He argued that "Haitians are commended for not forgetting that the first act toward the liberation of the slaves was taken by the functionaries of the Convention and that, whatever intentions they had, they had armed the blacks against the colonials".[35]

Also, because they regarded the Anglo-Saxons as boorish, harsh, crass and inferior to the French, during the US occupation of Haiti (1915–34) the Haitians' hatred for the Americans became very acrimonious and strident. An editorial in *La Petite Revue,* on 1 July 1930, cried out: "Haiti has a civilization, French, to be sure, but superior to whatever the US could offer her." Seven years later, *Le Temps* echoed the same sentiment when it declared on 12 July 1937: "It is said that Haiti imitates France. That is how it should be . . . without that suit of armor, without all those French traits that are inborn in us or that we have assimilated, we would have remained primitive Africans, and the US would have swallowed us in one gulp."[36]

This fascination with France and French culture and language has not been supported by all Haitian intellectuals. Dr Jean Price-Mars, for example, one among the most celebrated Haitian intellectuals, on many occasions denounced the "cultural bovarism" of the Haitian intellectuals and bourgeois class. Price-Mars and the indigenist Haitian writers decided to challenge the US influence on the country. These writers and intellectuals endeavoured to promote Africa and African culture as the true essence of the Haitians.[37] Among other actions they undertook, they elevated vodou to the status of an important and bona fide religion and fought for the recognition of Haitian Creole as the true language of the Haitians.

CONCLUSION

Even as they identify themselves with France, French culture and civilization, Haitians have never rejected their African roots. Even the mulattos, the light-skinned Haitians, have always celebrated their ties to black Africa. Moreover, because the Haitian revolutionaries achieved the unfathomable feat of successfully realizing the first and only slave revolt in modern history, Haitians have always presented themselves as the spokespersons for black people the world over. Conversely, Haiti has always loomed large in the blacks' imagination. In the 1820s, Haiti was called Africa's rising sun and the Haitian Revolution was credited with the efforts to regenerate Africa.

Africans have also accepted the role Haiti played in their own liberation even as Haiti continues to sink into a dire political and economic morass. For example, in a speech he delivered at the University of the West Indies in Jamaica on 20 June 2003, President Thabo Mbeki of South Africa acknowledged: "the victory of the African slaves in Haiti in 1804 is directly linked to the victory of the African oppressed in South Africa in 1994".[38]

During the last forty years, however, migration has affected the ways Haitians see themselves.[39] More Haitians now speak English or Spanish than French. Within the Haitian diaspora, there are clear signs of the decline of French as a means of communication among Haitian immigrants and people of Haitian origin. According to Saint-Fort:

Practically all the Haitian immigrants' community radio and television programs are in Creole; a great number of discussions that take place on the internet among Haitians happen in Creole; the bilingual education programs [for young Haitian immigrants] use English and Creole and not French, and personal communications among Haitians are in Creole. In addition, the second generation [Haitian immigrants' children] is not at all attracted by the French language. . . . thus, one must seriously question the future of the French language within the Haitian immigrant communities in the United States.[40]

Haitian immigrants are increasingly transferring their traditional love of and admiration for French culture and civilization onto other cultures. The most famous contemporary Haitian writer, Edwidge Danticat, writes and publishes in English and not French. As their stay abroad is extended, the immigrants and their children will become ever more incorporated into the host societies both culturally and socially. As the immigrant populations continue to grow and as contacts with their homeland increase in both quality and quantity, new transformations will surely occur in the Haitians' psyche wherever they happen to live.

However, it is rather difficult to predict for certain the nature and characteristics of the changes that sustained contacts between the Haitian diaspora and the sedentary populations will produce. What is certain, however, is that the Haitian Revolution will continue to play an important role in the world's political and social spheres. It is also evident, as Karl Marx had predicted, that not only the African masses in Africa and the African Diaspora but all oppressed people throughout the world will continue to study the Haitian Revolution to acquire a better understanding of their own national conditions and to empower them to respond more effectively to the challenges they face.

NOTES

1. See Ivan Hannaford, *Race: The History of an Idea in the West* (Washington, DC: Woodrow Wilson Center Press, 1996); Frank M. Snowden, Jr., *Blacks in Antiquity: Ethiopians in the Greco-Roman Experience* (Cambridge, Mass: Belknap Press, 1970).

2. Edward Long, cited in Ashley Montague, *Man's Most Dangerous Myth: The Fallacy of Race* (London: Oxford University Press, 1974), 37.

3. Chris Dixon, *African America and Haiti: Emigration and Black Nationalism in the Nineteenth Century* (Westport, Conn: Greenwood Press, 2000); also Léon D. Pamphile, *Haitians and African Americans: A Heritage of Tragedy and Hope* (Gainesville: University Press of Florida, 2001).

4. Spencer St John, *Hayti or The Black Republic* (Edinburgh: Ballantine Press, 1888), xi.

5. Carolyn Fluehr-Lobban, "Anténor Firmin: Haitian Pioneer of Anthropology", *American Anthropologist* 102, no. 3: xxxi; also Arthur de Gobineau, *De l'inégalité des races humaines* [The Inequality of Human Races] (New York: Howard Fertig, 1999).

6. Fluehr-Lobban, "Anténor Firmin", 459.

7. J. Michael Dash, *Haiti and the United States: National Stereotypes and the Literary Imagination* (New York: St Martin's Press, 1997), 8.

8. Karl Marx and Frederic Engels, *The German Ideology* (Moscow: Progress Press, 1976), 327.

9. Wendell Phillips, *Toussaint L'Ouverture* (Port-au-Prince: Imprimerie de L'État, 1950).

10. Pamphile, *Haitians and African* Americans, 8.

11. David Nicholls, *From Dessalines to Duvalier: Race, Colour and National Independence in Haiti* (Cambridge University Press, 1979).

12. Gordon Lewis, *Main Currents in Caribbean Thought: The Historical Evolution of Caribbean Society in Its Ideological Aspects, 1492–1900* (Baltimore: Johns Hopkins University Press, 1983).

13. Philip S. Foner, ed., *The Life and Writings of Frederic Douglass,* vol. 4 (New York: International Publishers, 1955), 138–39.

14. David Brion Davis, "Impact of the French and Haitian Revolutions", in *The Impact of the Haitian Revolution in the Atlantic World,* ed. David P. Geggus (Columbia, SC: University of South Carolina Press, 2001), 3–9.

15. Beauvais Lespinasse, "La civilisation noire et son avenir", in, *Ecrivains haitiens, première partie,* Dantès Bellegarde (Port-au-Prince: Henry Deschamps, 1950), 25–28.

16. Hannibal Price, *De la réhabilitation de la race noire par la République d'Haïti* (Port-au-Prince: Verrollot, 1900).

17. Edmund Paul, cited in Anténor Firmin, *The Equality of the Human Race* (Urbana: University of Illinois Press, 2002), 219.

18. Thomas Paul, *Columbian Sentinel,* 3 July 1824.

19. William Watkins, cited in Dixon, *African America and Haiti,* 31.

20. Elizabeth Rauh Bethel, "Images of Hayti: The Construction of an Afro-American *Lieu de Mémoire*", *Callaloo* 15, no. 3 (1992): 827–841.

21. Count de Vastey, cited in Nicholls, *From Dessalines to Duvalier,* 44.

22. Léon Audain, *Le Mal d' Haïti, ses causes et son traitement* (Port-au-Prince: Imprimerie Verollot, 1908), 47.

23. Anténor Firmin, *Lettres de St Thomas, études sociologiques, historiques et litteraires* (Port-au-Prince: Éditions Fardin, 1986).

24. Louis Joseph Janvier, *La République d'Haïti et ses visiteurs (1840–1882)* (Paris: Flammarion, 1883).

25. Normil G. Sylvain, "Manifeste", *La revue indigène* (July 1927).

26. Louis Joseph Janvier, *La République d'Haïti,* 57.

27. Dantès Bellegarde, "L'île d' Haïti, c'est la petite France d'Amérique", *Les Nouvelles,* 2 January 1923.

28. Demesvar Delorme, 1898, cited in Bellegarde, *Ecrivains haitiens,* 89.

29. Louis Joseph Janvier, et al., *Les detracteurs de la race noire et de la République d'Haïti* (Paris: Marpon et Flammarion, 1882).

30. Jean Price-Mars, *Ainsi parla l'oncle* (Paris: Imprimerie de Compiègne, 1928).

31. These movements and the expression of these ideologies were serious undertakings the Haitians took to resist attempts by the United States and the other hegemonic powers to subjugate the local bourgeoisie. It is important to be reminded that such movements and ideologies were propagated by well-educated blacks who were resisting their own exclusion from wealth and power in societies that were controlled directly and indirectly by European colonial powers. The fact that these elites were well educated and accepted the predominance of European culture yet were not accepted as partners by the creole or local elite groups caused them to reject, on the surface only, the premises of the superiority and dominance of Europe and European culture.

32. Léon Laleau, "Ainsi parla le neveu", in *Ainsi parla l'oncle,* Jean Price-Mars (Ottawa: LEMEAC, 1973), 12–13.

33. The few whites who had escaped the massacres that followed the Haitians' victory over the French troops could remain in Haiti only if they agreed to become "blacks".

34. Léon-François Hoffmann, *Bibliographie des études litteraires haitiennes 1804–1984* (Vanves, France: EDICEF, 1992).

35. Gislain Gouraige, *La diaspora d'Haïti et l'Afrique* (Ottawa: Editions Naaman, 1974), 52.

36. Léon-François Hoffmann, "Francophilia and Cultural Nationalism", in *Haiti: Today and Tomorrow, an Interdisciplinary Study,* ed. C.R. Foster and A. Valdman (New York: University Press of America, 1984), 57–86.

37. The 1946 Revolution, also called the *Noiriste* Revolution or the Indigenist Movement, was to some extent a revolt against this fascination with French culture. Some of the adherents to the movement sought to lead the Haitians to recognize the value of African culture and civilization and to embrace them as their own. Through the Faculty of Ethnology in Port-au-Prince, Haitian scholars conducted research to prove that before Europe, Africa had thriving civilizations and that the best way for Haitians to prove their pride in Africa was to see themselves as transplanted Africans.

38. Thabo Mbeki, "Address of the President of South Africa, Thabo Mbeki, at the University of West Indies, Kingston, Jamaica", 30 June 2003; http://www.dfa.gov.za/docs/mbek030701a.htm.

39. Nina Glick Schiller and Georges E. Fouron, *Georges Woke Up Laughing: Long-Distance Nationalism and the Search for Home* (Durham, NC: Duke University Press, 2001).

40. Hughes Saint-Fort, "Vers la disparition de la langue française dans les communautés linguistiques haïtiennes aux Etats-Unis?", *Haitian Times* 5, no. 48 (26 November–2 December 2003): 2.

CHAPTER 7

ANTÉNOR FIRMIN

HIS LEGACY AND CONTINUING RELEVANCE

CAROLYN FLUEHR-LOBBAN

INTRODUCTION

Anténor Firmin was a pioneering anthropologist in the nineteenth century, whose major work, *De l'égalité des races humaines (anthropologie positive),* was published in Paris in 1885 and was largely ignored as a foundational text in anthropology. The text has only recently been recovered, translated by Asselin Charles and introduced by me to an English language readership as *The Equality of the Human Races (Positivist Anthropology)* 115 years after its original publication.[1] The recovery of this text permits a re-examination of the foundations of anthropology and the impact of Anténor Firmin not only on Haitian anthropology but on American and Caribbean anthropology as well. It also invites an examination of Firmin's early pan-Africanist thinking. Anténor Firmin's work was inspirational to Jean Price-Mars, the founder of ethnology and folklore studies in Haiti, who spoke to his direct influence in his last work, a biography, *Joseph Anténor Firmin,* published posthumously in 1964.[2] Recent scholarship has examined the close relationship of Price-Mars to Melville Herskovits, the American founder of African and African-American studies, and also to the noted African Americans Katherine Dunham and Zora Neale Hurston, both students of Herskovits and Franz Boas.[3]

Although ignored in France, Firmin was never forgotten in Haiti, neither as a politician and diplomat nor as a scholar. Anténor Firmin and other scholar contemporaries, such as Louis Joseph Janvier and Hannibal Price, are remembered in Haiti as revered intellectuals to this day. This was how I learned about Firmin in 1988 when a Haitian student of mine, Jacques R. Georges, extolled *De l'égalité des races humaines* as I was lecturing about de Gobineau's *Essai sur l'inégalité des races,* indicating that it was a most compelling response to de Gobineau. *De l'égalité des races humaines* enjoyed something of a revival in Haiti in the second half of the twentieth century, with editions published in Port-au-Prince in 1963, 1968 and 1995.

G.R. Coultard noted, "Writers like Anténor Firmin, Hannibal Price, Claude McKay, George Padmore, and Jean Price-Mars were in the vanguard of the revaluation of African culture long before the nationalist awakening in Africa and before the concept of négritude was developed in the Caribbean."[4] Kwame Nkrumah acknowledged Firmin as a New World pioneer of pan-Africanism in a speech at the University of Ghana in 1964, while Aimé Césaire remembered Firmin in his *Discourse on Colonialism* as a nineteenth century "genius" whose writings were foundational to the négritude movement. In the United States, where Firmin was known to Negro elites, Booker T. Washington apparently advocated the publication of an American edition of *De l'égalité des races humaines* as early as 1902; however, the project was put on hold by the publisher Walter Hines. Firmin and Booker T. Washington met in Washington, DC, in 1908, and Firmin believed that they had much in common as those committed to uplifting the black race. By that time Firmin was in exile and fighting for his political life and he had asked Mr Washington for a loan of twenty-five thousand dollars, to which Washington replied that it was impossible.

In 1891 as minister of foreign affairs, Firmin staved off an American imperial advance to secure the Môle St Nicholas, culminating in a dramatic encounter between himself and the American consul to Haiti, Frederick Douglass. With this defining early experience with American imperialism, Firmin was able to be clear about the expansionist and colonial ambitions of the United States in the Caribbean.

Thus, Firmin was also an early pan-Caribbeanist who maintained active ties with regional fellow liberationists Ramón Betances and José Martí. His "Haiti y la Confederacíon Antillana", published in *Lettres de Saint Thomas* in 1910, referenced his recollection of a Parisian circle of Latin Americans whom Firmin knew during his stay in France in the 1880s, among them Torres Caicedo and Dr Ramón Betances.[5] Dr Betances had read *De l'égalité des races humaines* and was much impressed with it, while Firmin referred to him as "Padre de la Patria". Firmin advocated a confederation of the Antilles, as did these liberationists, and he warned his co-regionists against the "Gran República del Norte" which he often otherwise referred to as "the Giant to the North". With these Caribbean intellectuals, Firmin and the others were enthusiastic about the solidarity of the peoples of Latin American origin whose dream was the intellectual and moral emancipation of Latin America from national despotism and colonial exploitation.

The multiple dimensions of the legacy of Anténor Firmin are examined here – as a pioneering anthropologist who provided a critical view of race countering the racialist and racist physical anthropology of his day – as an early pan-Africanist and pan-Caribbeanist – and, finally, as a profoundly critical and deeply humanist writer whose prose is still evocative and provocative to this day.

PIONEERING ANTHROPOLOGIST

De l'égalité des races humaines (anthropologie positive) was published in Paris in 1885 while Firmin was in France as a Haitian emissary and as one of two Haitian members of the Paris Anthropology Society. Firmin was a member of the Society from 1884 to 1888, although apparently his name remained on the roster until years after death in 1911. Although he was a member of the Society who attended many of its meetings, his voice was effectively silenced by the racialist anthropological discourse dominant at the time and by his race. In the *Memoires* that provide a transcript of the Anthropology Society's deliberations, apparently Firmin rose to speak only twice, and on both occasions he was silenced by racist comments. He rose to challenge the biological determination of race that pervaded the prevailing physical anthropology of Paul Broca and others and was confronted by Clemence Royer (a pioneering woman of science who translated Darwin's *Origin of Species* into French), who asked Firmin if his intellectual ability and presence in the Society were not the result of some white ancestry he might possess. Firmin tells us in his own words in the preface to *The Equality of the Human Races* that he wanted to debate those who "divide the human species into superior and inferior races" but he feared his request would be rejected. "Common sense told me that I was right to hesitate. It was then that I conceived the idea of writing this book."[6] We now know that a signed copy conveying "Hommage respective a La Societé d'anthropologie de Paris, A. Firmin" was presented to the Paris Anthropology Society in 1885, and that no review or further mention of the book was made in the *Memoires d'Anthropologie,* the periodical of the Society, beyond a record of its having been received.

The publication date of 1885 of *De l'égalité des races humaines (anthropologie positive)* marks it as a pioneering text in anthropology well within the time framework of the other foundational texts in the field such as L.H. Morgan's *Ancient Society* (1877) and E.B. Tylor's *Anthropology* (1881).[7] Although Franz Boas, the father of American anthropology, began his "geographical" writings about Cumberland Sound and Baffin-land in 1884–85, he did not produce a synthetic work of anthropology until his *The Mind of Primitive Man,* in 1911, the year of Firmin's death; and that work by Boas contained a line of argumentation against the racialist and racist anthropology of the nineteenth century similar to that Firmin had developed more than a quarter of a century before.[8] By "racialism" I mean treating human physical or phenotypic difference in a scientific method or analysis; for example, the racialist measurement of differences in human crania. Racist ideas, by contrast, explicitly state differences of superior and inferior racial types.

Following the ideas of August Comte, Firmin applied positivist science to a critical examination of comparative craniometric data, noting their irregularities and the arbitrary means by which Paul Broca, Samuel Morton and other racialist scientists of the nineteenth century manipulated the numerical data to draw their foregone conclusions of racial separation, difference and ranking. After analysing various scholars' data on the cephalic index, measuring degrees of superior doli-chocephaly ("round heads") and inferior brachycephaly ("flat heads"), he concluded that this index provided anthropologists with insufficient ground for dividing the races into distinct groups.[9] Broca's facial index is also subjected to critical scrutiny whereby the most primitive black race may be close numerically to the Parisian! He subjects other indices – the nasal, the vertical, the orbital – to similar scrutiny, noting that a rational classification is impossible when the data used to generate them are "not only erroneous and irregular, but also often contradictory".[10] Their confusing and often conflicting craniological charts are more a source of entertainment to Firmin who admits he would normally dismiss them were they not taken so seriously by the anthropologists. Inspired by a greater mission, he wrote:

> Motivated by an insatiable thirst for truth and the obligation to contribute, no matter how modestly, to the scientific rehabilitation of the Black race whose pure and invigorating blood flows in my veins, I take immense pleasure in navigating through these columns of figures arranged with such neatness for the edification of the intellect.[11]

Firmin critically pursued the study of all of those "anthropological doctrines which have assumed the mantle of the august name of science while actually usurping its place".[12]

Not only do craniological measures fail the test of positivist science for Firmin, but so do all other racialized anthropometric devices and classifications, such as those dealing with hair and skin pigmentation that were likewise treated by Firmin as arbitrary and subjective. Firmin was among the first to locate skin colour with the substance melanin, constituted of "fine granules under the epidermis", giving the Ethiopian's skin its black hue.[13]

Nearly four decades before Franz Boas made a similar observation in *Race, Language and Culture* in 1924, Firmin devoted considerable effort to separating language from race, noting that language is an unreliable basis for the classification of race.[14] Firmin's signal contributions to an empirical and critical anthropology, especially as regards race, were lost to the mainstream development of European and North American anthropology in the formative years of the nineteenth century and thus to the decades of consolidation and growth of the discipline in the twentieth century.

FIRMIN'S LEGACY TO HAITIAN ANTHROPOLOGY: JEAN PRICE-MARS (1876–1969), HAITI'S PREMIER TWENTIETH-CENTURY ETHNOLOGIST

Admiration of Firmin by Haiti's premier ethnologist of the twentieth century, Jean Price-Mars, is clear. Price-Mars is the most obvious twentieth-century intellectual descendant of Firmin's anthropology, and he is rightly viewed as the founder of ethnological studies in Haiti. According to the late Magdaline Shannon, the translator of Price-Mars's classic work of Haitian ethnololgy and folklore, *Ainsi parla l'oncle* (*So Spoke the Uncle*), he "had early in life developed goals based upon the ideas of such leaders as Anténor Firmin and Hannibal Price".[15] Admiring the accomplishments of US Negroes, some of Price-Mars's earliest public lectures focused on the equality of human races, sounding so much like Firmin that President Nord Alexis accused Price-Mars of being a "Firminist" and said that his talk was "seditious".[16] This statement was made in 1906 while Firmin and the political Firminists were still actively opposing the Alexis government in Haiti. Firmin was forced into exile in St Thomas, where he died in 1911.

Price-Mars was, perhaps, able to do in 1920 what Firmin could not, or chose not, to do in 1885 – that is, to bring vodou into the academic realm of social science and comparative religion. He organized an historic conference on Haitian folklore at the Cercle Port-au-Princien, at which he introduced the serious study of vodou, gaining the respect of Haitian and French intellectuals. He drew upon Durkheim, enabling him to see vodou as a syncretistic blend of African animism and Roman Catholicism. Price-Mars's opening question in the now-classic work *Ainsi parla l'oncle* was, "What is folklore?" To this question he responded, "folklore is comprised of the legends, customs, observances which form the oral traditions of a people. And for the Haitian people, they are the fundamental beliefs upon which have been grafted or superimposed other more recently acquired beliefs." Uncle Bouqui is the prototypical Haitian storyteller: "Cric?" asks the storyteller, "Crac," replies the audience.[17]

The influence of Firmin on Price-Mars is acknowledged in many of his writings and especially in the last work of his long career, a biography, *Joseph Anténor Firmin*.[18] Both Price-Mars and Firmin were scholar-politicians in the Haitian (and Caribbean) way of not dividing the world of ideas from the world of politics. They were separated in age and time by a generation (Firmin, 1850–1911; Price-Mars, 1875–1964), yet both were committed to the proof of the equality of races. Price-Mars enjoyed a long and vital career as a scholar and politician. In addition to his being a founder of the Société d'Histoire et de Géographie d'Haiti, he also ran for President of Haiti in 1940, and in the 1950s he was appointed head of the Haitian delegation to the United Nations. During his long career he achieved more of the international recognition that Firmin's relatively briefer lifespan did not permit.

FURTHER INFLUENCE OF FIRMIN THROUGH PRICE-MARS TO MELVILLE HERSKOVITS

It is possible to connect not only the works of Anténor Firmin and Jean Price-Mars, but also the work of Jean Price-Mars to Melville Herskovits, a student of Franz Boas and the founder of African studies in America and of Afro-American anthropology.

Melville Herskovits was a protégé of Jean Price-Mars. Correspondence between them from 1928 to 1955 reveals a warm and affectionate professional relationship between the elder Price-Mars and the young Herskovits. It began as the American anthropologist developed an interest in Caribbean and South American Negroes, after his original studies of the American Negro, and later when he planned a period of research in Haiti. Price-Mars responded generously to Herskovits's requests for assistance in the field and he responded to his questions about Haitian ethnology as he encouraged the young American scholar. Herskovits conducted several months of fieldwork in Haiti in 1934 with Price-Mars arranging for the visit, hosting Herskovits and his wife, selecting the field location of Mirebalais, assisting with housing and introductions, and providing a senior ethnologist's advice, perspective and scholarly resources. This resulted in the publication in 1937 of Herskovits's classic *Life in a Haitian Valley*, in which he credits Price-Mars and his colleague J.C. Dorsainvil with critical assistance:

> Aid and inspiration were derived from many friendly conversations with two out-standing students of Haitian folk-life, Dr Price-Mars and Dr J.C. Dorsainvil. My indebtedness to the works they have published on the subject is shown by the references to their publications given at the end of this volume, for their researches must be accepted as basic by any serious investigator of Haitian customs. Their cordial advice to a fellow-student constitutes one of the most pleasant memories of this fieldwork.[19]

This published acknowledgement of Price-Mars is corroborated in his private correspondence:

> September 26, 1934 Melville Herskovits to Jean Price-Mars
> . . . I do want to write and tell you how much I enjoyed the time I spent with you while I was in Haiti and also to convey to you my appreciation of the material aid you gave me in making possible our research in Mireabalais. Just as it would not have been possible without your aid to have got my films through the customs so our work would have been less productive without the help which General Cantave gave me as a result of my having been introduced to him by means of the card from you which I carried. (best wishes on your senatorial and presidential campaigns).

Price-Mars's desire to have *Life in a Haitian Valley* translated suggests his contin-ued interest in Herskovits's work. Herskovits nominated Price-Mars for membership in the American Anthropological Association in 1933. Scholarly associations in Haiti were formed by Jacques Roumain (*Masters of the Dew*, 1944), who was the founder of the Bureau d'Ethnologie in Port-au-Prince in 1941. In the same year Price-Mars founded the Institut d'Ethnologie and was president until 1947, occupying the chair of Africology and sociology. Jacques Roumain and Normil Sylvain founded *La Revue Indigène* in 1927, inspired in part by the Harlem Renaissance literary movement and with the intent of critiquing the Haitian elite's fawning adherence to French literature, while embracing Haitian indigenous culture as Price-Mars had urged.

Price-Mars received other American students of anthropology, including. in 1935 Katherine Dunham, whom he helped with her work in Afro-Caribbean dance as a new subject of research in anthropology, and George E. Simpson (as recollected in Simpson's Introduction to the 1983 edition of *So Spoke the Uncle.*[20]

Anténor Firmin, Pioneer in Négritude and Pan-Africanist Scholarship

Although Firmin's *De l'égalité des races humaines (anthropologie positive)* was lost to francophone anthropology, it was nonetheless recognized among pan-Africanist and vindicationist scholars of colour in Haiti, the Caribbean and the United States. Although Jean Price-Mars is often credited with being the founder of *noirisme,* and Senegalese President Leopold Senghor hailed him as the "Father of Négritude",[21] others acquainted with Firmin's earlier tome see his pan-Africanist thought as pioneering. Pradel Pompilus subtitled his study of Anténor Firmin's thought *Le champion de la négritude et de la democratie haitienne.*[22] It is entirely possible that Firmin and others of Haiti's nineteenth-century intellectual elite laid the primary foundation for what became the négritude movement. Jean Price-Mars's homage to Firmin in his biography of him may be considered such an acknowledgement as he saw similarities between Firmin and the twentieth-century Senegalese pan-Africanist, Cheikh Anta Diop.

Firmin's work should be considered as a precursor to pan-Africanism and the négritude movement. Four chapters in *The Equality of the Human Races* speak directly to the primary role played by the black race in world history and civilization, including "Egypt and Civilization", "Intellectual Evolution of the Black Race in Haiti", "Evolutionary Pace of the Black Race" and "The Role of the Black Race in the History of Civilization". Indeed, the entire book reveals Firmin to be *noiriste,* without arrogance or apology. Added to his scholarship is a documented history of activism. Firmin attended the first Pan-African Congress in London in 1900, which W.E.B. DuBois also attended, and he was present at the second congress in 1909. Kwame Nkrumah acknowledged Firmin as a New World pioneer of pan-Africanism at a speech at the University of Ghana in September 1964 as he extolled the works of Africans and scholars in the Diaspora who "believed in and urged the necessity of writing about Africa from the point of view of African interests and African assumptions and concepts and not from the point of view of Europeans and others who have quite different interests . . ." He continued:

> And let us not forget the important contributions of others in the New World, for example, the sons of Africa in Haiti such as Anténor Firmin and Dr Jean Price-Mars, and others in the United States such as Alexander Crummell, Carter G. Woodson, and our own Dr DuBois.[23]

It is possible that Nkrumah learned about Anténor Firmin through his close relationship with Jean Price-Mars. While many white and black intellectuals see Price-Mars as the greatest of Haitian intellectuals, and attribute to him the title of "father of négritude", he never acknowledged this claim. He lived well into the second half of the twentieth century and witnessed both the end of European colonialism in Africa and the postcolonial rise of ideological and political négritude. Price-Mars was unanimously chosen as president of the first Congress of Black Writers and Artists held in Paris in 1956, when he was ninety years of age, and presidents Ahmed Touré of Guinea and Leopold Senghor at Conakry proclaimed him "the incomparable Master".

At the end of his remarkable life, he paid his respects to Anténor Firmin in a biography of his intellectual predecessor, *Joseph Anténor Firmin,* chronicling his life as scholar, diplomat, patriot and politician. Devoting one chapter to Firmin as an *homme de science,* he extolled the importance of the scholarly contributions made in *De l'égalité des races humaines.* He referred to Firmin as a prodigy and marvelled at the remarkable achievement of writing a book of its scope in only eighteen months, the sort of work that it would take others years of research and reflection to accomplish. He noted that Firmin and Louis Joseph Janvier, the two Haitian members of the Paris Anthropology Society, were subjected to the racist ideas of French anthropology that pronounced them inferior. Yet, knowing this to be a false science, he nonetheless embraced the potential of anthropology, and this is how he came "to his vocation as an anthropologist".[24] Price-Mars remarks especially on Firmin's critique of anthropometry and craniometry, noting that had the world heeded his ideas the tragedy of "Hitlerism" or Nazism might have been avoided. He pointed to Firmin's recognition of Egypt as an African civilization, including presciently referencing Nubia and Meroë in Sudan in his praise of ancient Africa. He intimated the fate of obscurity that befell Firmin's book, whose arguments provoked a "scandal" in Europe, so much did they represent a break with the prevalent ideas of his time. As mentioned above, he suggested a close linkage with the ideas of Cheik Anta Diop's *Nations Négres et Culture* as well as the work of Basil Davidson, *Africa before the Europeans,* both popular books in the 1960s when *Joseph Anténor Firmin* was published. While acknowledging Firmin as "pioneering" among Haitian scholars, Price-Mars also mentions others in this constellation of scholarly greats, including Beauvais Lespinasse, author of *Histoire des affranchis de Saint-Domingue,* and Hannibal Price, who wrote *De la réhabilitation de la race noire par la République d'Haïti,* from whom Price-Mars had taken his name.[25]

FIRMIN AND PRICE-MARS ON AFRICA AND AFRICANS

The knowledge of the two scholars of Africa and Africans can be contrasted. Firmin was largely ignorant of the African continent of his day, recalling that much of the African interior had yet to be fully explored and mapped at the time of the writing of *De l'égalité des races humaines* in 1885. The Berlin Congress dividing the continent amongst the major European powers had occurred the year before, in 1884. Myths, inferior peoples, and tales of monstrosity characterized European views of Africa. Lacking accurate knowledge of the present and adhering to the dictates of science, Firmin declared, "I want to limit myself to generally known fields where serious discussions can be conducted with evidence and verification."[26] Thus, he turned to Africa's glorious past in support of his anti-racist theory. He devoted much attention to the ancient Nile Valley, recognizing the achievement of Nubia (Ethiopia) as well as the better-known Egypt, understanding well ahead of his time the rivalry between the two separate, yet fraternal, civilizations.

By contrast, more than four decades later, Price-Mars used Haitian folklore as a key to Haiti's African past and present links. Price-Mars referenced Africa of "the Congo, the Sudan, Dahomey", while Firmin conjured the ancient Nile, Egypt, Ethiopia – from "Memphis to Meroë" – in support of Africa's contribution to the civilization of the black race. Price-Mars rejected the "Dark Continent" characterization, relying upon works of Joseph Deniker, W.E.B. DuBois and Maurice Delafosse.

In *So Spoke the Uncle,* he portrays the manner in which, like a geologist in a process of recovery, peasant life could uncover the vestiges of ancient African customs, beliefs and mores sifted through a French sieve. Moreover, he told the story in Creole through the words and sentiments of Haitian masses. Both Price-Mars and Firmin emphasized the importance of Creole as transitional to French in Haitian education, and both saw in the American Tuskegee approach of self-determination an example for Haitian development.

Both Haitian scholars legitimated the study of Africa on its own terms. Further, they exerted a major effort to rehabilitate Haitian culture for itself and for the world by valourizing not only Haitian intellectuals and folklore, but the past and present grandeur of Africa. Price-Mars was less equivocal than Firmin was in his day that contemporary African culture was as great a source of pride in Africa as its glorious past.

FIRMIN ON SLAVERY:
HIS ENCOUNTER WITH FREDERICK DOUGLASS

Anténor Firmin was well acquainted with Frederick Douglass's *Slave Narrative,* which he quoted at length, from 1845, forty years before the publication of *De l'égalité des races humaines.* Rather than citing the portions of the *Narrative* that deal with Douglass's beatings and the general brutality wrought upon the slaves to which he bears witness, Firmin quoted Douglass's account of the transformative moment of resistance against the slave-breaker Covey.[27] Firmin saw Douglass as America's most illustrious "mulatto", judging him by Haitian racial standards not as "black" – as would be the case with the American one-drop rule – but by the account of his own birth by his enslaved black mother and white father of indeterminate identity, but likely his mother's master.

This prior knowledge and sympathy with Douglass makes the encounter between the two over the Môle of St Nicolas – Douglass as consul general of the United States in Haiti and Firmin as minister of foreign affairs – all the more interesting and dramatic. Minister Firmin said "No" to the American request – relayed through Ambassador Douglass but played out with US gunboats in Port-au-Prince harbour, and in the end both men were disgraced – Frederick Douglass for his failure to deliver the Môle and Minister Firmin for even entertaining the question. Firmin wrote vigorously against slavery as the institution related to the doctrine of the inequality of races. He contrasted the more "timid" pro-slavery ideas of the non-slaveholding nations of Europe with the unapologetic defence of slavery in the United States. He noted that pro-slavery sentiments were to be found alike among anthropologists who counted themselves as monogenists (espousing a single origin of humanity) or polygenists (theorizing multiple and unequal origins of humans).

> The anti-philosophical and anti-scientific doctrine of the inequality of the races rests on nothing more than the notion of man's exploitation by man. Only the American school has shown any honesty and consistency in its support of the doctrine, for its proponents have never hidden the interest that they have had in its promotion.
>
> While accepting the idea of the plurality of species and their comparative inequality, the European scientist will protest against slavery in magnificent tirades. . . . Broca, for example, who does not hesitate to say what he thinks of the Ethiopian black, indignantly raises his voice against slavery.[28]

Firmin's empathy with the condition of enslavement is deep and profound, whether he is discussing racial myths of docility, indolence or feigned ignorance in the face of the brutal dominance of slave master over slave. He extolled especially the accomplishments of Haiti's *métis* (mixed-race persons) triumphing over their suffering as "mulattos". His focus on the fecundity and biological vigour of the New World's racially mixed persons was meant to challenge the "scientific" view of many anthropologists and other scientists of the infertility of the offspring of black and white. More amused by this assertion than agitated, he pointed to the vigorous, hybrid populations of New World societies, including the growing populations of Haiti and the Dominican Republic, as examples that racially mixed people reproduce as well as any other. The fact was that few black voices on the subject of race were to be heard, which was one of the stated reasons for Firmin's book. Responding to the assertion by de Quatrefages that black people sweat less than white people, he speaks with authority on the subject:

> I am Black and nothing distinguishes me anatomically from the purest Sudanese. However, I transpire abundantly enough to have some idea of the facts. My congeners are not beyond the laws of nature. I shall not bother to discuss the issue of the putative sui generis odor that is supposedly a particular characteristic of the Negro race. The idea is more comical than scientific.[29]

Firmin says all of this and more about slavery and its effects upon the Negro mind, body and soul as he looks to a future when the educated "Ethiopian" will read into the past of human history and pass his own judgement upon what has been done to him and what he has done to others.

Instead of harbouring hatred in his heart, he will generously spread the inexhaustible love of which he is naturally endowed, so much so that those who do not know the rich and varied qualities of his temperament will read into it a feminine trait even as they behold him at his most masculine behavior. Facing the other races, he will remember his days of humiliation under the yoke of slavery, when he was forced to pay with his sweat for the luxurious way of life of the sybaratic colonizer. As he reviews the past he will remember that there was a time when . . .the children of Seth and Japheth were themselves under the harsh rule of his Black ancestors. The gigantic monuments which are the glory of Egypt had been built with the labor of Whites from the East and the West. Humanity is one in time as it is in space; the injustices of past centuries echo those of the present centuries.[30]

This passage reveals the grand historical perspective that Firmin easily referenced and the halcyon days of black rule in antiquity, but the passage also reveals the essential humanism that underlies Firmin's *The Equality of the Human Races.*

ANTÉNOR FIRMIN'S
PRESCIENT POSTCOLONIAL LITERARY ANALYSIS

Firmin's generation of Haitian scholars was already three or four generations post independence when their many remarkable works were written during the last decades of the nineteenth century. As they were writing in the first black republic to free itself simultaneously from both slavery and colonialism, it is not surprising that Firmin, or others before him, would develop an early postcolonial perspective in their writing.

Several chapters of *The Equality of the Human Races* are devoted to a critique of historical European thought regarding "the Negro". Chapter 18, "Religious Myths and Words of the Ancients", contains a systematic critique of Christianity with its "white angels" and "black devils"; its White Jesus ("to make him likeable"), and the inborn Curse of Ham. Firmin made excellent use of his knowledge of classical Greek and Latin (standard parts of a nineteenth-century Haitian education) by revealing the benign and non-racist views of these ancients regarding the Africans/Ethiopians in their midst. He thus presages the work of Frank Snowden in *Before Color Prejudice,* published in 1983,[31] and, like Snowden, he makes liberal use of the words of the ancients. From *The Iliad* he cites a quotation about the character of the Ethiopians: "Jupiter came down yesterday toward the Ocean to attend a feast in the land of the Ethiopians who are renowned for their justice, and all the gods followed him."[32] What greater tribute to a people, notes Firmin, than to have the gods follow them!

From Latin literature Firmin examines Ovid's *Fastes,* in which the issue of skin complexion is clearly raised involving the dark Ariadne and the god Bacchus. Ariadne worries that her black skin may be a disadvantage before a rival with a white complexion, but Bacchus "embraces her, and oblivious to her black skin he says to her, 'Let us go to heaven. You shall share not only my bed, but my name.' "[33] Firmin admires Shakespeare's *Othello* for its emphasis both on the relevance and irrelevance of race in the love story of Othello and fair Desdemona. Shakespeare puts these words on her lips: "I saw Othello's visage in his mind." In other words, Firmin argued, she loved the moral and intellectual man beyond colour or physical features.[34]

In his concise chapter 13, "Prejudices and Vanities", Firmin pens a scathing critique of Western philosophy, from Buchner ("the Negro's brain is smaller, more animal-like"), to Müller ("the Negro is an excellent imitator, but he is in a complete state of inferiority"), to the notorious de Gobineau ("Negroes occupy the lowest rung of the ladder"). But he is careful also to include liberals of their age, as there are always competing ideas; thus he noted Hegel's argument that slavery is irrational because negroes are members of the human race, and Louis Figuier's identification of "many Negroes who are intellectually superior to Europeans".[35] Upon this review, Firmin asks the essential question: "How did it happen that so many prominent men, individuals of great intellect, scientists and scholarly inventors of bold theories, free-thinking philosophers, could adopt this strange notion of the inferiority of Blacks?" To this question he provides an answer that still holds relevance for the present era:

> the notion of the inequality of the races is so deeply rooted in the minds of the most enlightened men of Europe that they seem incapable of ever discarding it. There must be, then, certain extrinsic causes which are alien to science but which have such a stranglehold on the minds of the most intelligent men that they are intellectually paralyzed. To explain satisfactorily the persistence of this notion of the inequality of the races, we must identify those influences and try to understand how they could motivate people to hold onto a wrong opinion in the face of the most convincing evidence to the contrary.[36]

CONCLUSION

Anténor Firmin was a pioneering anthropologist, pan-Africanist, early critical race theorist, and prescient scholar in what has become postcolonial studies in the latter part of the twentieth century. Haitian scholars such as Anténor Firmin and Jean Price-Mars have been marginalized from the canon of anthropology and other Western scholarly disciplines not only by the revolutionary tradition of Haiti and by race, but by their scholarship in the French language, with the global dominance of English. Both are signal figures in the intellectual legacy of the Haitian Revolution, with Jean Price-Mars as the better-known *noiriste* and pan-Africanist, while Anténor Firmin is the less well-known but acknowledged intellectual predecessor of Price-Mars. In my view, Firmin should be received not only as a pioneering anthropologist but also as an early pan-Africanist in the formative period of this movement. His work can also be considered as pioneering to the much later postcolonial studies movement during the second half of the twentieth century. These features of the intellectual legacy of *The Equality of the Human Races* make it remarkable and still as relevant to the twenty-first century as it was for the nineteenth century.

Finally, I was struck by the congruence between sentiments expressed by Price-Mars[37] and Firmin's last lines of *The Equality of the Human Races,* both quoting Victor Hugo: "Every man is man", with Firmin completing this thought with the "divine instruction" to "love one another".[38] This intergenerational message from Firmin and Price-Mars to the present generation offers a core value of common human heritage, respect and, finally, love that addresses the scholarly humanism of both Firmin's and Price-Mars's scholarship.

NOTES

1. Anténor Firmin, *De l'égalité des races humaines* (Paris: Cotillon, 1885); Anténor Firmin, *The Equality of the Human Races,* trans. Asselin Charles, introduction by Carolyn Fluehr-Lobban (New York: Garland Press, 2000; paperback edition, Urbana: University of Illinois Press, 2002).

2. Jean Price-Mars, *Jospeh Anténor Firmin* ([Port-au-Prince?] Haiti: Imprint Séminaire, 1964).

3. Kevin Yelvington, "Pioneers Marginalized by Race" (paper presented at AAA Centennial panel, American Anthropological Association, New Orleans, 2002).

4. G.R. Coulthard, *Race and Colour in Caribbean Literature* (London: Oxford University Press, 1962), 117.

5. Anténor Firmin, *Lettres des Saint Thomas* (Paris, 1910).

6. Firmin, *De l'égalité des races humaines,* liv.

7. Edward Burnett Tylor, *Anthropology: An Introduction to the Study of Man and Civilization* (1881; reprint, 1902).

8. Franz Boas, *The Mind of Primitive Man* (New York: Macmillan, 1911).

9. Anténor Firmin, *The Equality of the Human Races,* 100.

10. Ibid., 108.

11. Ibid., 102.

12. Ibid., 108.

13. Ibid., 118.

14. Ibid., 120–35.

15. Magdaline W. Shannon, *Jean Price-Mars, the Haitian Elite and the American Occupation, 1915–35* (New York: St Martin's Press, 1996), 163.

16. Ibid., 21.

17. Jean Price-Mars, *Ainsi parla l'oncle* (France: Impremerie Compiègne, 1928); and Jean Price-Mars, *So Spoke the Uncle,* trans. Magdaline Shannon (Washington, DC: Three Continents Press, 1990), 13, 17.

18. Price-Mars, *Jospeh Anténor Firmin.*

19. Melville Herskovits, *Life in a Haitian Valley* (New York: Alfred A. Knopf, 1937), x.

20. George E. Simpson, Preface, in *So Spoke the Uncle,* Jean Price-Mars, trans. Magdaline Shannon (Washington, DC: Three Continents Press, 1990).

21. Jean Fouchard, Introduction to the English edition, in *So Spoke the Uncle,* Jean Price-Mars, trans. Magdaline Shannon (Washington, DC: Three Continents Press, 1990).

22. Pradel Pompilus, *Anténor Firmin par lui-même, Le champion de la négritude et de la démocratie haïtienne* (Port-au-Prince: Edition Pegasus, 1988).

23. Kwame Nkrumah, speech (delivered at the first meeting of the editorial board of the *Encyclopedia Africana,* University of Ghana, 24 September 1964).

24. Jean Price-Mars, *Jospeh Anténor Firmin,* 148.

25. Hannibal Price, *De la réhabilitation de la race noire par la République d'Haïti* (Port-au-Prince: Imprimerie J. Verrollot, 1900).

26. Firmin, *The Equality of the Human Races,* 401.

27. Ibid., 323–33.

28. Ibid., 140.

29. Ibid., 61–63.

30. Ibid., 447.

31. Frank Snowden, *Before Color Prejudice* (Cambridge, Mass.: Harvard University Press, 1983).

32. Firmin, *The Equality of the Human Races,* 420.

33. Ibid., 421.

34. Ibid., 423.

35. Ibid., 326–27.

36. Ibid., 328.

37. Jean Price-Mars, *Lettre ouverte au Dr René Piquion* (Port-au-Prince, 1967).

38. Firmin, *The Equality of the Human Races,* 451.

CHAPTER 8

RE-CREOLIZING SWING
ST DOMINGUE REFUGEES IN THE *GOVI* OF NEW ORLEANS

KEITH CARTWRIGHT

> *When objects are taken off an altar to be introduced into*
> *ritual action, or when they are moved from one ritual arena*
> *to another, they are first swung from side to side, or the people*
> *carrying the objects turn around and around themselves, often*
> *with the sacred pots or bottles perched on their heads. When*
> *the yams were cut and ready to be cooked, Madame Jacques's*
> *daughters were told to pick them up and* balanse, *balance,*
> *dance by turning round and round, as they headed up the stairs*
> *to the kitchen. To "balanse" in Haitian Creole does not mean to*
> *achieve equilibrium. It means to activate or enliven, to dance*
> *in a back-and-forth way. To raise energy by playing with con-*
> *flict and contradiction is to "balanse". Balancing is a way of*
> *exposing the true nature of something by bringing it within the*
> *forcefield of clashing energies and contradictory impulses.*
>
> – Karen McCarthy Brown, "The Ritual Economy of Haitian Vodou"

As we grow more attentive to Kamau Brathwaite's description of creolization as "a cultural action – material, psychological, and spiritual" – the Haitian Revolution demands renewed study as one of the most profoundly creolizing cultural actions of New World experience.[1] After chattel "servants" successfully resisted the zombifica-tions of colonial rule by acting, in part, upon the inspiriting authority accessible to them as *serviteurs* (servants) of the vodou *lwa* (spirits), the entire plantation complex felt reverberations of Haiti's "rebalancing" swing. Something material, psychic and spiritual of Haiti's revolutionary cultural action inhabits American consciousness, particularly the (sub)consciousness of unity and disunity in the United States. We can gain some sense of this from Edgar Allan Poe's "The Raven", a poem so singularly canonical in American literature that it has been recited by school children, recast in rock lyrics and used to provide the moniker of a professional sports team. Tellingly, readers have been slow to recognize the Haiti-informed hauntings of Poe's plantation South in this poem featuring an "ebony bird", a "thing of evil" that escapes "from some unhappy master whom unmerciful Disaster / Followed fast and followed faster till his songs one burden bore". The raven's "tempest tossed" arrival "On this home by Horror haunted" to throw "his shadow on the floor" can not be cut free from the material, psychological and spiritual balancing acts of the Haitian Revolution. From atop "the pallid bust of Pallas", his repeated call of "nevermore" gives voice to what Édouard Glissant has described as "the unstoppable conjunction" of creolization and "the damnation of those who fight it".[2]

According to Alfred Hunt, it was in reaction to the St Dominique revolution and through increasing censorship and restrictions on black agency "that the South began to erect its intellectual blockade against potentially dangerous doctrines".[3] While the eastern seaboard of North America felt the fallout of the Haitian Revolution, receiving as many as twenty-five thousand St Domingue refugees (including the Florida exile of one of the insurrection's key initiators, Jorge Biassou), it was in Louisiana that St Domingue's cultural actions continued to move with the kind of dynamism that had caused an embattled Napoleon to offer the Louisiana territory for US purchase.[4] If the Haitian Revolution's creolizing forces imparted a spirit of dread closure to Poe's "The Raven", some of these same forces – material, psychological and spiritual – filled what Ishmael Reed has called "the Govi of New Orleans".[5] Attending to ways in which New Orleans has served as a *govi* (one of the clay vessels housing *lwa* and ancestral spirits, and from which these spirits may speak), this chapter focuses on the unique "housing" that New Orleans offered to St Domingue's migrant *lwa* or "saints" and the manner in which they thrived to inspirit early jazz and open the city's populace (along with the world's) to moments "When the Saints Go Marching In". The substantial presence of St Domingue refugees in New Orleans worked to re-creolize a creole city that has been described as "perhaps the most seething ethnic melting pot that the nineteenth-century world could produce".[6] Migrating *lwa* dancing in the heads of Louisiana-bound *serviteurs* found balancing agency in rites that eventually moved from serving the spirits to serving the more secular jazz spirit of swing. This chapter's effort to go to the mouth of the *govi* of New Orleans, however, calls for difficult acts of listening to subalternized voices that are most often poorly represented, if recorded at all, in our available texts. We may find creole orientation in voodoo's polyrhythmic "remix" of the diverse bodies of knowledge that entered its embodying repertoires as we essay a Haiti-informed reading of New Orleans's francophone literature.[7] Early accounts of voodoo rites and the emergence of jazz can help us chart crossroads of aesthetics and performance connecting these two often spectacular realms of Afro-Creole authority. Finally, when such "archeological" sources are brought into confluence with more recent African-American literature invoking New Orleans's Legba-ruled hermeneutics – complemented by theoretical applications based in Afro-Atlantic ritual and music – we may gain a perspective balanced enough to see how Haitian *govi* served so powerfully as melting pots of the spirits of many nations that their attendant rites of swing were uniquely prepared to house the New World (and new World) creolizations moving to and from New Orleans.

The Franco-Creole and Afro-Creole cores of New Orleans were sustained in the nineteenth century by a single event: the St Domingue migration to Louisiana, about which George W. Cable writes "it might be easier to underestimate than to exaggerate the silent results of an event that gave the French-speaking classes twice the numerical power with which they had begun to wage their long battle against American absorption".[8] While Louisiana's Afro-Creole culture owes much to its foundational Senegambian slave presence, the mass migration from St Domingue (with 9,059 refugees coming in the final wave of exodus from Cuba during the last nine months of 1809) revitalized and re-creolized it.[9] Following the 1809 arrival of 2,731 whites, 3,102 free people of colour, and 3,226 slaves, the population of New Orleans increased to 6,331 whites, 4,950 free people of colour, and 5,961 slaves.[10] Coming just six years after the Louisiana Purchase and more than doubling New Orleans's francophone creole population and black majority, the St Domingue migration allowed French (or Franco-Creole) speakers to remain a majority presence until around 1830 and likely enabled New Orleans to hold onto its uniquely French and Caribbean heritages of language, culinary arts, religion, music and its three-caste racial society.[11] As Paul Lachance's study of antebellum Louisiana marriage contracts has shown, "Saint-Domingue refugees were not only an important addition to the number of free persons of color living in New Orleans, but also to the wealth of the group" as "female refugees of color arrived with more property than local free women of color had been able to accumulate".[12] New Orleans's free black populace, most of whom could claim St Domingue descent, possessed land and wealth in amounts and numbers well beyond the reach of any other black population in the United States. The St Domingue migration bolstered the independence of Afro-Creole communities and fostered Franco-Creole and Afro-Creole models of agency, education and activism that would sustain unique modes of performance and authority embodied in vodou, that would offer resistance to crude anglophone codes of segregation via Plessy versus Ferguson, and that would help swing the new jazz sounds of modern time. This city, whose recent Afro-Creole mayors have been descendants of St Domingue migrants, offers an early nineteenth-century model of urban multiculturalism that has grown familiar to contemporary Americans. Haitian contributions to New Orleans's cultural gumbo have indeed been key.

St Domingue emigrés both re-Africanized and re-creolized the whole material, psychological and spiritual matrix of New Orleans. The power of the improvisational aesthetics of assemblage that migrated from St Domingue in the heads of the *lwa*'s servants is well conveyed in Donald Cosentino's discussion of contemporary Haitian altars:

> To look at a Vodou altar cluttered with customized whisky bottles, satin pomanders, clay pots dressed in lace, plaster statues of St Anthony and the laughing Buddha, holy cards, political kitsch, Dresden clocks, bottles of Moët-et-Chandon, rosaries, crucifixes, Masonic insignia, eye-shadowed kewpie dolls, atomizers of Anais-Anais, wooden phalli, goat skulls, Christmas tree ornaments, Arawak celts . . . is to gauge the achievement of slaves and freemen who imagined a myth broad enough and fabricated a ritual complex enough to encompass all this disparate stuff.[13]

Cosentino repeatedly utilizes the currency of jazz analogies to give readers a sense of the sophistication of a demonized religion's sacred arts. He notes David Byrne's description of vodou altars as "'visual jazz, constantly reworked and reactivated'" and practitioners' reinterpretations of Catholic lithographs and iconic hagiography: "The process is centripetal, pushing out into new forms like a jazz riff."[14] If jazz serves as valourizing analogy for maligned vodou, we may also see that vodou has worked as primitivist analogue for the syncopating powers of jazz. Whether from a *Ladies' Home Journal* (1921) attack on swing's origination as "the accompaniment of the voodoo dancer, stimulating the half-crazed barbarian to the vilest deeds", or whether we find it in Sidney Bechet's homage to a Congo Square drumming grandfather who sought the praisesongs of a voodooist "to throw out the devils and bring down powers", jazz's swinging power has been tied to fantastic figurations of voodoo.[15] We would do well to look more attentively to the St Domingue-informed crossroads of vodou and swing. There we may find musical energizing of the individual/collective body in ritual practice, creating meaning and community through the rhythmic integration of the "mindful body". In nineteenth-century New Orleans writing we may begin to see how Louisiana voodoo rose from cross-currents of Catholicism, Senegambian *nyama,* masonic rites, spiritualism, revolutionary Romanticism, carnivalesque performance and an already agglutinating Haitian vodou in a manner that divined the birth of jazz.[16]

Pre-revolutionary St Domingue provides the setting of "Le Mulâtre" (1837) by Victor Séjour, the New Orleans-born son of a free man of colour from St Domingue. The story of a slave's vengeance against his planter-father, "Le Mulâtre" offers a sympathetic representation of vodou alongside precursory modes of jazz funeral rites. In a scene where vodou practitioners bury the central character's Senegal-born mother, we see that "[e]ach of them, having blessed the remains of the deceased, kneels and prays; for most of the negro races, despite their fetishism, have profound faith in the existence of God", and "[w]hen this first ceremony is finished, another one, no less singular, commences" with "songs, and then funeral dances!"[17] An important element in the creolization of relations with the dead in Haiti and Louisiana was the rise of nineteenth-century spiritualism. Spiritualist seances and mesmerism emerged as popular forces, engaging black mediums such as the New Orleans blacksmith J.B. Valmour and white mediums such as Charles Testut on common ground.[18] Testut's "new age" novel *Le Vieux Saloman* (1872) evokes a freemasonry-informed spiritual-ist organization that stretches from Louisiana across North America, Europe and the Caribbean in its abolitionist activity, working to free "those who possess men as well as . . . those possessed".[19] While Testut's work depicts effectively the spir-itual activities linking the black and white creole intellectual elites, Alfred Mercier's *L'habitation Saint-Ybars* (1881) engages Afro-Creole life more intimately, provid-ing dialogue in gumbo French and acknowledging a fuller, "swinging" range of creolized authority in Louisiana. The white creole protagonist grows up listening to the banjo music of his nurse's Bambara father while the nurse learns classical repertoires on the piano. Much of the gothic storyline is tied to the body and blood of a phenotypically white slave woman whose mixed-race grandmother "was raised by a good master . . . who came here after the disasters of Saint-Domingue".[20] While Mercier embraced much of the Afro-Creole cultural matrix shaping the social and spiritual fluidities of swing, Marie Augustin, a Louisiana-born descendant of St Domingue exiles, underscored needs for strict mastery in her novel *Le Macandal: Episode de l'insurrection des noirs à St Domingue* (1892). Published in the peak year of lynchings in the United States, Augustin's narrative takes up the question of whether "the blood of Macandal may engender anything other than a monster".[21] Her novel dramatizes an inevitable reversion to orgy and terroristic savagery as Macandal's Paris-educated but unrehabilitated son directs Bois Caïman's "monstrous ceremony", which is "impregnated with an electricity charged from the agglomeration of these human bodies". The rest of the novel is anticlimax, leading ultimately to the killing of the would-be rehabilitators, to a flotilla of surviving exiles with their loyal servants and to a last look upon St Domingue as winds push them "toward the hospitable shores of Louisiana".[22]

George W. Cable's *The Grandissimes* (1880) treats voodoo in sharper detail than the Franco-Creole fictions do, noting "an oblation of beer sweetened with black molasses to Papa Lebat, who keeps the invisible keys of all the doors".[23] An exotic alterity moving between fear and longing pervades Cable's representation of voodoo's swinging rites. In one ritual he perceives "a frightful triumph of body over mind", but later observes the physical education which draws a servant of the spirits to "turn, posture, bow, respond to the song, start, swing, straighten, stamp, wheel, lift her hand, stoop, twist, walk, whirl, tip-toe with crossed ankles, smite her palms, march, circle, leap – an endless improvisation of rhythmic motion to this modulated responsive chant".[24] In similar but more appreciative vein, Karen McCarthy Brown has described how practice of Haitian vodou works past "the mind/body splitting that has characterized Western thought and, further, assumes that an appreciation for the embodied minds of human beings – or better, their mindful bodies – is crucial if one is to understand what it means to be human in the world".[25] Voodoo's supple resistance to white supremacist inflexibility comes across in powerful counterpoint when Cable's white centre, Frowenfeld, reacts with dread as "the cathedral clock struck twelve and was answered again from the convent tower; and as the notes died away he suddenly became aware that the weird, drowsy throb of the African song and dance had been swinging drowsily in his brain for an unknown lapse of time". Swinging in spite of itself to voodoo pulsings and subalternized modes of knowledge, the novel's gothic core lies in the Haiti-haunted story of Bras Coupé's rebellion recalled by the book's primary voodoo priestess, who "had heard of San Domingo", and knew "the lesson she would have taught . . . was Insurrection".[26] What the book also conveys is a feel for the transformative power of pre-jazz music and dance in New Orleans.

Against the gothic threat of repetition of "the lesson of St Domingue" lay the desire attached to the tourist-drawing spectacular Afro-Creole roots of creole identity as seen in Cable's work and particularly in Alcée Fortier's *Louisiana Folk-Tales* (1895), which presents Compé Lapin (Brer Rabbit) as an icon of authority. Rabbit, whose "mouth was so honeyed that no one could refuse him anything", the master drummer who plays the creole balls and makes the strongest gris-gris, is a spectacular performer of sacred, secular and transpositional rites.[27] New Orleans spectacles, the balls, the opera and particularly Mardi Gras received the formative energies of St Domingue refugees and contributed to the symbiotic performative realms of voodoo and swing. Tending towards complexly dialogized hybridizations, carnival created, according to Cable, "gorgeous, not to say, gaudy, tableaux drawn through the streets under the glare of blazing petroleum and frequent lime-lights, on tinselled cars, by draped teams, to the blare of brass music and the roar of popular acclamation, in representation of one or another of the world's great myths, epics, or episodes", all of which he could dismiss as "make-believe art, frivolous taste, and short-sighted outlay".[28] Mardi Gras's early "make-believe art" shared a performative assemblage aesthetic – and almost certainly, brassy syncopations – with the ritual *konesans* (knowledge) of voodoo practitioners, who according to Mintz and Trouillot had "successfully 'patched' what *had* been believed to what *would* be believed" and whose spirit-work had been similarly dismissed.[29] New Orleans's Caribbean aesthetic of patchwork spectacle, with its double emphasis on continuity and freshness, was well honed by voodoo's incorporating rites of swing.

Prior to the influx of St Domingue refugees, Louisiana's Afro-Creole spiritual practices were most deeply shaped by Senegambian slaves in dialogue with Catholicism and other African/Afro-Creole/colonial practices. With the ascension of Sanité Dédé, a free "quadroon" from St Domingue, as New Orleans's first-recorded voodoo queen during the 1820s, Haitian vodou appears to have taken solid root in New Orleans. She is credited with establishing St John's Eve (June 23) as the major fête of the ritual calendar and with choosing Pontchartrain's shores as the annual meeting place.[30] A fifteen-year-old white, brought to Dédé's spirit-house on Dumaine Street one night in 1825 by a "West Indian" servant, recalled witnessing possessions induced by the ritual *konesans* swinging a sheepskin drum, a bone-drummed barrel, a gourd *asson,* a banjo and a ritually balanced snake moving a "lithe, tall black woman, with a body waving and undulating . . . . to sway on one and the other side" as the lead drummer sang: "Houm! Dance Calinda! / Voudou! Magnian ! / Aie! Aie! / Dance Calinda !" Even at this earliest recorded New Orleans voodoo ceremony "half a dozen white men and two white women" were submitting to a St Domingue priestess and the spirits (particularly Danballa) she served.[31]

While Sanité Dédé, New Orleans's first recorded voodoo priestess, was born in St Domingue, the key figure in the popularization of the religion, Marie Laveau, was most likely New Orleans–born. Married in 1819 to the St Domingue emigré Jacques Paris, she became known as "the Widow Paris" after Paris's disappearance. She then entered into a relationship with another St Domingue emigré, Christophe Glapion (around 1826–27), emerging soon thereafter as New Orleans's pre–eminent *mambo*. Under Laveau voodoo appears to have permeated all strata of creole society, and while guarding private rites for initiates and sincere or "paying" seekers, she developed the annual festival of St John's Eve as a carnivalesque attraction. Robert Tallant asserts that the St John's rites "became, under Marie's direction, a little like 'shows' staged for the benefit of the curious whites, particularly the police and the newspaper reporters".[32] Marie's daughter, Marie II, continued the spectacular nature of St John's Eve, bringing "great crowds" to the lake, according to one reporter in 1872, for feasts and rites that continued until dawn.[33] Tallant states, "To go see Marie Laveau became one of the things a tourist in New Orleans must do, just as he was supposed to eat once in each of the famous restaurants and attend a performance at the French Opera House."[34] Voodoo's spectacular exposure spread its rhythms and inspiriting dance. An Irish-Louisianan who lived along the lakefront recalled her mother's tales of the fêtes: "The police would come out some-times, but she – that Laveau woman – would hoodoo them and they would take off their clothes, too. Can you imagine all them people, white and colored, dancing around like devils, and all of them naked as jaybirds?"[35] Voodoo's kinetic power (along with the vexing tone of exoticized alterity that accompanies most historical accounts) appears well grounded in pre-revolutionary St Domingue as observed by Moreau de Saint-Méry, who writes of practitioners dancing there "to the edge of consciousness" and adds that "never has any man of the constabulary, who has sworn war upon Voodoo, not felt the power which compells him to dance and which without doubt has saved the dancers from any need for flight". Having watched vodouists "spin around endlessly", Moreau was savvy enough to see that these physically and psychically energizing balancing acts, given their utterly independent authority to convert legally possessed "things" into *serviteurs* possessed by master *lwa,* "can be made into a terrible weapon".[36]

Marie Laveau is credited with reinvesting voodoo practice with the spiritual glamour of Catholicism's material culture and iconography. Still her service to the saints worked to feed Haitian *lwa,* as Josephine Green's memory of Legba rites makes clear:

> All the people wit' her was hollerin' and screamin', "We is goin' to see Papa Limba! We is goin' to see Papa Limba!" My grandpa go runnin' after my ma then, yellin' her, "You come on in her Eunice! Don't you know Papa Limba is the devil?" But after that my ma find out Papa Limba meant St Peter, and her pa was jest foolin' her.[37]

We hear of Legba's *serviteurs* entering the lake, circling, holding hands and singing as food is tossed to "Papa La Bas". Another informant recalled a song her aunt learned from Marie: "St Peter, St Peter, open the door, / I'm callin' you, come to me ! / St Peter, St Peter, open the door" and added that "Marie Laveau used to call St Peter somethin' like 'Laba' " and "called St Michael 'Daniel Blanc,' and St Anthony 'Yun Sue' ".[38]

Succeeding the first Marie Laveau and competing with the second, Malvina Latour apparently worked to remove some of the Catholic iconography from voodoo ritual.[39] Rites described from Latour's era share core Afro-Creole practices with contemporary Haitian vodou and Cuban santería, as the description of the design of a St John's Eve altar in 1884, featuring a cloth placed on the floor with candles at the corners, suggests: "on the cloth, there was a shallow Indian basket filled with weeds, or, as they call them, *herbes.* Around the basket were diminutive piles of white beans and corn. . . . outside of all several saucers with small cakes in them."[40] Dance instrumentation included a two-string African-style fiddle and skin-covered gourds drummed in rhythms ritually punctuated by "mistings" of liquor sprayed by mouth into the candles' flame. C.D. Warner, attending a ceremony in 1885, describes the process of rapping invocations on the floor, offering candles and brandy on the altar and dashing libations on the floor before stepping into the "shuffle" of a dance. Responding to this collective "swing", believers were misted in brandy sprayed from the mouth of an initiating elder who, as in Haitian practice, washed their heads, "shampooing them" before spinning each in acts of ritual balancing.[41]

Although the voodoo leaders' authority over multiethnic ritual "houses" suggests a unique Afro-Creole agency that prefigures much of what jazz would swing into accomplishment, Congo Square is more often invoked by jazz historians and musicians themselves "as the originating locus of American jazz".[42] Saxophone pioneer Sidney Bechet opened his autobiography with the story of an enslaved grandfather who used to "beat out rhythms on the drums at the square – Congo Square they called it. . . . No one had to explain notes or feeling or rhythm to him."[43] Faced with the rhythms, feelings and knowledge of masses of potentially revolutionary slaves from St Domingue, the New Orleans City Council moved in 1817 to sanction Congo Square as the site for slaves' Sunday dances (which had previously been held in diverse locations), allowing for simultaneous release of enslaved black energies and for their policed observation. The earliest detailed description of the Congo Square dances, from an 1819 entry in Benjamin Latrobe's diary, suggests how much its dance and music must have shared with the voodoo rites led by Sanité Dédé in 1825. Latrobe notes several simultaneous ring dances utilizing antiphonal patterns of music and song along with instrumentation consisting of a banjo prototype, percussive gourd instruments and a variety of drums such as the one played by "an old man [who] sat astride of a cylindrical drum about a foot in diameter, & beat it with incredible quickness with the edge of his hands & fingers".[44] Accompanying Latrobe's careful drawings of the instruments and his wonder over an "extraordinary . . . incredible noise" comes requisite Kantian remastery of the sublime in his dismissal of the scene as "brutally savage . . . dull & stupid".[45] A repeating pattern emerges: white supremacist "reason" remasters encounters with the slave sublime but also tends to be swung by it.

Congo Square soon became a well-policed tourist attraction. As one enthusiastic arrival advertised, "[e]very stranger should visit Congo Square. . . . once at least, and, my word for it, no one will ever regret or forget it".[46] Herbert Asbury insists that "sometimes there were almost as many white spectators surrounding the square to watch the slaves 'dance Congo' as there were black dancers" and adds that "[e]ven in earlier days a Congo dance was considered one of the unique attractions of New Orleans; visitors were always taken to see the slaves at play".[47] Any jazz history that turns to Congo Square for narratives of origin also alerts us to the originating ways in which the jazz freedoms of chattel possessions have been circumscribed by policed, tourist stagings and commodifications.[48] Such stagings are indeed a key part of the story, but we should also look to the underground and public rites of voodoo for the *govi* of jazz's ancestral spirits. Musicians and dancers moved fluidly between the public Congo Square proceedings (which appear to have been discontinued some time after 1835) and the more private voodoo rites – with St Domingue emigrés playing key roles in both arenas. While Marie Laveau may have presided over the Congo Square gatherings as well as over voodoo rites, key differences of authority and agency exist between the Congo Square dances and voodoo services. The Congo Square gatherings were official slave meetings held under the watchful eyes of police and white spectators. Voodoo rituals were often officiated by free people of colour, and whites tended to be *participants* in voodoo perhaps even more often than they were spectators, thereby submitting to Afro-Creole authority in a manner unparalleled in any other arena. Furthermore, the "swinging" music of voodoo "houses" continued well after Congo Square had fallen silent, providing inspiriting sources of rhythms located in the swaying, syncopating individual/collective bodies swung and possessed by *lwa*.

Before swing became a jazz-age noun, it was a verb of ritual, syncopating movement. Brent Edwards refers to swing "in its verb form" as "paradigmatic black cultural *action* or *process*".[49] We may find a verbal equivalent in Haitian vodou and the act of "balancing" or swinging ritual objects and bodies in order to raise their energy, thereby enlivening and heating things up. Karen McCarthy Brown has observed that vodou ritual action calls for objects and bodies to be "balanced", swung back and forth: "To *'balanse'* in Haitian Creole does not mean to achieve equilibrium" but rather "to activate or enliven, to dance in a back and forth way".[50] The ritual necessity of swinging individual and congregational bodies in order to raise their energy and heat things up comes across well in the numerous descriptions of "balancing" acts in New Orleans voodoo. According to an observer of an 1885 rite, after a ritual head washing, a celebrant lifted a *serviteur*, "spun him round a half a dozen times, and then sent him whirling". He notes how the dance's "rhythmical shuffle, with more movement of the hips than of the feet, backward and forward, round and round, but accelerating . . . as the time of the song quickened and the excitement rose in the room . . . made it almost impossible for the spectator not to join in the swing of its influence".[51] Swing provides much of what makes belief and ritual *konesans* possible. One learns to serve the spirits by learning to embody the ritual spirit of swing. Writing of santería drumming, Katherine Hagedorn remarks that it is "swing" that "propels the sound forward, and that excites a physical reaction from listeners. . . .

if you don't move the room, you won't bring down the *santo* [saint]".[52] This ritual swing is clearly a widespread Afro-Atlantic phenomenon, but we must attend to the particularly intense refinement and insistence upon polyrhythmic swing in the St Domingue–informed voodoo worship unique (in the nineteenth-century United States) to the New Orleans area.

Vodou rites balance those who serve the spirits through a ritual swinging that heats things up and works to avoid the chattel ideal of zombifying stiffness, an inflexibility that too often accompanies the mind/body splittings of religions or disciplines of the book.[53] Sharing local spiritedness and *konesans,* early New Orleans swing freed players – as Louis Armstrong observed in his autobiography, *Swing That Music* (1936) – "to be able to leave that score and to know, or 'feel,' just when to leave it and when to get back on it". The key would be to activate "something new swinging into the music to make it 'hot'", a term used "when a swing player gets warmed up and 'feels' the music taking hold of him so strong that he can break through the set rhythms and the melody and toss them around as he wants without losing his way". Heating things up and swinging them, vodou balancing acts prepare the head to become "horse" of the *lwa.* Armstrong insists "when you've got a real bunch of swing players together in an orchestra, you can turn them loose for the most part. 'Give 'em their head', as they say of a race horse. They all play together, picking up and following each other's 'swinging'."[54] This well-tested manner of ritually unloosing and remixing bound bodies and repertoires could embrace any material, following voodoo's exemplary hermeneutic lead. The New Orleans drum great Baby Dodds speaks, for instance, of hearing the Buddy Bolden and John Robichaux bands "play classics in swing", and says of those transitional days, "they didn't call it jazz, but they called it swing".[55]

From the dislocating diasporas of the slave trade to those of St Domingue, New Orleans and current global migrations, rites of swing have answered re-locating needs for family, fraternity and sorority. Answering Homi Bhabha's recent call for a "subaltern secularism" in a way that remains not altogether divorced from spirituality, black Atlantic soul musics nourish and form a sense of migrant community that, like the vodou family described by Karen McCarthy Brown, "is both the occasion for and the product of its own ritual activity".[56] Paul Gilroy's influential response to a globally creolizing "slave sublime", the Black Atlantic's "politics of transfiguration", has called attention to this ethos that "points specifically to the formation of a community of needs and solidarity which is magically made possible in the music itself . . . on a lower frequency where it is played, danced, acted, as well as sung and sung about, because words . . . will never be enough to communicate its unsayable claims to the truth".[57] A song from a Brooklyn *manje yam* ceremony points to this capacity for reassembling networks of need and solidarity:

Lafanmi sanble,	The family is assembled,
Sanble nan.	Gathered in.
Se Kreyol nou ye,	We are Creoles,
Pa genyen Ginen anko.	Who have Africa no longer.[58]

Voodoo provided unique means for St Domingue emigrés and local Afro-Creoles to wield an authority that could "balance" multi-ethnic ritual families in Louisiana. While voodoo thrived in the nineteenth century under the leadership of St Domingue immigrants such as Sanité Dédé, it proved difficult to sustain against North American forces that have long demonized it. Its secular offspring, jazz, did emerge, however, from the old polyrhythms, from the dances of Congo Square, from funeral second lines, Masonic orchestras and local jukes to balance a counterculture *to* and *of* modernity, shaping a global vernacular by sampling and reassembling a circum-Caribbean mix.

Any honest discussion of a creole religion like Haitian vodou or a musical form like jazz cannot look in a single direction for origins, must keep in mind Glissant's notion of creolization as "confluence", and finds much of its subaltern agency unrecorded, poorly documented, misrepresented and "undisciplined".[59] This is the ultimate case of the history of voodoo in New Orleans and the early mixings of jazz styles. Still we may note certain shared aesthetics of assemblage, embodying swing, a polyrhythmic antiphonal perspective described by John Miller Chernoff as "profoundly pluralistic", allowing for symbiosis between "the aesthetic conception of multiple rhythms in music and the religious conception of multiple forces in the world", an open orientation that has provided much of the agency of creolization, for "there is always an in-between, always a place to add another beat".[60] St Domingue refugees, coming from what was the most Africanized colony in the New World to double the population of North America's creole city, added another beat in-between, allowing Papa LaBas and the other "saints" to inform a vibrant crossroads sense of swing that has been best documented by the African-American poets and novelists who have been its most committed *serviteurs*.

Lwa of the crossroads, Legba holds an "authority over mix and transition" that, as Nathaniel Mackey writes, has "made him especially relevant to the experience of transplantation brought about by the slave trade" and to those in need of his "mediatory skills".[61] It is this Haiti-informed voodoo hermeneutics that Louisiana-born poet Yusef Komunyakaa embraces in his own jazz-based poetics. He asserts, "Jazz discovers the emotional mystery behind things; it provides a spiritual connection to the land, reconnecting us to places where its forms originated" and adds "[i]t's easy to recognize contemporary American culture in the graceful shadows swaying with the night in Congo Square. They committed an act of sabotage merely by dancing to keep forbidden gods alive."[62] One can read a similar respect for diasporic forms and spiritual content in Zora Neale Hurston's work, whether in her Haitian fieldwork on vodou, in her writing of *Their Eyes Were Watching God* in Haiti, or while initiating with five New Orleans voodoo "doctors" before working with Luke Turner, who recalled how they used to "beat the drum with the shin bone of a donkey and everybody dance like they do in Hayti".[63] The ability of Ralph Ellison to see around corners also owes much to New Orleans, "home of mystery", and to the creolizing bounce of its swing, that "slightly different sense of time. . . . its nodes, those points where time stands still or from which it leaps ahead".[64] Ellison slips into the breaks of Storyville's "Basin Street Blues", that "street where the dark and light folks meet", as an initiating touchstone for a process by which Minton's Playhouse in Harlem might also become "the source of the mystery", "a shrine" where "an audience initiated and aware" might sway with the musicians' rites of "apprenticeship, ordeals, initiation ceremonies, of rebirth".[65] New Orleans's red light district is replaced by voodoo as a deep locus for the creation of ritual family, a process whereby "[t]hose who have been initiated into the mysteries and have passed the *boule zen* (trial by fire) are born anew as *ounsi kanzo* (initiated by fire)".[66] Ellison praises the New Orleans-born gospel singer Mahalia Jackson as "the high priestess [who] sings within the heart of the congregation as its own voice of faith". Hers is "an art which swings".[67] Then turning to voodoo-jazz hagiography to make a *lwa* of "the legendary Bird", Charlie Parker, and noting how " 'legend' originally meant 'the story of a saint' . . . often identified with symbolic animals", Ellison reveals how much of his own authorial power stems from ritual *konesans* of jazz re-creolizations of the *lwa*.[68]

Legba's agency finds a most tricksterish literary engagement in Ishmael Reed's *Mumbo Jumbo* (1972), which traces the untraceable *lwa* "Jes Grew" from its "entrance into the Govi of New Orleans" to Chicago, New York and beyond.[69] Jes Grew, like early jazz, is seen by those who resist it as a "psychic epidemic" spreading from an assumed "local infestation area" of Congo Square, and its priests are often jazzmen such as Charlie Parker, "for whom there was no master adept enough to award him the Asson".[70] Jes Grew's creolizations and syncopations unsettle those who would stop the contagion, for "it's nothing we can bring into focus or categorize; once we call it 1 thing it forms into something else".[71] It is this difficulty in pinning down creolizing mystery, its material, psychological and spiritual agency, that Reed under-scores in *Mumbo Jumbo*'s embedded epigraphs, beginning with Louis Armstrong's description of second line dancing, "*The spirit hits them and they follow*"; moving to Hurston's description of the birth of new *lwa* in Haiti, "Some *unknown natural phenomenon* occurs which cannot be explained, and a new local demigod is named"; to James Weldon Johnson's awareness that "the earliest Ragtime songs, like Topsy, 'jes' grew'".[72] In spite of Jes Grew's creole mulitiplicity of origins, Reed locates its subaltern powers most firmly in New Orleans soil via Haiti as signified in the name of Jes Grew's key *serviteur,* PaPa LaBas, who works out of Mumbo Jumbo Kathedral and maintains "22 trays which were built as a tribute to the Haitian loas that LaBas claimed was an influence on his version of The Work". Asserting "'We serve the loas'", LaBas admits, "I don't know the extent to which the Haitian aspects of The Work can be translated here."[73]

Mumbo Jumbo's primary assumption, however, is that this translation has already occurred, originating most substantially "in the Govi of New Orleans" that allowed jazz and blues to each become "a loa that Jes Grew", a "*gros-ben-age* of the times, that aura that remains after the flesh of the age has dropped away".[74] The demographic and cultural translations that took place following the 1809 St Domingue migration to New Orleans had a re-balancing effect on Louisiana creole culture that would be difficult to overestimate. The city's slave and free Afro-Creole populations were more than doubled and received dynamic individuals and ritual families importing com-plexly creolizing experiences of St Domingue and Cuba. Anglo-American authorities received this influx with a fear of the Haitian Revolution's material, psychological and spiritual contagion. Much of the dread terror "shadowing" a poem like Poe's "Raven" marks the reaction of the nation's violent culture of fear to the revolutionary precedent of St Domingue and the subsequent repression of that knowledge and fear in the face of an ultimately unpossessable chattel population. *Mumbo Jumbo* presents the US occupation of Haiti from 1915 to 1934 as a defence of plantation-style monocultures and an "attempt to kill Jes Grew's effluvia by fumigating its mias-matic source". Resisting the Marines' "Holy War in Haiti", the book follows a group of powerful Haitian vodou priests, Harlem freemasons, artists, and the hoodoo work of PaPa LaBas, all collaborating to feed Jes Grew's re-emergent agency in North America. Noting how "our loas adapt to change", the Haitians seek to encourage Jes Grew's jazz *lwa* and allow potential ritual family members of any race or class "to go out of their minds so that spirits could enter their heads".[75]

The refinement of means to go out of the head, to "be in that number / when the Saints go marching in", emerges as one of the richest "translations" enabled by the St Domingue emigrés in New Orleans. As Joan Dayan writes, "For the possessed, that dance is not a loss of identity but rather the surest way back to the self, to an identity lost, submerged, and denigrated."[76] This self, like the music, is quite fluid, moving through a plenitude of "sainted" *lwa,* ancestors, guardian "angels" and componential aspects of "soul".[77] With so many "saints" (and such a symbiotic "polyrhythmic" complex tying individual identity to ancestral, familiar, wild and unborn forces), we may understand the fear behind the culture wars, the increasingly cornered desire to honour a single canon or singularly fixed identity or perspective. While vodou's demonized rites swing-ing individual/collective bodies work, in the words of Laënnec Hurbon, to "evoke our own strangeness to ourselves, as human beings: they bring us to *das Unheimlich,* to the 'disquieting strangeness' of which Freud speaks", we may see that they also "open the path to the encounter, to intercultural comunication".[78] The events and creolizations that pushed St Domingue out of its head reached a uniquely transformative inten-sity. Entering New Orleans's diasporic *govi,* the swinging agency of vodou incorporated Afro-Creole innovations of form by which the material, psychological and spiritual content of the "master" cultures was transposed and by which New World cultures and identities have been perpetually reassembled. The events of the Haitian Revolution stand as a landmark to such balancing acts. We must recognize finally that Haitian crossings to New Orleans have meant a thing or two to what swings US and global cultures as well.

NOTES

1. Edward Brathwaite, *The Development of Creole Society in Jamaica* (Oxford: Oxford University Press, 1971), 296.

2. Edgar Allan Poe, *The Complete Tales and Poems of Edgar Allan Poe* (New York: Random House, 1965), 944–46; Édouard Glissant, *Faulkner, Mississippi,* trans. Barbara

Lewis and Thomas C. Spear (Chicago: University of Chicago Press, 1999), 30. Poe's poem has been revamped in music by the Alan Parsons Project and has inspired the naming of the National Football League's Baltimore Ravens. For a fuller reading of Poe's Haitian shadow and of the Haitian presence in American gothic writing, see Keith Cartwright, *Reading Africa into American Literature* (Lexington: University Press of Kentucky, 2002).

3. Alfred P. Hunt, *Haiti's Influence on Antebellum America: Slumbering Volcano in the Caribbean* (Baton Rouge: Louisiana State University Press, 1988), 114.

4. Douglass R. Egerton, *Gabriel's Rebellion: The Virginia Slave Conspiracies of 1800 and 1802* (Chapel Hill: University of North Carolina Press, 1993), 47; Jane Landers, *Black Society in Spanish Florida* (Urbana: University of Illinois Press, 1999), 209–17. An assessment of President Jefferson's debts to the Haitian revolutionaries for making the Louisiana Purchase possible is offered in Joseph J. Ellis, *American Sphynx: The Character of Thomas Jefferson* (New York: Vintage, 1998), 246–47.

5. Ishmael Reed, *Mumbo Jumbo* (1972; reprint, New York: Atheneum, 1988), 6.

6. Ted Gioia, *The History of Jazz* (New York: Oxford University Press, 1997), 7.

7. "Voodoo orthography" raises a number of creolized, creolizing difficulties. I prefer the increasingly standard "vodou" for Haitian religious practice, and I use the historically popular (but also much denigrated) word "voodoo" when referring to Louisiana practice. As for the vodou/voodoo spirits, I use the Haitian Creole "*lwa*", but a number of the authors I cite use the French "*loa*", which was at one time more pervasive in the literature.

8. George W. Cable, *The Creoles of Louisiana* (New York: Scribner's, 1884), 138.

9. A path-breaking study of the foundational role played by Senegambian slaves in the formation of Louisiana creole culture has been offered us by Gwendolyn Midlo Hall, *Africans in Colonial Louisiana: The Development of Afro-Creole Culture in the Eighteenth Century* (Baton Rouge: Louisiana State University Press, 1992). Figures for St Domingue migration to New Orleans are given by Paul F. Lachance, "The Foreign French", in *Creole New Orleans: Race and Americanization,* ed. Arnold R. Hirsch and Joseph Logsdon (Baton Rouge: Louisiana State University Press, 1992), 105.

10. Ibid., 111–12. See also Caryn Cossé Bell, *Revolution, Romanticism, and the Afro-Creole Protest Tradition in Louisiana 1718–1868* (Baton Rouge: Louisiana State University Press, 1997), 37–38.

11. Lachance, "The Foreign French", 117.

12. Paul Lachance, "Were Saint-Domingue Refugees a Distinctive Cultural Group in Antebellum New Orleans? Evidence from Patterns and Strategies of Property Holding", *Revista/Review Interamericana* 29, nos 1–4 (1999): 191.

13. Donald Cosentino, "Imagine Heaven", in *Sacred Arts of Haitian Vodou,* ed. Donald Cosentino (Los Angeles: UCLA Fowler Museum of Cultural History, 1995), 27.

14. Ibid., 28; Donald Cosentino, "It's All for You, Sen Jak!" in *Sacred Arts of Haitian Vodou,* ed. Cosentino, 255.

15. Anne Shaw Faulkner, "Does Jazz Put the Sin in Syncopation?" in *Riffs and Choruses:*

A New Jazz Anthology, ed. Andrew Clark (London: Continuum, 2001), 40; Sidney Bechet, *Treat It Gentle* (New York: Hill and Wang, 1960), 10.

16. For a discussion of "mindful body" and ritual embodiment in the practice of vodou, see Karen McCarthy Brown, "The Ritual Economy of Haitian Vodou", in *Sacred Arts of Haitian Vodou,* ed. Cosentino, 205, 220–23. For studies of cultural components in the development of New Orleans voodoo, look to Hall, *Africans in Colonial Louisiana* on Senegambian *nyama*; and on the merger of Catholicism, spiritism, freemasonry, romanticism, opera and carnival in vodou and voodoo, look to Cosentino, *Sacred Arts of Haitian Vodou,* and also to Bell, *Revolution, Romanticism, and the Afro-Creole Protest Tradition in Louisiana.*

17. Victor Séjour, "The Mulatto", in *The Norton Anthology of American Literature,* ed. Henry Louis Gates and Nellie Y. McKay (New York: Norton, 1997), 290.

18. On Valmour and Testut, see Bell, *Revolution, Romanticism, and the Afro-Creole Protest Tradition in Louisiana 1718–1868,* 205–7. Bell also notes the Haitian studies and travels of the Afro-Creole poet/spiritist medium Nelson Desbrosses (pp. 215–16), and provides summary highlights of the publication *Le Spiritualiste de la Nouvelle Orléans,* which debuted in 1857, printing spiritual communiqués and editorials that contested Louisiana's increasingly conservative Anglo-controlled church authority (pp. 208–15).

19. Charles Testut, *Le Vieux Saloman; ou Une Famille d'esclaves au XIXe siecle* (New Orleans: No. 200 Rue Chartres, 1872), 96.

20. Alfred Mercier, *L'habitation Saint-Ybars, ou maitres et esclaves en Louisiana* (Montreal: Guerin littérature, 1989), 87.

21. Marie Augustin, *Le Macandal: Episode de l'insurrection des noirs a St Domingue* (New Orleans: Imprimerie Geo. Muller, 50, rue Bienville, 1892), 2; http://www.centenary .edu/french/macandal1.html (accessed 11/10/2003).

22. Ibid., 14, 39.

23. George W. Cable, *The Grandissimes* (1880; reprint, American Century Series, New York: Hill and Wang, 1968), 131.

24. Ibid., 40, 306.

25. Brown, "The Ritual Economy of Haitian Vodou", 217.

26. Cable, *The Grandissimes,* 96, 184.

27. Alcée Fortier, *Louisiana Folk-Tales in French Dialect with English Translations* (New York: American Folklore Society, 1895), 5, 110, 13.

28. A classic text on the carnivalesque's "complexly dialogized" hybridizations is Mikhail M. Bakhtin, *The Dialogic Imagination,* trans. Caryl Emerson and Michael Holquist (Austin: University of Texas Press, 1981), 82; George W. Cable, *The Creoles of Louisiana,* 315–16.

29. Sidney Mintz and Michel-Rolph Trouillot, "The Social History of Haitian Vodou", in *Sacred Arts of Haitian Vodou,* ed. Cosentino, 127.

30. Herbert Asbury, *The French Quarter: An Informal History of the New Orleans Underworld* (New York: Knopf, 1936); and Robert Tallant, *Voodoo in New Orleans*

(1946; reprint, New York: Collier Books, 1965) give accounts of Sanité Dédé's leadership of voodoo rites in New Orleans. Jessie Gaston Mulira, "The Case of Voodoo in New Orleans", in *Africanisms in American Culture,* ed. Joseph E. Holloway (Bloomington: Indiana University Press, 1990), offers a synthesizing account of New Orleans voodoo and speaks to Sanité Dédé's foundational role. Wonda L. Fontenot, *Secret Doctors: Ethnomedicine of African Americans* (Westport, Conn.: Bergin and Garvey, 1994) focuses its research on rural Louisiana healing practices and is rich in evidence for Haitian legacies. Finally, Luisah Teish, *Jambalaya: The Natural Woman's Book* (San Francisco: Harper and Row, 1985) presents information that Marie Laveau may have arrived in New Orleans from St Domingue. Teish, a New Orleans–born santería priestess, received this information from a spirit, and though her spirit communiqués push against the boundaries of what is admissible as scholarly evidence, her rationale for preferring the spiritual voice over textual authorities speaks to some of the difficulties my own essay faces: "Any time I am given a choice between the word of a spirit and that of white men writing about black women in the 1800s, I will listen to the spirit and face the consequences" (p. 168).

31. Asbury, *The French Quarter,* 264, 261.

32. Tallant, *Voodoo,* 74.

33. Ibid., 90.

34. Ibid., 103.

35. Ibid., 92.

36. Moreau de Saint-Méry, *A Civilization That Perished: The Last Years of White Colonial Rule,* selection reprinted in *Libète: A Haiti Anthology,* ed. Charles Arthur and Michael Dash (Princeton: Marcus Wiener Publishers, 1999), 321, 322.

37. Tallant, *Voodoo,* 67.

38. Ibid., 75–76, 111.

39. Ibid, 140.

40. Asbury, *The French Quarter,* 278. Similar ritual or altar designs may be found in photographs in Karen McCarthy Brown, *Mama Lola: A Voodoo Priestess in Brooklyn* (Berkeley and Los Angeles: University of California Press, 2001), 42; and in Hector Delgado, "From the Sacred Wild to the City: Santería in Cuba Today", in *Sacred Possessions: Vodou, Santería, Obeah and the Caribbean,* ed. Margarite Fernández Olmos and Lizabeth Paravisini-Gebert (New Brunswick, NJ: Rutgers University Press, 1997), 102, 104, 112–13 and especially 118.

41. Tallant, *Voodoo,* 40, 42.

42. Catherine Gunther Kodat, "Conversing with Ourselves: Canon, Freedom, Jazz", *American Quarterly* 55, no. 1 (2003): 2.

43. Bechet, *Treat It Gentle,* 6.

44. Dena J. Epstein, *Sinful Tunes and Spirituals: Black Folk Music to the Civil War* (Urbana: University of Illinois Press, 1977), 97 (quotation).

45. Ibid., 97 (quotation).

46. Ibid., 134 (quotation).

47. Asbury, *The French Quarter,* 242.

48. On Congo Square's role in the ongoing story of jazz stagings and commodifications, see Kodat, "Conversing with Ourselves". Marie Laveau appears to have presided over both Congo Square and voodoo stagings as mentioned in Tallant, *Voodoo,* 66.

49. Brent Edwards, "The Seemingly Eclipsed Window of Form: James Weldon Johnson's Prefaces", in *The Jazz Cadence of American Culture,* ed. Robert O'Meally (New York: Columbia University Press, 1998), 590.

50. Brown, "The Ritual Economy of Haitian Vodou", 222.

51. Tallant, *Voodoo,* 42, 40 (quotations).

52. Katherine Hagedorn, *Divine Utterances: The Performance of Afro-Cuban Santería* (Washington, DC: Smithsonian Institution Press, 2001), 131. See Jon Michael Spencer, *Re-Searching Black Music* (Knoxville: University of Tennessee Press, 1996), on his concept of "theomusicology", an idea borrowed in large part from Léopold Senghor.

53. Laënnec Hurbon, "American Fantasy and Haitian Vodou", in *Sacred Arts of Haitian Vodou,* ed. Cosentino, 192, explores the idea of zombification as chattel ideal; and Karen McCarthy Brown, "The Ritual Economy of Haitian Vodou", in *Sacred Arts of Haitian Vodou,* ed. Cosentino, 222, offers an insightful look at vodou's ritual use of the body.

54. Louis Armstrong, *Swing That Music* (1936; reprint, New York: De Capo Press, 1993), 30, 31, 31–32.

55. Larry Gara, *The Baby Dodds Story: As Told to Larry Gara* (1959; reprint, Baton Rouge: Louisiana State University Press, 1992), 12.

56. Homi Bhabha, "Unsatisfied: Notes on Vernacular Cosmopolitanism", in *Postcolonial Discourses: An Anthology,* ed. Gregory Castle (Malden, Mass.: Blackwell Publishers, 2001); Brown, "The Ritual Economy of Haitian Vodou", 210.

57. Paul Gilroy, *The Black Atlantic: Modernity and Double Consciousness* (Cambridge, Mass.: Harvard University Press, 1993), 37. I am deeply indebted to Gilroy's thought throughout this chapter as I follow his lead in examining musical (and inspiriting) counter-cultures of modernity.

58. Brown, "The Ritual Economy of Haitian Vodou", 207.

59. Édouard Glissant, *Caribbean Discourse,* trans. J. Michael Dash (Charlottesville: University of Virginia Press); Walter Mignolo, *Local Histories/Global Designs: Coloniality, Subaltern Knowledges, and Border Thinking* (Princeton: Princeton University Press, 2000) feeds my understanding of how "undisciplined forms of knowledge . . . were reduced to subaltern knowledge by colonial disciplined knowing practices" (p. 10).

60. John Miller Chernoff, *African Rhythm and African Sensibility: Aesthetics and Social Action in African Musical Idioms* (Chicago: University of Chicago Press, 1979), 155, 156, 158.

61. Nathaniel Mackey, "Sound and Sentiment, Sound and Symbol", in *The Jazz Cadence of American Culture,* ed. Robert O'Meally (New York: Columbia University Press, 1998), 613–14.

62. Yusef Komunyakaa, ed., Radiclani Clytus, *Blue Notes: Essays, Interviews, and Commentaries* (Ann Arbor: University of Michigan Press, 2000), 4.

63. Zora Neale Hurston, *Mules and Men* (New York: Harper and Row, 1990), 193.

64. Ralph Ellison, *Invisible Man* (1952; reprint, New York: Vintage, 1972), 484, 8.

65. Ellison, *Shadow and Act* (1964; reprint, New York: Signet, 1966), 200–201, 205–6, 206.

66. Joan Dayan, *Haiti, History, and the Gods* (Berkeley and Los Angeles: University of California Press, 1995), 101.

67. Ellison, *Shadow and Act,* 216, 214.

68. Ibid., 219.

69. Reed, *Mumbo Jumbo,* 6.

70. Ibid., 16.

71. Ibid., 4.

72. Ibid., 7, 11, 11.

73. Ibid., 28, 40, 52.

74. Ibid., 6, 128, 20.

75. Ibid., 214, 147, 137, 213.

76. Dayan, *Haiti, History, and the Gods,* 74.

77. See Alfred Métraux, *Voodoo in Haiti,* trans. Hugo Charteris (New York: Schocken, 1972), 153–56, 257–65; and Maya Deren, *Divine Horsemen: The Living Gods of Haiti* (Kingston, NY: Documentext, 1970), 24–27, on componential soul in vodou.

78. Hurbon, "American Fantasy and Haitian Vodou", 197.

CHAPTER 9

HAITI AND THE HAITIAN REVOLUTION IN THE POLITICAL DISCOURSE OF NINETEENTH-CENTURY TRINIDAD

BRIDGET BRERETON

The extraordinary events in St Domingue/Haiti between 1791 and 1804 resonated everywhere in the Caribbean and the New World, a terrible warning to slaveholders and an inspiration to enslaved people and other oppressed groups throughout the Americas. Trinidad was much more directly affected by the turbulence of the revolutionary years in the Lesser Antilles – Martinique, Guadeloupe and Grenada especially – than in St Domingue, and far more émigré whites and free coloureds arrived from the former islands. In comparison with Jamaica, Cuba or the United States, Trinidad received only a few refugees (white, mixed-race, enslaved) fleeing the devastating conflicts in the "pearl of the Antilles". But the island's elite had become predominantly French in the 1780s and 1790s, mainly through migration from the eastern Caribbean; by the time of the British seizure of Trinidad from Spain in 1797, French landowners and slaveholders (white and mixed-race) dominated its social and economic life. This ensured that the Haitian Revolution would have special resonance in nineteenth-century Trinidad, despite its geographical distance; the memory, the terror, the "lessons" and the inspiration of "San Domingo" would continue to live in the minds of many of its inhabitants for decades after 1804.

As Mimi Sheller has argued, the collection of stories which made up the "Haytian Fear" helped whites in the Caribbean (and elsewhere) to articulate their claims to racial supremacy and civilization; at the same time, black or brown political leaders used very different stories of Haiti's independence to promote movements for social and political change in the region. Writing about Jamaica, Sheller shows that Haiti was central in the development of a "shared counter-discourse of

African identification and Caribbean solidarity", which was dialectically linked to the whites' "Haytian Fear" narrative. Together they shaped "symbolic mappings of Haiti in the competing racial discourses of multiple contenders for public opinion". And in general, as David Geggus writes, Haiti became a "crucial test case for ideas about race and about the future of colonial slavery", acquiring "an exemplary or symbolic value, fuelling both sides of the anti-slavery debate" – and of the post-slavery debates on the capacity of ex-slaves and black people for self-government and civilization. Certainly the leaders and intellectuals of nineteenth-century Haiti saw their nation as a universal symbol of African regeneration and racial equality; on this point, at least, black and mixed-race Haitians were almost always in agreement.[1]

THE REVOLUTIONARY YEARS, 1791–1815

News of the terrifying events in St Domingue which began in 1790–91, as well as the turmoil in the French Windward islands, much closer to home, must have reached Trinidad (and everywhere else in the Americas) via letters, newspapers and verbal accounts from refugees, seamen and travellers. Published accounts of the "Horrors of San Domingo" – which always meant massacres of whites by rebellious blacks, not vice versa – were also influential, especially Bryan Edwards's frequently reissued work, with its lurid accounts of "unspeakable atrocities and scenes of horror". Two books published in 1805 presented more balanced accounts of the Haitian struggles, those by Marcus Rainsford and Pierre McCallum. McCallum's polemic, which was mainly devoted to a denunciation of Thomas Picton, Trinidad's first British governor, probably circulated quite widely in the island, but it was Edwards's sensational reporting which set the tone for the "Haytian Fear" narrative as it developed in the English-speaking world.[2]

Of course the great rebellion quickly became the favourite argument of pro-slavery forces against any "agitation" or discussion of reforms or changes in the slave system. But others derived a different "lesson" from the events in St Domingue: that the high concentration of native Africans in that colony was the root cause of the "servile war" and consequent ruin. Influential policymakers and abolitionists argued persuasively that in the interests of British West Indian security, to avoid the same kind of "conflagration", further importations of enslaved people from Africa should be stopped. Trinidad, a recent British acquisition with a great deal of uncultivated land, was right at the centre of this debate in the

early 1800s. James Stephen, Henry Brougham and others believed that the proliferation of native Africans in the years before 1791 had caused the blacks' triumph
in St Domingue. To fill up Trinidad with masses of Africans could only expose the
island to the same dangers and jeopardize the security of all the British colonies. With
the Haitian Revolution seen as mainly the work of native Africans, the conclusion was
obvious: abolition of the slave trade (but not emancipation of the slaves). The importation
of new slaves from Africa to the "conquered colonies", including Trinidad, was prohibited
in 1806. The "Haytian Fear" had acted to prevent the further development of Trinidad
towards a classic slave society with a huge majority of enslaved persons.[3]

Anxiety about the security of Trinidad, greatly heightened by the news from
St Domingue, actually pre-dated the British capture of the island. The Spanish
governor, J.M. Chacon, and royalist French refugees from the Windward Islands
already in the island by 1792–94, were determined to prevent the arrival of black
or mixed-race persons from St Domingue, especially if they had military back-
grounds. Both Chacon and the Cabildo (the municipal council of Port of Spain)
protested against the plan by the Cuban authorities to settle Jean-François and
his men in Trinidad. Jean-François had fought with great success for the Spanish
crown as auxiliary troops in both parts of Hispaniola in 1793–95, so he was if
anything counter-revolutionary in his politics. But he was a black military leader
from St Domingue; he was definitely not wanted in a "Colony, where the seeds
of Revolutionary Principles have not only taken root but in several instances have
been seen to send forth shoots", as the Cabildo put it. Chacon more briefly said
he would have been an "idiot" to have allowed such men into Trinidad; and all
144 of them were returned to Cuba in July 1796. Chacon was forced to surrender
the island to the British in 1797, and Picton, his successor, continued to worry
about contamination from the rebel colony, his fears no doubt heightened by news
of two serious slave plots on the Caribbean coast of New Granada (Colombia) in
1799, both apparently led by free coloureds from St Domingue. No wonder that
Picton was alarmed at the arrival, early in 1800, of nearly three hundred "uni-
formed" black men under the Compte de Rouvray. Despite protests again from the
Cabildo and from the "Inhabitants", Picton allowed them to land, "with the exception of certain San Domingo Chiefs and their wives who had been active in all the
atrocities committed in that miserable Island; conceiving that Persons of the above
Description would not be admitted without hazarding the Peace and Tranquillity
of the Island, I thought it my Duty to refuse them".[4]

By contrast, Picton generally welcomed the arrival of émigré white planters from St Domingue, often with their slaves. In some cases, he was instructed by London to assist refugees who had served in the armed forces under British command during the occupation of St Domingue between 1793 and 1798 and were being resettled under official auspices in Trinidad. Even before the British evacuation in 1798, the idea of shipping such men to Trinidad and giving them land grants there had been under discussion, especially when the Jamaican Assembly made clear its objection to allowing large numbers of slaves to enter that island along with their refugee "owners". Though far fewer émigrés came to Trinidad than to Jamaica, among them were men who became powerful members of the island's elite and who helped to shape the "Haytian Fear" in the society.[5]

One of these was Charles-Joseph, Compte de Loppinot, who arrived in Trinidad in 1800 with several men and women he claimed to hold as slaves. Probably born in French Canada, he was a wealthy coffee planter in the Grand'Anse (Jérémie) area of southern St Domingue by 1781, and commandant of Port-au-Prince in 1790. He was a strong counter-revolutionary with a military background and excellent connections with the exiled royalist elite, links which secured for Loppinot the designation as "governor-general" of St Domingue by the future Louis XVIII (1793). Not surprisingly, he served with the British forces during their occupation of the colony, and was evacuated with them to Jamaica in 1798; he was one of the émigrés specially assisted to resettle in Trinidad as a reward for his military services. Loppinot tried to set up as a sugar planter at Orange Grove, but failed; then he established a flourishing cocoa estate, La Reconnaissance, in the area which still bears his name. His military experience ensured that he played a prominent part in the local militia, of which he was brigadier-general (1806); his royalist connections also made him politically influential, and he served on the Council of Advice from 1813 until his death in 1819. That Loppinot never gave up the dream of restoring Haiti to French rule and slavery is shown by a remarkable correspondence he carried on, from Trinidad, in 1814. Once the Bourbons had been restored, he reminded the king and his brother of his appointment back in 1793 as "governor-general" and proposed that France should undertake a military campaign to subjugate the errant colony and restore slavery, so that he could resume his office! Absurd though this sounds – and sensibly enough, neither the king nor his brother replied to Loppinot's several letters – the Bourbon restoration was the signal for thousands of bitter and vengeful refugees, in France and elsewhere, to pressure the new government to "take back" Haiti. Many anticipated a war of extermination, to be followed by the massive importation of Africans as slaves. The Bourbon government soon abandoned any such notion; but the *anciens colons* like Loppinot, with links to the ultra-royalist party, refused to give up their hopes until the French recognition of Haiti in 1825.[6]

Another influential émigré was Jean Charles, Baron de Montalembert (also spelled Montalambert). Like Loppinot a leading counter-revolutionary with royalist connections, he owned a sugar plantation in the Cul de Sac, near Port-au-Prince; he became the most important French military officer serving with the British forces in the campaigns of 1794–98, commanding a "legion" composed mainly of émigré officers and men. During these campaigns, Montalembert acquired an apparently well-deserved reputation for ruthlessness (against republicans of all kinds, but especially black and coloured ones) and venality, amassing a large fortune for himself. He seems to have arrived in Trinidad in 1801, purchasing the Coblenz sugar estate in St Ann's and stocking it with 150 "well seasoned" slaves from Jamaica (perhaps originally from St Domingue). When many of these unfortunates died mysteriously, poisoning was suspected; special "poison tribunals" modelled on those of Martinique were set up to deal with the accused and hand out savage punishments. Men like Loppinot and Montalembert, bitter about their losses and defeats in St Domingue and ruthless towards both slaves and free coloureds, helped to ensure that the memory of Haiti remained alive in Trinidad.[7]

This resonance of the Haitian Revolution was especially damaging for Trinidad's large and important free coloured community. As Geggus notes, "contemporaries often attributed the destruction of St Domingue not to the slaves who accomplished its destruction, nor to the political and social divisions that weakened white resistance, but to the bitter struggle between white and brown", and saw the free coloureds' demand for equality and civil rights as the start of all the "horrors" that followed. In Trinidad, all the free coloureds of French-Caribbean origins (the majority) were tainted by the implications of this interpretation of the revolution. "For years after the St Domingue uprising", James Millette writes, "white patriots continued to see, or said they saw, the spectre of slave revolt behind every attempt by the free coloured to extend the area of his freedom". In 1802, Picton described the "French free coloureds", nearly three thousand strong, as "a dangerous Class which must gradually be got rid of"; in 1803, just before he left the island, he insisted that many if not most of them were "refugees from the Insurged Islands, where they had borne Arms" and participated in "Jacobinical outrages and violation". The Cabildo concurred, describing most of the free coloureds as "the scum of the Revolution", whose "arrogance" made its members fear the spread of insurrection as in St Domingue; the attorney-general believed that the "overbearing insolence of this class" was increasing (1803), making him fear the imminent outbreak of "the massacres and conflagrations that have marked San Domingo". This, then, was "the model of thinking about free coloured violence" in Trinidad, Carl Campbell argues: "a free coloured rebellion would inevitably end in a slave rebellion". When a few free coloured men signed a mildly worded petition in 1810, the governor claimed to believe that it might have been "the first step towards the commencement of the same enormities in this Colony, for it was precisely by such a beginning that the dreadful scenes which took place . . . in St Domingo were preceded". "No amount of peaceful behaviour could shake the stereotype of the subversive free coloured", Campbell concludes; the "shadow" of the Haitian Revolution haunted this group at least until 1815, if not much longer.[8]

Campbell is probably correct in his argument that the whites in Trinidad feared the free coloureds more than the slaves in the late 1700s and early 1800s. But they were distinctly agitated by the discovery of a slave "conspiracy" in the Carenage district west of Port of Spain in December 1805 which seemed to have the clearest possible links to the Haitian Revolution. The suspected plotters were said all to have come from the French colonies, including Haiti, and suspicions were aroused by remarks and taunts made to policemen and other whites "to beware lest they suffer the same fate as in San Domingo". The governor, Thomas Hislop, had no doubt that the intention was "a general massacre" of whites and coloureds on Christmas Day and that by his prompt measures, he had "avoided a most Dreadful Event and such Diabolical Scenes as characterised the Outbreak in San Domingo". His fears were heightened by news of a planned "Insurrection of the negroes" in Guadeloupe at the same time, apparently headed by "Chiefs . . . said to belong to San Domingo".[9]

But the Haitian link seemed to be most strikingly proven by a verse and couplet of a French Creole song which the conspirators are said to have sung, and which was reproduced by L.M. Fraser in his history of Trinidad, published in 1891. Fraser, who had married into a prominent French creole family, may well have relied on oral tradition for the words of this "seditious ditty":

Pain nous ka mangé
C'est viande beké
Di vin nous ka boué
C'est sang beké
Hé St Domingo, songé St Domingo.

The plotters held a "blasphemous Mass" and as the bread and wine were administered, they said: "Songé, pain z'autes ka mangé c'est viande beké; di vin z'autes ka boué c'est sang beké." Fraser translates this as: "Remember, the bread you are eating is white man's flesh; the wine you are drinking is white man's blood." Since Fraser seems to be the sole source for the song and incantation, we must, of course, admit that they might be at least in part the product of contemporary hysteria about the Haitian Revolution, conveyed to Fraser many decades later by descendants of the slaveholders of 1805. Yet there remains a strong possibility that the plotters did, indeed, celebrate their knowledge of what had happened in Haiti, and their dream of a world turned similarly upside-down in Trinidad, in song and even in a parody of the mass.[10]

The conspiracy, real or imagined – for E.L. Joseph, who lived in Trinidad from around 1820 and wrote his history of the island only three decades after the event, was very sceptical about its significance or even its reality – was brutally suppressed. As Fraser points out, "some of the members of [the Council] had actually witnessed the horrors of servile insurrection; to all, the details of the revolt of the slaves in St Domingo were familiar". None was in doubt, like Hislop, of the need to save themselves, and all near and dear to them, from "fire, pillage and rapine". A contemporary wrote from Trinidad about "the explosion of a volcano here as well as at San Domingo which would have completely overwhelmed not only the British but all the other Colonies". Swift "trials" were followed by savage punishments. Three (maybe four) plotters were hanged, then decapitated; their heads were exposed on poles, their bodies hung up in chains, close to their estates. Many others were brutally flogged and mutilated, some were banished from Trinidad for life, others forced to wear heavy chains or iron rings for long periods. All these actions were endorsed by the British government, which congratulated Hislop and his Council for their swift action to save Trinidad from disaster. So did the free coloureds, ever anxious to "prove" their loyalty. The "Haytian Fear" ensured the reprisals would be brutal, even though not a single person had been harmed, not a stalk of cane had been burned, by the "plotters". Yet knowledge of what had happened in Haiti could not be suppressed.[11]

TRINIDAD AND HAITI DURING THE YEARS OF AMELIORATION AND EMANCIPATION

During the campaigns to "ameliorate" and then to end slavery in the British colonies (1823–38), Haiti occupied a central place in the public discourse on the future of these Caribbean societies. Both sides exploited Haiti's propaganda value for all it was worth; the dangers of emancipation, or of not emancipating, were inexorably linked with the events in St Domingue/Haiti. The apparent association between anti-slavery and rebellion, between emancipation and massacre, was a serious obstacle for the abolitionists, and proslavery writers made much of what they saw as Haitian decline, barbarism and ruin after 1803. Contesting interpretations of Haiti and the Haitian Revolution, in short, were very much at the forefront of the British and Caribbean discourse on the slavery issue during the 1820s and early 1830s. But with emancipation achieved in two stages between 1834 and 1838, Haiti began to "fade from view"; as Geggus puts it, "Haiti ceased to be a political issue at the same time as it lost its propaganda value as the sole post-slavery society in the Caribbean."[12]

In Trinidad, the island's leading newspaper, the *Port of Spain Gazette,* disseminated a considerable amount of "news and views" about Haiti in the 1820s and early 1830s; its coverage declined markedly after 1834. As in the case of the Jamaican press at this period, the *Gazette* frequently carried extracts on Haiti from British, US and Jamaican newspapers; it also featured a French-language section which often included extracts from French periodicals, as well as editorials and letters in that language, on Haitian affairs. On the whole Haiti enjoyed considerable salience in the political discourse of Trinidad's literate elite, to judge from the island's leading newspaper, in the period of slave amelioration and emancipation.

Through extracts from foreign papers, editorials, articles and letters, in both English and French, the *Gazette*'s readers were kept informed of the events leading up to, and following, France's recognition of Haitian independence in 1825 and the punitive "indemnity" imposed as the price.[13] The development of commercial links between Haiti, France, Britain and the Caribbean colonies was also covered by the newspaper. At the end of 1825, it reproduced a very long piece (from a US paper) detailing the provisions of a new tariff issued from Port-au-Prince, making one wonder if Trinidad merchants were trading with Haiti at this time. This same issue reproduced, in French, another long article: the report of the minister of the marine and colonies to the King of France on the events leading to the recognition of Haitian independence. In 1826, the *Gazette* reported on the Treaty of Amity and Commerce between Haiti and Britain, and reproduced a letter from a British merchant in Port-au-Prince, who noted that "the resources of St Domingo [*sic*] are by no means contemptible, but the extravagance of government expenditure and the payments to France have crippled us sadly for a time".[14]

As we have seen, some members of Trinidad's influential French creole elite were former St Domingue proprietors, and the whole group probably sympathised with the losses of the *anciens colons*. The *Gazette* often reported on issues related to the claims of these people to compensation for their vanished properties. Following French recognition of Haiti, the king appointed a commission to propose how the *anciens colons* should make claims and what should be the procedures for distributing the sums allocated to it; these developments were reported in both the English and French sections of the paper, the editor on one occasion writing that he included such reports "en raison de l'intérêt que plusieurs de nos lecteurs peuvent y trouver". Very little came of these attempts to secure compensation for individual ex-proprietors, and the *Gazette* reported on the bitter disappointment of the many St Domingue colons in France and elsewhere at what they saw as a betrayal by the French government. Its editor commented that this disappointment would be shared by the *anciens propriétaires* resident in Trinidad, but that he had never believed in the likelihood of compensation. By 1838, when a new treaty between France and Haiti was concluded, the editor was clear that there was no further hope of redress for the few *anciens colons* still living, or their heirs; the French government had "sacrificed" them and ignored their protests.[15]

A very different kind of claim for compensation, arising out of the Haitian Revolution, was reported in the *Gazette* just months before the final end of slavery in 1838. An ex-slave (apprentice) named Justine Joseph sued for the discharge of her apprenticeship and a large sum (two thousand pounds) in compensation. Born in Africa, a "Congo", she had been taken to St Domingue as a child and became the property of the Compte de Loppinot on his coffee estate near Jérémie. She was one of the many "loyal slaves" who were shipped to Trinidad with Loppinot in 1800, and ended up on his La Reconnaissance estate. Loppinot died in 1819, and she (along with the estate) had been purchased by W. Gillman, against whom the suit was filed. Her case was that in 1794, living in St Domingue, she had been freed by the decrees of the French government and therefore she had been held in slavery illegally ever since. Her counsel, and Gillman's, referred at length to historical works on the revolution, including Bryan Edwards's: to establish the facts about the two emancipation decrees of 1793 and 1794 (for the plaintiff); and to show that Jérémie in the south was under British occupation from 1793 on and the decrees were never enforced there (for the defendant). In fact, the Grand'Anse region where Loppinot's estate was situated was the "least affected by the Revolution", according to Geggus; the emancipation decrees were dead letters and few planters in the district lost slaves, especially around Jérémie itself. The court, headed by Chief Justice George Scotland whose sentiments were generally anti-slavery, found that Justine was in fact free before and on 1 August 1834; she must be discharged from her apprenticeship and the defendant was ordered to pay costs and damages of two pounds (presumably the small sum was in recognition of the fact that Gillman had no culpability in the original denial of her freedom). The reports of this interesting court case must have reminded readers of the revolutionary years and the involuntary removal of many "slaves" from St Domingue to Trinidad with their "owners".[16]

Much of the coverage of Haitian affairs in the *Gazette* in these years illustrates how the country became a metaphor and a propaganda point in the discourse on slavery and abolition. The newspaper often reproduced reports of debates in Parliament in which speakers made "St Domingo" a central argument for or against amelioration and emancipation, or articles in British or French periodicals and propaganda pamphlets which did the same thing. In many cases the paper was simply reporting on metropolitan debates, but from time to time editorials or articles by locals reflected the place of Haiti in the slavery discourse in Trinidad specifically. In one interesting editorial, the writer rebuked the rival paper (the *Trinidad Standard*) for advocating "colonial resistance" against Britain over the slavery question (in 1828). The *Standard* had argued that Trinidad could successfully resist "a numerous and powerful enemy from a more temperate region [Britain]" with "very small numbers of seasoned and determined troops". What examples was the reader referred to? asked the *Gazette* editor. "The revolution in St Domingo – the Maroon war in Jamaica – the insurrections of Grenada, of St Vincent, of Barbados and of Demerara!" This was seditious and mischievous nonsense from "unruly spirits, who have nothing to loose", the editor concluded. In 1833, as emancipation approached, a local who wrote in French and signed his pieces "DF" argued in several articles that Britain must learn from the Haitian disaster; fanatical abolitionism ruined St Domingue and could do the same in the British colonies. Haiti showed that false humanitarian theories led only to "la licence et le brigandage". And the country's experience since 1804 showed conclusively that sugar could not be grown with free labour; Boyer's attempts to reintroduce Toussaint's Code Rurale had failed, a free man could not be forced to labour on a sugar estate if he had alternatives.[17]

But not everyone assumed that Haiti was a good predictor of what would happen in the British colonies after emancipation. Writing in 1838, a few months before the end of apprenticeship, the editor of the *Gazette* meditated on whether the freed people would become "useful cultivators of the soil and industrious citizens". He stated firmly,

> The revolution of St Domingo should not be cited as bearing on the question; the freedom of Hayti was conceived in phrenzy, born amid wars, and baptised with blood. At the end of the wars of St Domingo, all property, all capital, was ruined, all civilisation was driven from her shores; the result has been that from slaves, the negroes of St Domingo have become barbarians – formerly they crouched beneath the scourge, they now are ruled by the bayonet. There is no more analogy between the revolt of St Domingo and the emancipation of the slaves of the British West Indies, than there is between the French revolution, at the end of the last century, and the late reform in Parliament.

This common-sense dismissal of the "lessons of Haiti" argument contrasts strongly with DF's gloomy predictions.[18]

That the "pearl of the Antilles" had been ruined by the revolution, that Haitians after independence were ignorant, indolent and barbaric, was an article of faith among the defenders of slavery in the Caribbean and elsewhere. Much of the coverage of Haiti in the *Gazette* reflects this element in the slavery discourse. "The agreeable state of a community of Emancipated Blacks", wrote the editor in 1826, "who have secured their *freedom* by a series of the most barbarous and atrocious murders and outrages, may be pretty well judged by the following extract of a letter from America." The letter, describing a Haiti where anarchy reigned, the soldiers terrorized everyone and agriculture was declining, was "extremely interesting, not only as intelligence to those who have any notion of going thither" – a hint that some Trinidad free coloureds were contemplating emigration – "but as exhibiting the state of a Black popular emancipation". Jamaican and US newspapers were sometimes quoted to show the "barbarism" of rural Haitians, given over to voodoo orgies, child sacrifice and cannibalism, utterly indolent as agriculture and trade collapsed. A good example is a reproduction of an 1834 letter from a US naval officer, originally published in the *American Advertiser*. It painted a lurid picture of desolation and collapse, especially in and around Le Cap, where the inhabitants were "too lazy to do anything but eat, drink and sleep". Apart from a few better-off and educated persons, "the large majority are but little better informed than the same number of monkeys". A refreshingly different note was struck by the *Gazette's* editor (probably the historian E.L. Joseph) in 1838, reporting that a private letter from "St Domingo" stated that all was tranquil, and commenting, with reference to the recent treaty with France, "we know not if all men, even barbarians, are born diplomatists; certain we are that in all protocols, treaties, or other diplomatic intercourse, the dark statesmen of St Domingo [*sic*] have ever shewn themselves fully equal to those opposed to them".[19]

In the tense years before emancipation, fears of slave revolt haunted the slave owners of the British colonies; memories of the Haitian Revolution, as well as the risings in Barbados (1816), Demerara (1823) and Jamaica (1831), heightened these fears. The largely French or French creole slave owners of Trinidad were especially inclined to "remember Haiti" whenever something seemed to be brewing. There were rumours of slave unrest in the Diego Martin area in October 1823, at a time when the "amelioration" proposals were under discussion and a major revolt had just taken place in Demerara. A commission was established to try the arrested plotters, but (perhaps surprisingly) the evidence failed to establish any kind of planned rising and all the accused were released. Much alarm was nevertheless expressed about the "appalling Consequences, which Experience has taught may follow from the commission of this Offence" (slaves plotting to secure their freedom). In general, the French slave owners seemed more anxious about slave unrest than their British (or Spanish) counterparts. French planters like St Hilaire Begorrat and A.V. St Bresson, who gave evidence to the Trinidad Council's Committee to Investigate the Negro Character (1825), were clearly obsessed about the possibility of a slave rising and concerned at the public debates about the new laws. The French planters placed the highest premium on security and public calm, remembering only too well that the St Domingue disaster had begun with debates about reforms and privileges.[20]

Another wave of panic about slave unrest swept Trinidad in 1832–33, just before emancipation. The *Port of Spain Gazette* rarely failed to predict dire consequences from the most trivial signs of disobedience or "insolence" from slaves. A planned strike on a group of estates in the Naparimas, early in 1832, might have led to much worse – "to subsequent horrors, which are too well known to require recapitulation and which afford so useful a lesson upon the subject of 'delay' and 'neglecting to adopt timely precautions' ". Enormously exaggerated reports of the

Jamaican revolt in December 1831 (5,000 free persons killed, 15,000 slaves killed, 106 plantations destroyed) were reaching the editor at the same time, of course only increasing the sense of panic. Two unrelated fires on estates in the Naparima district in March 1832 provoked a *"Gazette Extraordinary"* published on a Sunday, full of hysterical language: "The die has been thrown – the work of devastation has commenced – Heaven only knows where it will stop!" All in the Naparimas was "terror and alarm"; Trinidad would soon suffer "a second edition of the horrors lately enacted in Jamaica". Subsequent articles claimed that only the hand of Providence had averted "a tragedy . . . the bloodiest in the history of Trinidad". "Multitudes of our negroes in a state of mutiny – estates wantonly and maliciously burned – our slave population encouraged to ———— [*sic*] But the picture is too frightful for contemplation." The slaves of Savanna Grande (Princes Town) were said to be only awaiting the rains to make roads impassable to put their "diabolical plans" into operation. It is hard not to see the "Haytian Fear" behind this hysterical reaction to what were, objectively, very minor signs of slave unrest, at a time when slave owners themselves were holding regular indignation meetings and talking wildly about resistance to Britain.[21]

Of course, fears of disorder or worse on and after 1 August 1834, were at least as pronounced in Trinidad as elsewhere in the British Caribbean. And there was a near-riot in Port of Spain on 1 August, when hundreds of apprentices, including many old men and women, converged to protest their new status, shouting "point de six ans" and loudly complaining that they had not been given "full free". Most whites, and certainly the editor of the *Gazette,* wanted martial law to be declared and the troops called in to fire on the crowd; both the governor, and the colonel commanding the troops, refused, earning several severe rebukes from the newspaper. Interestingly, another British officer, who witnessed the scene and later wrote a description of the day's events, commented "for about a week to ten days after August 1st, 1834, the inhabitants (many of them) were very apprehensive of insurrection and revolt; the French were the most alarmed. A lady, who had been driven from St Domingo at the early part of the French Revolution, told me that the troubles in that Island, commenced by deputations of old persons coming forward in the first instance; and, that consequently, when she heard of the assemblage before the Government House, she dreaded lest similar horrors to those formerly perpetrated at St Domingo were on the eve of being committed in Trinidad." Marking the final end of apprenticeship, 1 August 1838 passed altogether quietly, but some whites did fear a rising, especially the French with their St Domingue nightmare.[22]

We noted that Trinidad's free coloureds, ever since the 1790s, had been seen as potentially subversive, at least in part because it was believed that the Haitian Revolution had begun with the coloureds' campaign for equality and civil rights. This association haunted them well into the 1820s. When their leader in this period, Jean-Baptiste Philippe, wrote a treatise setting out their claims in 1824, he referred to Haiti in an impressive peroration which ends the work. Philippe justified the revolution as a struggle for freedom, while deploring the "horrid scenes" and "unbridled rage" which swept over the land and wishing that the same end could have been accomplished peacefully. He concluded:

> My Lord, I am no advocate for insubordination, rebellion, or massacre; my design in reverting to the scenes in St Domingo, is far from a wish to evince any exultation at the preludes to, or the issue of, that contest. I myself would not desire to see freedom obtained at the price of so much carnage, atrocity and crime. But again, the retrospect of that mournful period should present a lesson of moderation and equity; should humble the pride of despotism; should inculcate to legislators that every branch of a public is equally entitled to justice; that no privileges should be accorded to a part which is inconsistent with the happiness and the prosperity of the whole.[23]

It was, of course, politically astute, and prudent, to distance himself and his campaign for free coloured equality from the violent events in St Domingue/Haiti. But in 1824 Haiti was under a coloured president (Boyer), was governed mainly by *anciens libres* or their sons, and was inviting foreign black or mixed-race emigrants to settle. To many among the French-speaking free coloured community of Trinidad (to which Philippe belonged), Haiti must have seemed attractive; perhaps, as Campbell writes, "he saw the revolution there as a mulatto revolution in a mulatto controlled country". That some Trinidad free coloureds did emigrate to Haiti is suggested by Philippe's comment that their numbers were increasing "in spite of the late numerous emigrations to St Domingo", which had slowed down population growth in 1823–24. Such emigrants could claim Haitian citizenship on arrival, under the republican constitution, as persons of African descent. We know that some free coloureds of Martinique and Guadeloupe emigrated around this time; and so did several thousand free African-Americans in the 1820s, specifically encouraged by the Boyer government. Trinidad's free coloured leadership did not seem to have the close links with Haiti which their Jamaican counterparts developed, both before and after 1838. But like them, Philippe and the community he spoke for might well have seen Haiti in the 1820s, not only as "a powerful symbol of freedom and African progress, [and] . . . the capacity for black self-government", as Sheller puts it, but also as a possible haven for persecuted free coloureds who happened to be French-speaking.[24]

CREATING A COUNTER-DISCOURSE: HAITI AND THE COLOURED RADICALS, 1840s–1850s

Haiti remained "an important and contested symbol in post-emancipation struggles, central to the racial projects of various contenders", writes Sheller; competing narratives of that country were used to construct alternative political and ethnic "maps" of the Caribbean. Haiti was significant to Jamaica's mixed-race leaders from Edward Jordan and Robert Osborn in the 1830s to G.W. Gordon in the 1860s. In Trinidad, an important coloured radical leader of the mid-nineteenth century, George Numa Dessources, showed a consistent interest in Haiti in the two newspapers which he owned or edited between 1845 and 1852, the *Spectator* and the *Trinidadian*. Dessources probably had a family link to Haiti; he may have been a grandson, or other relative, of the "General" Dessources (a white *colon*) who led a corps of black Volunteers or Chasseurs which fought for the British in the campaigns of 1794–98. He went to Jamaica after the British evacuated St Domingue, but he may have subsequently come to Trinidad; his son, Nelson Dessources, died in Port of Spain in 1838, a planter of Irois in the south of the island. George Numa was born, apparently in Trinidad, in 1819, certainly of mixed race, probably to a slave-owning free coloured family. He was educated in Britain and France and wrote in both English and French in his newspapers. He may have known the "General"; he prefaced a short story he published in the *Trinidadian* in 1851 with a note stating it was told to him by "le Chevalier Des Sources, alors capitaine au régiment des voluntaires Des Sources" and manager of a plantation in the Artibonite. G.N. Dessources took a strongly anti-government line in his newspapers, championed popular causes, defended both coloureds and blacks (ex-slaves) against their detractors, and led a movement for black/brown emigration from Trinidad to Venezuela in 1852–54. Returning to Trinidad when this failed, he died there in 1880.[25]

There was considerable coverage of, and comment on, Haitian affairs in the *Spectator* and the *Trinidadian*; many extracts from French, British, US and Jamaican papers were carried, and there were frequent articles about Haiti published in the French-language section of these papers, which was quite extensive.

Many items reporting on current events in the republic were carried in the *Spectator* in 1846–47, in both languages; in one, Dessources indicated that a degree of scepticism was required in "reading" some of these reports: "On se plaît à donner une couleur odieuse à tout ce qui sort de cette république naissante; l'on doit accepter avec réserve les nouvelles qui en viennent."[26]

In his second paper, the *Trinidadian,* this extensive coverage of Haiti continued. Many items appeared on the growing persecution by President Soulouque of coloured leaders in 1848, culminating in the killing of several. Dessources often commented editorially on these developments, showing considerable familiarity with Haitian affairs, urging scepticism towards the more lurid accounts of massacres, but also revealing a deep sympathy for coloured victims of Soulouque's "tyranny". He consistently rejected any tendency to portray Haitian politics as uniquely violent or bloodthirsty, pointing out that in Europe, several great nations had also been convulsed by bloody revolutions and civil struggles (1848). The violence which was, in fact, meted out to Haitian coloureds was the work of a despot and a madman (Soulouque), not a genocidal attack by blacks against coloureds – and there was more than one Soulouque in Europe. In one French-language editorial, Dessources wrote that he had never believed that the attacks against coloureds amounted to a civil war based on "caste" hatreds – between blacks and coloureds; instead, he saw them as struggles of the poor and deprived against the people with property and education, mostly coloureds, comparable to the fierce class conflicts which were convulsing Europe, and especially France, in 1848. If there was anything consoling in contemplating the excesses in Haiti, it was to think that the attacks on the "gens de couleur" had no other source than "cette folie du communisme. Quel serait l'avenir des Antilles, s'il en était autrement!" The *Trinidadian* reported on Soulouque's assumption of an imperial crown as Faustin I, generally unsympathetically, and criticized his attempts to subjugate the Dominican Republic by force of arms. A brief article in French marked the death of Boyer, in exile, in 1850; he was a remarkable head of state and an honest politician. In 1851, Dessources reproduced a balanced and thoughtful article from the Jamaican *Morning Journal,* which argued that the turmoil and near-anarchy experienced in Haiti since the fall of Boyer (1843) was due to the devastation of the revolution, the violent "birth" of the new state, and misgovernment since the coup against Boyer. The "lesson" for Jamaica – and for Trinidad, commented Dessources – was to educate the people, to enlighten them gradually so that self-government was both possible and safe.[27]

In addition to this substantial coverage of current events in Haiti, Dessources used his newspapers to examine the history of the revolution there and to probe its meanings for the post-emancipation project of radical Caribbean politicians like himself. He reproduced without editorial comment a long article from the French journal *La Presse,* titled "Des Révolutions de Saint-Domingue", which took a gloomy view of Haiti's post-1804 history: the expulsion or massacre of the whites, and the persecution of the coloureds, had eradicated all signs of "civilisation" among the people, who had relapsed into barbarism. But his own editorial comments on the history of Haiti were more positive. For instance, he reproduced (in French) correspondence between Pétion and Bolívar and argued that Pétion would come to be seen as the equal of Washington and Bolívar himself, when ignorant prejudices against people of African descent had disappeared. The "horrors" of the revolution, Dessources argued, were caused by the worse horrors of slavery, and it would take several generations for social harmony (between blacks and coloureds) to be established, granted the cruelties of slavery and the devastation of the years of civil war. In another editorial article, Dessources admitted that he could not entirely approve of the clause in the Haitian constitution which prohibited white ownership of land, because he believed it would have the effect of retarding the growth of the economy and, indeed, of "civilisation". Yet, considering the bloody past – still a living memory for the older Haitians – and the cruelties of the *anciens colons* ("le débris du grand drame Haitien"), he argued that revoking the prohibition could not be considered until at least two generations had passed away. He believed that Haiti was poised to enter an era of improvement – a hope which was shaken by the later rise of Soulouque and the attacks on coloured leaders. Like so many others of African descent in the Americas, Dessources looked to Haitian history to find black icons and great men whose deeds could "vindicate" the moral and intellectual capacities of the race. Toussaint was everyone's great icon, and Dessources added Pétion and Boyer – but not Dessalines or Christophe.[28]

For Dessources, Haiti and its history were powerful metaphors and symbols of immediate relevance to his political and racial projects in post-emancipation Trinidad. They might be "used" by his opponents: when he or his colleagues argued for political changes and social reforms, they were often accused of wanting to stir up turmoil and class or racial divisions which might lead to another Haiti. The "Haytian Fear" could be manipulated by powerful white elites and conservative forces generally to hold back changes which sought to give African Trinidadians more political rights and social equality. But Haiti was also a symbol of black redemption and a beacon of hope for people elsewhere in the Caribbean, who were now free but were still denied political, economic and social rights. And Dessources often used the Haitian Revolution as an example of what could happen when liberty was denied to oppressed people and violence seemed the only redress for those who were cruelly persecuted.

Whenever he publicly advocated reforms, Dessources complained in 1847, "quelques sots disent à de plus sots qu'eux que nous voulons faire une *St-Domingue* du pays, etc etc"; if he spoke of grievances, "on dira que nous avons tort, que nous sommes révolutionnaires, etc etc". Three years later he returned to this point, this time in an English editorial:

> Whenever a disturbance takes place in the West India Islands a cry of alarm is raised, and Haiti pointed at as a bloody example of the danger of negro emancipation. Whenever we call for the introduction of the elective franchise in the Legislature, Haiti is cited as an instance of the impossibility of self-government being judiciously exercised by the African race. Not one step is made towards certain parties, not one word spoken, not one wish expressed for a better state of things, but St Domingo is on their lips as an irrefragable argument in opposition to our demands. St Domingo is, in fact, the bugbear of the enemies of political progression in the Colonies.

In France, Dessources pointed out, the enemies of reform pointed to the excesses of the Terror; in the Caribbean, reformers were accused of wanting to reproduce "les orgies d'Haiti dans sa fièvre des premiers jours de liberté". In 1851, Dessources took issue with the editor of the conservative *Port of Spain Gazette,* which had accused him of "wishing to assume in this Island the character of Soulouque!": "It is a new verse of his old favourite lamentation, by means of which he is anxious to persuade the authorities *at home* that the opposition in this country has anti-British tendencies! – that we dream but of revolutions, massacres, blood, and death!"[29]

Dessources was in no doubt that the "Haytian Fear" was alive and well in mid-nineteenth century Trinidad, if primarily as a useful propaganda point rather than an anticipation of actual danger. Opponents of political reforms to give a share of legislative power to the island's black and coloured population predicted "revolutions, massacres and blood". "Haiti, the nightmare of every conscience-stricken European or colonist, is pointed at as an instance of the fatality of granting such authority to whomsoever is warmed by a particle of African blood." Why, Dessources asked, did they focus on Haiti when so many European countries had recently experienced anarchy and bloody civil disorder? And "would Haiti be what it now is, if the cruelty of its former owners had not banished from the aborigines and Africans every feeling of sympathy and humanity?" But the "nightmare of Haiti" was too useful to be put to rest. In 1850, a New York paper published what purported to be a letter from "A Planter" writing from Port of Spain. It lamented that the consequences of a planned removal of British troops from the island would be "direful": "the terrible scenes of St Domingo, etc, will be enacted here". Relations between blacks and whites were tense, and "an opportunity alone is wanted for the far more numerous blacks to exterminate the few whites remaining". If the troops really were removed, "your humble correspondent will fly on the first intelligence, and thus try to save his throat from being cut, and his family from brutal outrage". Dessources reproduced this letter, and wrote an editorial dismissing it as a piece of crude propaganda concocted by "an enemy of Reform". He wrote:

> The reaction of those men who regret Slavery and oppose themselves to the amelioration of the emancipated classes, presents always to the Government the eternal example of St Domingo. St Domingo is the canvass on which they embroider all their dark reveries against Reform. The slightest effort of the liberal party appears to them a rallying cry – an echo of the frightful orgies of St Domingo.

But it was slavery that caused the "excesses" of the revolution, and since slavery no longer existed in Trinidad, they could never recur there. "Let us keep in mind the example of St Domingo, but, only as a warning of what may be produced by odious oppression"; let "the men of the reaction" beware: "They are making use of a dangerous weapon, which sometimes bursts in the unskilful hands of those who overcharge it."[30]

For Dessources, the "lesson of Haiti" was that prolonged and brutal oppression would lead inevitably to bloody revolution and all its "excesses". This was a theme he frequently took up in his newspapers. What happened in Haiti, and in Europe during the "Year of Revolutions" (1848), was the inevitable result of long years of arrogant oppression. It was his duty to warn oppressors closer to home of these facts, he wrote – for which he was, of course, accused of extremism and "menacing language". Unspeakable cruelties against the slaves, and persecution of the free coloureds, produced the anarchy and bloodshed of the Haitian Revolution; in 1848, France, "most polished nation of civilised Europe, was deluged in the blood of her best citizens". The example of Haiti showed the folly and crime of a government withholding freedom from a people. In an 1850 editorial, Dessources put his argument into the mouth of Sir William Molesworth, a liberal British politician whose views on colonial government he admired:

> He is not one of those who will speak of Haiti as an instance of the consequences of power in the hands of the people; but he will show it as a living monument of the direful evils which a cruel and tyrannic Government bequeaths to a country. He will fearlessly proclaim that the people become barbarians when their rulers have been inhuman, and he will warn the latter that to oppress the former, is to accumulate the engines of vengeance.[31]

The importance of Haiti as symbol and metaphor for contesting discourses in Trinidad was highlighted by the visit early in 1850 of John Candler, a British representative of the antislavery movement who had published a book on the black republic a few years earlier. He spoke at a public meeting in Port of Spain. "The supporters of slavery", he was reported as saying, "were bold enough to plead for it on the ground of it leaving the people happier than freedom could make them; and they said to us look at St Domingo! He had looked at St Domingo again and again" – he had lived there for several months – and ten years ago, the people were "physically speaking, well-off". Their "moral" condition was "low", but "as a nation they had proved themselves more fit for self-government than many of their white neighbours of the western world" (that is, the Latin American republics). Haiti had "many glaring faults, and its present government was unhappily one of despotism; but as compared to the time of slavery the land might be truly said to be a happy one. Emancipation in Haiti was no failure, but had proved an immense boon to the emancipated people." Dessources thanked Candler for disproving most of the "calumnies heaped on that unhappy country, and on the persecuted race" which lived there; his sober testimony rebuked "certain Trinidad prophets who have ever been endeavouring to make St Domingo synonymous with anarchy, bloodshed etc".[32]

It is unlikely that many whites (or coloureds) in mid-nineteenth century Trinidad actually lived in fear of massacre and mayhem from the ex-slaves who surrounded them. But responses to a fairly minor popular riot in Port of Spain in 1849 (the "Prisoner Riot") do suggest that the "Remember Haiti" slogan was still current and perhaps lay behind official and upper-class reactions. For two days early in October 1849, crowds protested against new prison regulations which seemed to make it compulsory for persons in jail as debtors to have their heads shaved, and do hard labour, as was the case for common criminals. Several hundreds protested outside the Red House (the seat of the legislature), the situation seemed menacing to the authorities, the Riot Act was read and the police fired, killing two persons and injuring several. Though the protest was quickly and easily repressed, a few cases of apparent arson on estates in the countryside suggested that unrest had spread, though very briefly, outside the city.

Dessources consistently argued in the *Trinidadian* that the violence by the mob was wrong and indefensible, the result of their ignorance; but that some outbreak of popular passion was inevitable, granted the oppression endured by the black population for so long. He was soon accused of helping to incite unrest, which he denied, while not seeking to conceal his sympathy for the "popular cause" though not for the actual rioting. But especially interesting are the echoes of the "Haytian Fear" in the language which W.H. Burnley, the leading spokesman for the conservative forces in Trinidad, used in the Council debate on the riot. He spoke of the "barbarism" of the population, the "menacing language" of the "incendiaries", the terror of the respectable inhabitants:

> What was the situation of Agricultural Proprietors at the present moment? Why they went to bed every night under the apprehension that their estates would be burnt down before the morning, from some pique on the part of their labourers . . . What was the situation of respectable families in this Town of Port of Spain on the night of the 1st of October? Women and children, left alone in their houses, whilst their husbands and fathers were doing duty as special constables, in the midst of ferocious rioters! In their fears they expected nothing less than being burnt, or assassinated, in their beds. – These fears proved exaggerated, but they were bitterly felt, and a life of suspicious fears is more intolerable than death itself. How many respectable men on that occasion had sworn that this was not a country fit to live in, and that one and all would abandon it, when their affairs were wound down?

Burnley painted a lurid picture of island-wide insurrection, the jail issue a mere pretext to

> stir up the passions of the labouring population throughout the length and breadth of the Colony – to have induced the most distant villages to send forth bands armed with bludgeons, cutlasses and firearms . . . a body of incendiaries from Port of Spain to set fire to canes and burn down houses and works in the rural districts . . .

Burnley solemnly assured the Council:

> Sinister faces were seen unknown to the Police and inhabitants and menacing cries were heard savouring of the worst periods of Jacobinical France . . . And amongst the rioters now under arrest, was one who boasted of being a relative, a brother he [Burnley] believed, of Soulouque, the present Emperor of Hayti!

Of course, in a whole series of editorials, Dessources dismissed this tirade as carefully calculated hysteria and lurid fiction from a former slave owner who openly regretted emancipation. But it seems clear that Haiti was a powerful influence behind these reactions, however calculated, to a minor riot in which not a single person was actually harmed by the rioters.[33]

The "Haitian nightmare" certainly lost much of its resonance in Trinidad in the second half of the nineteenth century. Fear of violence from the African Trinidadians receded; perhaps it was the Indian immigrants who were the more dangerous group – as Donald Wood writes, "Cawnpore joined Haiti as a precedent for a possible massacre of the whites and coloured men of property." A.H. Gordon, the governor, in 1869 described Trinidad's blacks as "the quietest and most inoffensive people it has ever been my lot to meet with". The only possible disturbances to the island's tranquillity, he thought, might come from the Indian and Chinese immigrants concentrated on the sugar estates. His friend Charles Kingsley, who stayed with him in Trinidad in 1869–70, took a similar line:

> As long as the Negroes are decently loyal and peaceable, and do not murder their magistrates and drink their brains mixed with rum, nor send delegates to the President of Hayti to ask if he will assist them, in case of a general rising, to exterminate the whites – tricks which the harmless Negroes of Trinidad, to do them justice, never have played, or had a thought of playing . . .

then "we" must tolerate their impertinence and indolence. The "Haytian Fear" had receded, it seemed.[34]

The brief quotation from Kingsley hints at the strongly racist tone of much of the European discourse on the Caribbean in the later part of the century, informed by the pseudoscientific racism of the era. Influential books about Haiti, notably that by Spencer St John, offered lurid pictures of a people given over to voodoo, devil or serpent worship, human sacrifice and cannibalism – in a word, all sorts of "African barbarities". J.A. Froude took a very similar line (he was clearly influenced by the first edition of St John's work), and both authors saw the state of Haiti in the 1880s as proof positive that blacks could not govern themselves and that Britain should not cede any further political rights to her non-white colonial populations. Writing of political agitation for reform in 1887–88, Froude thought that the black Trinidadian

> knows what has happened in St Domingo. He has heard that his race is already in full possession of the finest of all the islands. If he has any thought or hopes about the matter, it is that it may be with the rest of them as it has been with St Domingo, and if you force the power into his hands, you must expect him to use it.

Revolutionary violence by the blacks was no longer a threat, at least in Trinidad, but Haiti continued to provide a useful argument for the opponents of political reform.[35]

It was the African-Trinidadian intellectual J.J. Thomas who, in his reply to Froude, deflated his "ghastly imaginings" that granting the franchise to educated blacks and coloureds would unleash in Trinidad a repetition of events in Haiti. "With regard to the perpetual reference to Hayti," Thomas wrote, "because of our oneness with its inhabitants in origin and complexion, as a criterion for the exact forecast of our future conduct, this appeared to us, looking at actual facts, perversity gone wild in the manufacture of analogies." The circumstances of blacks in the British West Indies, in the 1880s, were utterly different from those of the founders of the black republic. Yet Froude claimed to believe that

> in spite of being free, educated, progressive, and at peace with all men, we West Indian Blacks, were we ever to become constitutionally dominant in our native islands, would emulate in savagery our Haytian fellow-Blacks who, at the time of retaliating upon their actual masters, were tortured slaves, bleeding and rendered desperate under the oppressors' lash – and all this simply and merely because of the sameness of our ancestry and the colour of our skin!

For Thomas, this was merely to rehash all the "old pro-slavery prophecies" in the service of a reactionary political creed. It was a common-sense dismissal of the "Haytian Fear" and the Haiti analogy altogether.[36]

NOTES

ABBREVIATIONS

TTHS	Trinidad and Tobago Historical Society Publications Number
POSG	*Port of Spain Gazette*
Trin	*Trinidadian*
Spec	*Spectator* (Trinidad)
CO	Colonial Office
WO	War Office

NB All citations of newspapers refer to nineteenth-century dates

1. M. Sheller, *Democracy after Slavery: Black Publics and Peasant Radicalism in Haiti and Jamaica* (London and Oxford: Macmillan, 2000), 71–73; D.P. Geggus, "Haiti and the Abolitionists", in *Abolition and Its Aftermath*, ed. D.Richardson (London: Frank Cass, 1985), 114; D.P. Geggus, "British Opinion and the Emergence of Haiti, 1791–1805," in *Slavery and British Society, 1776–1846*, ed. J. Walvin (London: Macmillan, 1982), 146–48; D. Nicholls, *From Dessalines to Duvalier* (London: Macmillan, 1988), 5, 34, 36, 66. Cf. also D.B. Davis, "Impact of the French and Haitian Revolutions", in *The Impact of the Haitian Revolution in the Atlantic World,* ed. D.P. Geggus (Columbia, SC: University of South Carolina Press, 2001), 4–5.

2. B. Edwards, *An Historical Survey of the French Colony in the Island of St Domingo* (London: John Stockdale, 1797), esp. 63–92, 116–18; O.M. Blouet, "Bryan Edwards and the Haitian Revolution", in Geggus, *Impact,* 44–57; P.F.McCallum, *Travels in Trinidad During the Months of February, March and April 1803 (*Liverpool: 1805), esp. 115–24, 313–31; M. Rainsford, *An Historical Account of the Black Empire of Hayti* (London: Albion Press, 1805), esp. chapters 4 and 5; Geggus, "British Opinion", 128–45.

3. C. Fergus, "British Imperial Trusteeship: The Dynamics of Reconstruction of British West Indian Society with special reference to Trinidad & Tobago" (PhD diss., University of the West Indies, St Augustine, 1995), 132–39, also 177–93, 443–44; G. Matthews, "Slave Rebellions in the Discourse of British Anti-Slavery" (PhD thesis, University of Hull, 2002), 86–88, 185–87; J. Stephen, *The Crisis of the Sugar Colonies* (1802; reprint, New York: Negro Universities Press, 1969), esp. 117–78, 202; H. Brougham, *An Inquiry into the Colonial Policy of the European Powers* (1803; reprint, New York: Augustus M. Kelley, 1970), 2: esp. 141–56, 300–302.

4. J. Noel, "Spanish Colonial Administration and the Socio-Economic Foundations of Trinidad, 1777–1797" (PhD thesis, University of Cambridge, 1966), 152–53, 300–301; TTHS 696, Minutes of Cabildo 14/3/1796; D.P. Geggus, *Haitian Revolutionary Studies* (Bloomington and Indianopolis: Indiana University Press, 2002), 179–203; A. Helg, "A Fragmented Majority", in Geggus, *Impact,* 157–75; TTHS 525, Picton to Dundas, 1/5/1800, WO 1/94.

5. D.P. Geggus, *Slavery, War and Revolution: The British Occupation of Saint Domingue, 1793–1798* (Oxford: Clarendon Press, 1982), 271–72; J. Millette, *The Genesis of Crown Colony Government: Trinidad, 1783–1810* (Curepe, Trinidad: Moko, 1970), 99–101; TTHS 525, in note 4.

6. Geggus, *Slavery,* 62, 73, 273, 421, 424; K.S. Wise, *Historical Sketches* (London: Historical Society of Trinidad and Tobago, 1938), 3: 51–59; M.R. Pocock, *Out of the Shadows of the Past* (Hastings, Sussex: The author, 1993), 288–300; Geggus, "Haiti and the Abolitionists", 117–21.

7. Geggus, *Slavery* (many references all through); K.S. Wise, *Historical Sketches* (Port of Spain: Trinidad Historical Society, 1936), 2: 90–94; V.S. Naipaul, *The Loss of El Dorado* (Harmondsworth: Penguin, 1973), 196, 221, 276.

8. Geggus, *Slavery,* 37–44; Millette, *The Genesis of Crown Colony Government,* 33–34, 113; TTHS 181, Picton to Hobart 18/2/1802, CO 295/2; TTHS 986, Address by Picton to Council 14/4/1803, CO 295/5; G. Carmichael, *The History of the West Indian Islands of Trinidad and Tobago* (London: Alvin Redman, 1961), 63–65; C. Campbell, *Cedulants and Capitulants: The Politics of the Coloured Opposition in the Slave Society of Trinidad* (Port of Spain: Paria, 1992), 30–33, 71, 127–35, 145–48, 160, 180–82.

9. TTHS 879 Hislop to Castlereagh 17/12/1805, CO 295/11; TTHS 880 Hislop to Castlereagh 19/12/1805, CO 295/11; TTHS 881 Hislop to Castlereagh 8/1/1806, CO 295/14; TTHS 882 Hislop to Edward Coke, Private, 8/1/1806, CO 295/14; Carmichael, 76–77.

10. L.M. Fraser, *History of Trinidad* (1891; reprint, London: Frank Cass, 1971), 1: 268–72.

11. See notes 9 and 10; also E.L. Joseph, *History of Trinidad* (1838; reprint, London: Frank Cass, 1970), 229–30; G. Besson and B. Brereton, *The Book of Trinidad* (Port of Spain: Paria, 1992), 90–91; A. de Verteuil, *Begorrat Brunton: A History of Diego Martin 1784–1884* (Port of Spain: Paria, 1987), 72–73 and The Plates, 3 (n.p.); Naipaul, *Loss of El Dorado,* 291–99.

12. Geggus, "Haiti and the Abolitionists", 129–37.

13. *POSG* 21/9/25, 24/9/25, 26/10/25, 23/11/25, 7/1/26, 7/6/26, 24/6/26, 22/7/26, 20/9/26, 28/4/27, 25/7/27.

14. *POSG* 7/12/25, 1/4/26, 22/11/26, 9/12/26.

15. *POSG* 9/11/25, 8/4/26, 28/6/26, 23/4/28, 3/4/38, 23/6/38.

16. *POSG* 23/2/38, 6/3/38; Geggus, *Slavery,* 65, 234–45, 311.

17. *POSG* 19/4/26, 26/4/26, 3/5/26, 31/5/26, 7/6/26, 7/3/27, 17/5/28, 8/2/33, 22/3/33, 26/3/33, 23/7/33, 11/10/33, 1/11/33. The writer who signed his French-language articles "DF" has not been identified.

18. *POSG* 9/2/38 (editorial).

19. *POSG* 24/5/26, 31/5/26, 10/1/27, 5/5/27, 27/9/28, 15/8/32, 30/9/34, 10/2/35, 13/4/38.

20. CO 295/59 Woodford to Bathurst 5/11/1823; de Verteuil, *The Plates,* 3 (n.p.); Millette, *The Genesis of Crown Colony Government,* 113; CO 295/66 Report of the Committee of Council to investigate the Negro Character, 20 April 1824.

21. *POSG* 15/2/32, 7/3/32, 24/3/32, 25/3/32 (Gazette Extraordinary), 7/4/32, 11/4/32, 18/4/32, 6/6/32, 9/6/32, 9/11/32, 30/4/33.

22. *POSG* 5/8/34, 8/8/34, 12/8/34, 16/9/34, 24/10/34; Besson and Brereton, *The Book of Trinidad,* 169–70; Lieut.-Col. Capadose, *Sixteen Years in the West Indies* (London: 1845), 1: 66–67; *POSG* 3/8/38; D. Wood, *Trinidad in Transition: The Years After Slavery* (London: Oxford University Press, 1968), 47.

23. Jean-Baptiste Philippe, *A Free Mulatto* (1824; reprint, Port of Spain: Paria, 1987), 194–97; Campbell, *Cedulants and Capitulants,* 246–47.

24. Campbell, *Cedulants and Capitulants,* 247; Philippe, *A Free Mulatto,* 175; Nicholls, *From Dessalines to Duvalier,* 71, 90; A.N. Hunt, *Haiti's Influence on Antebellum America* (Baton Rouge: Louisiana State University Press, 1988), 158–71; Sheller, *Democracy after Slavery,* 75–81.

25. Sheller, *Democracy after Slavery,* 80, 85, 227–37; for Dessources (sometimes spelled Des Sources) and his relatives, see: Geggus, *Slavery,* 130, 165, 224–25, 274, 289, 439; *POSG* 13/2/38: Death Notice; *Trin* 9/4/51; Pocock, *Out of the Shadows of the Past,* 198–203; M. Toussaint, "George Numa Dessources, the Numancians, and the effort to form a colony in Eastern Venezuela, circa 1850–1854" (paper presented at thirty-third Conference of Caribbean Historians, St Augustine, Trinidad, 2001).

26. *Spec* 7/1/46, 25/3/46, 4/4/46, 2/5/46, 27/2/47, 1/9/47, 13/11/47.

27. *Trin* 10/6/48, 14/6/48, 17/6/48, 12/7/48, 12/8/48, 16/8/48, 22/8/48, 25/10/48, 16/12/48, 3/1/49, 10/1/49, 27/1/49, 11/7/49, 28/7/49, 29/7/49, 31/10/49, 5/6/50, 7/8/50, 14/8/50, 28/8/50, 12/10/50, 28/5/51, 1/7/52, 9/2/53.

28. *Spec* 24/1/46, 21/10/46, 31/10/46, 16/12/46, 8/8/46, 26/5/47.

29. *Spec* 6/1/47; *Trin* 4/11/48, 23/1/50, 23 and 27/3/50, 23/7/51.

30. *Trin* 1/6/50, 30/10/50.

31. *Trin* 24/2/49, 16/3/49, 23/1/50, 6/7/50.

32. *Trin* 23/1/50. Candler's book was *Brief Notices of Hayti: With its Condition, Resources and Prospects* (1842).

33. For the 1849 riot, see: *Trin* 3/10/49, 6/10/49, 10/10/49, 24/10/49, 7/11/49, 10/11/49, 17/11/49, 15/12/49, 19/12/49, 26/12/49, 29/12/49; *POSG* 2/11/49, 6/11/49: Council of Government, 1 and 2/11/49; Besson and Brereton, *The Book of Trinidad,* 302–4; Wood, *Trinidad in Transition,* 175–77; D. Trotman, "Protest in Post-Emancipation Trinidad: The Prisoner Riots of 1849" (paper presented at fifteenth Conference of Caribbean Historians, Mona, Jamaica, 1983); D. Trotman, "Capping the Volcano: Riots and Their Suppression in Post-Emancipation Trinidad" (unpublished paper, 2003), 5–8.

34. Wood, *Trinidad in Transition,* 154; Gordon to Granville 24/5/1869 (Secret), CO 295/247; C. Kingsley, *At Last a Christmas in the West Indies* (1871; reprint, London: Macmillan, 1900), 245.

35. S. St John, *Hayti or The Black Republic* (1884 and 1889; reprint, London: Frank Cass, 1971), esp. chapters 4–7; J.A. Froude, *The English in the West Indies* (1888; reprint, New York: Charles Scribner's, 1906), 88–89, 181–88, 340–48; B. Brereton, *Race Relations in Colonial Trinidad, 1870–1900* (Cambridge: Cambridge University Press, 1979), 196–97.

36. J.J. Thomas, *Froudacity* (1889; reprint, London: New Beacon, 1969), 52–55, 164–65.

Chapter 10

The Travelling Revolutionary
Situating Toussaint Louverture

Charles Forsdick

Even a cursory survey of the many biographies devoted to Toussaint Louverture during the two centuries since his death reveals these texts' over-reliance on a series of recycled anecdotes – stories disseminated initially through an oral tradition, but progressively granted credence as they were repeated in print. Percy Waxman, author of *The Black Napoleon,* claimed "so little trustworthy 'source material' exists that it is extremely difficult for one with no gift for fiction to attempt a complete story of his life".[1] Although C.L.R. James (with undoubted accuracy) dismissed this account as a "superficial book",[2] its author was sufficiently astute and self-aware to acknowledge the fictionalization and mythologization to which his object of study had been – and would, in his own contribution to the tradition, continue to be – subject. French national and colonial archives contain, of course, empirical evidence: invaluable documents, including Toussaint's own correspondence, that illuminate the final years of his life, details of which nevertheless remain lacunary and whose interpretation depends on a historiographic tradition that tends to marginalize Haiti in the story of a European revolution. It is, however, Toussaint's life before 1789 that remains particularly obscure: his son Isaac Louverture's memoirs contain few details regarding this period; and, beyond a number of contradictory references in civil registers, documentation relating to the first five decades of Toussaint's life appears to be non-existent. It is the gaps of knowledge relating to this period that have lent themselves to speculation. Details of the then Toussaint Bréda's education, acquisition of Latin and exposure to the (in this context, neatly prophetic) writings of l'Abbé Raynal have been repeated so often that they have achieved the status of orthodoxy, providing a teleological explanation of the ex-slave's rise to prominence. This emphasis on Toussaint's exceptionalism – namely on his formation and differentiation from his black Haitian peers under the influence of contemporary metropolitan intellectual trends – has led to a journey tradition that associates these influences with the future revolutionary's purported actual travel to France, as if contact with texts alone was not enough to guarantee his credentials as an activist of Enlightenment. An article on Toussaint's life before 1789 explores and debunks a number of these journey narratives that place him in France as, variously, slave, estate manager and fifty-year-old manumittee learning to read and write; it ascribes these traditions to hearsay or to cases of mistaken identity.[3] What these travel stories nevertheless underline is the role of the journey as a defining element of Toussaint's biography, a biography in which authentic itineraries – his parents' from West Africa to St Domingue, his own from St Domingue to Joux – play a major role.

In posthumous interpretations of Toussaint, it is in particular the transatlantic deportation to the Château de Joux that has achieved a privileged, even iconic status. Interpretations shift to match the contexts of representation, ranging from an early nineteenth-century French sense of retributive justice imposed on the traitorous ex-slave to a more widespread emphasis on the white-shrouded alienation of the black tragic hero.[4] It is, however, with the posthumous itineraries by which the meanings of Toussaint have been freighted that this chapter is concerned. Toussaint's reaction to Abbé Raynal's call for "ce grand homme à qui la nature sera redevable de ses enfants vexés, opprimés et tourmentés" [that great man to whom nature will be indebted on behalf of its offended, oppressed and tormented children] is regularly cited in accounts of the revolutionary's rise to power.[5] There is, however, in the same passage from *L'Histoire philosophique des deux Indes,* a subsequent comment regarding this future black Spartacus that might be presented as equally prophetic and more rel-evant to concerns underpinning this chapter. When Raynal claims that "ils élèveront partout des trophées en son honneur" [everywhere future generations will raise trophies in his honour], it is as if he alludes already to the often celebratory and increas-ingly complex freighting of Toussaint through a wide range of differing contexts. For only rarely have historical figures achieved a transcultural significance comparable to that of the Haitian revolutionary; Toussaint is one of very few characters who, like and yet perhaps more so than his contemporary Napoleon, have persisted in the popular imagination; he has inspired writers and thinkers in a variety of historical situations; he has been mythologized, allegorized and instrumentalized in a number of ideological and moral causes. Cast as the leader of the first successful slave revolt in history, Toussaint is seen to have pushed the Enlightenment project to logical limits unimagined in France itself, transforming Haiti, at certain points of its revolutionary struggle, into the hub of more generalized transatlantic activity. The impact of such an international influence may appear to have been neutralized by the revolutionary's ignominious and solitary death in French custody at Joux, but Toussaint's demise marked instead the beginning of two centuries of transnational reinterpretations that, with celebrations of the bicentenary of his death in 2003, show no sign of abating. To borrow Roland Barthes's terms, Toussaint as a "phenomenon" remains unrecoverable, reduced to a collection of manuscript letters, references in official reports and private diaries, and a series of recycled anecdotes and quotations; even his remains have been dispersed, and relics once believed authentic proven to be unidentifiable. It is rather to Toussaint as a dynamic "myth", travelling between contexts and constantly renewed, that subsequent interpreters have had access.[6]

Active on the other side of the Atlantic (but also so heavily guarded in his journey across France to the Jura that his presence at Joux was itself subject to wild contemporary speculation), Toussaint remained either absent from or invisible to contemporary French commentators, who provide some of the first extant accounts of him. These, published in the period around Toussaint's death, reflect nevertheless the shifts of interpretation that will characterize the next two centuries. By 1802, the Republican general and consul-general, only recently fêted for his patriotic (that is, pro-French) zeal, had been transformed as Haiti approached independence into the figure of an anti-Napoleonic "nègre atroce" [horrifying Negro],[7] whose previous adherence to the ideals of 1789 was dismissed by Dubroca as hypocrisy and naked ambition: "un exemple frappant des crimes où peut conduire l'ambition, quand la probité, l'éducation et l'honneur n'en répriment pas les excès" [a striking example of the crimes to which ambition may lead when integrity, education and honour do not suppress its excesses].[8] Although any contemporary Haitian responses to Toussaint remain difficult to gauge, especially in the light of his increasingly troubled relationship with the leaders such as Dessalines who would eventually lead Haiti to independence, a British reaction to French demonization is already clearly apparent. One pamphlet, produced shortly after his death at Joux ("the murder of this great and good man") clearly responds to Dubroca ("one of his bitterest defamers") by denouncing the victim's "merciless oppression" at the hands of Napoleon.[9]

The anonymous author (revealed in a subsequent 1814 edition to be the abolitionist James Stephen), presenting Toussaint's agrarian policies in a utopian light and skating over issues such as his desertion and betrayal by former comrades, produces an anti-Napoleonic tract prefiguring a long comparative tradition that brings together the two Napoleons, French and Haitian, white and black.[10] Such a Manichean approach was perpetuated in the European Romantic tradition, whose adoption and transformation of Toussaint is epitomized by Wordworth's evocation of the revolutionary's incarceration "alone in some deep dungeon's earless den".[11] As Cora Kaplan explains, early nineteenth-century European translations of Toussaint, particularly in their emphasis on Joux and their deflection of attention from the actual conditions of slave revolt, transform the revolutionary into a martyr and instrument of the abolitionist cause, often underlining his exceptionalism and perpetuating certain pigmentocratic assumptions relating to ethnic groups in Haiti.[12] The instrumentalization of Toussaint and his yoking to a variety of ideological imperatives thus began shortly after his death; his memory was henceforth a contested territory.

The nineteenth century also witnesses the internationalization of Toussaint. While re-appropriated by a series of Haitian nation-building poets and dramatists (for instance, by Vendenasse Ducasse, Charles Moravia), who challenged the negative portraits produced by mulatto historians such as Saint-Rémy, the revolutionary was also adopted as a principal exemplum in North American debates surrounding abolition (for instance, by John R. Beard and Wendell Philips). In the context of an emerging recognizably modern racism, Toussaint operated as a reflection of proto-Negritudinist black dignity, challenging hierarchical understandings of ethnicity and any resultant primitivist denigration of blackness. In a largely undervalued and unexplored text, for instance, Anténor Firmin challenges Gobineau's theses of inequality, and presents Toussaint as "le plus merveilleux exemple de l'étonnante et prompte évolution qu'avaient subie les Africains transportés en Haïti" [the most wonderful example of the astonishing and swift evolution experienced by Africans on their transportation to Haiti].[13] Firmin's work incorporates Toussaint into anthropological and philosophical debates that, although rooted in Haitian examples, transcend the immediate Caribbean or francophone context and assert him as a figure with international valency.

Throughout the twentieth century, despite Toussaint's persistence as a key character in Haitian literature, associated in particular with literary contributions to the creation of a consensus of commemoration,[14] it is this international dimension that is firmly asserted. With Haiti subject to US occupation, Toussaint continued to provide a national model of past glory and future potential, an interpretation that emerges clearly from the hagiographic overtones of Auguste Nemours's numerous historical publications; yet Nemours is equally to be associated, albeit obliquely, with an internationalist Toussaint, for it was to him that C.L.R. James turned during his visits to Paris in the early 1930s (of which more below) for an understanding of the military aspects of the Haitian Revolution. *The Black Jacobins,* while it is a document rooted firmly in the political turmoil of the interwar period, remains a key point of reference in studies of the Haitian Revolution, not least because it reinvigorated enquiry into the events with its challenge to the dominant traditions of French revolutionary historiography. There is a risk, however, that any privileging of James's Toussaint eclipses a more entangled set of contemporary representations. *The Black Jacobins* is in itself a complex product, resulting from James's transatlantic journey to Britain and the politicization to which this displacement led; in writing it, James is motivated by initially literary ambitions, rooted in its author's daily contact with the working class community of the Lancashire town of Nelson, but is to be seen at the same time as part of "the West Indies . . . speaking for itself to the modern world".[15] But *The Black Jacobins* must also be read in relation to a global network of seemingly disparate yet loosely interconnected interwar engagements with Toussaint, who figures prominently in the Harlem Renaissance (especially in Jacob Lawrence's Haitian Revolution series), in the Parisian emergence of négritude (Aimé Césaire's elevation of Toussaint in *Cahier d'un retour au pays natal*), and in a number of contemporary Soviet representations (Anatolii Vinogradov's *The Black Consul,* of which Eisenstein, in a brief yet intensive period of activity, planned to make a film).[16] Added to these is an additional series of seemingly freestanding biographies – by Otten, Rüsch and Waxman – appearing within several years of each other, suggesting that Toussaint served as a means of exploring a series of interwar concerns relating to ideology, culture and race.[17]

This roughly sketched network of creative representations contains connections, some concrete (Paul Robeson, for example, appeared on the London stage in 1936 in the dramatic version of James's history, but had also visited Moscow in 1934 to discuss the Eisenstein project), others more speculative (both James's and Césaire's Toussaints emerge at once from transatlantic displacement and their experience of 1930s Paris, although it seems unlikely that the two actually met), which need to be examined carefully. And although it is the 1930s that perhaps witnessed the most diversified and intensive engagement with Toussaint, other periods are also characterized by these competing representations: the two decades following the Second World War, for instance, continued to witness Haitian re-readings (for example, Raphaël Tardon's), supplemented by the assertion of a francophone Caribbean Toussaint (in works by both Césaire and Glissant) that explores the ambiguities of the region in a period of rapid global decolonization, as well as the West African perspective provided (slightly later) by Dadié's *Iles de tempête*.[18] In addition to these were published several English-language versions, ranging from a pedagogically paternalistic appropriation (in W.M.A. Jones's *Black Emperor*) to the transformation of Toussaint into Left-Book-Club hero (in Ralph Korngold's *Citizen Toussaint*);[19] and the bicentenaries of both Toussaint's death and Haitian independence (following closely on his highly suspect recruitment to the French Republican philanthropic cause in the 1998 celebrations of one and one-half centuries of the second abolition of slavery) have themselves triggered a series of new representations and interpretations, both textual and ceremonial.[20]

It must be stressed that, for all its neatness, any such chronological presentation of the posthumous refigurings of Toussaint during the two centuries since his death ignores the complexity of the processes in question. The "travelling" Toussaint has resulted in a process of sedimentation, both intertextual and intercultural, whereby accumulated interpretations have formed the many layered and constantly evolving figure into which the revolutionary has been transformed. This image of layering is central to any understanding of the ways in which the historical character has been mythologized and instrumentalized: it permits a vertical or diachronic approach to such processes, underlying the progressive shifts on which they depend, whilst at the same time underlining the importance of those horizontal or synchronic readings that signal competing interpretations that might co-exist at any given moment. Sedimentation remains, however, an uneven process, belying neat geometric models, for the excavation of one layer of meaning can unexpectedly reveal another and create connections between culturally, geographically and historically distinct moments. The convenient linearity by which histories of representation are often guided is replaced by a more complex recognition that such a series of interpretations is based on interdependency and interconnectedness, with impact transformed to such an extent by the context and ways in which each is presented that any claims of organic progression become unfounded.

Perhaps one of the most useful starting points in any such exploration of Toussaint is Edward Said's concept of "traveling theory" (as developed in an article first published in *Raritan* in 1982, included in *The World, the Text and the Critic,* and subsequently revisited in a 1994 essay).[21] Said's reflections on this concept allow, I shall argue, an attenuated consideration of the translation of Toussaint between a range of different contexts (restricted here to the twentieth century) and an assessment of the implications of such transfer for his initial revolutionary impact. In its first formulation, "traveling theory" considers the circulation of ideas and the impact – in terms of gains and losses – that such displacement between contexts involves. Said identifies four elements in such a process: the initial circumstances of emergence of an idea; the distance crossed in its transfer; the new context into which it is received with varying degrees of resistance and acceptance; and the transformed idea as it is translated into a different cultural, geographical and historical context. By focusing on issues of representation and institutionalization, Said asks what happens when a theory or idea is instrumentalized and undergoes multiple displacements, with the transformed idea itself serving in turn as a new point of origin. His example is Lukács's analysis of reification in *History and Class Consciousness,* the transfer of which from 1919 Budapest to (in the work of Lucien Goldmann) mid-twentieth-century Paris and finally (in the work of Raymond Williams) to later-twentieth-century Cambridge is seen in terms of dissipation, degradation and domestication. There is no critique of borrowing, which is accepted as an intellectual necessity, rather an emphasis on the importance of recognizing both current context and point of origin. Transfer is seen in terms of the loss of insurrectionary power and of revolutionary impact; for Said, when an idea first emerges, it possesses a worldliness or organic connection to lived experience that is lost as it is progressively distanced from its origins. Such a dissipatory teleology is eschewed in Said's corrective "Traveling Theory Reconsidered", in which he considers alternative trajectories; in Adorno and Fanon's respective engagements with Lukács, there emerges an alternative form of "traveling theory gone tougher, harder, more recalcitrant", as if borrowing has become (in Said's terms) a more intransigent and re-invigorating process of "affiliation", whereby initial impact is not so much repeated as re-ignited in different contexts and situations.[22]

Said's revisiting of his earlier essay is an implicit response to James Clifford's critique that the first statement of "traveling theory" was predominantly modernist: "an all-too-familiar story of immigration and acculturation".[23] Extending Said's ideas to a postcolonial context, Clifford emphasizes "the feedback loops, the ambivalent appropriations and resistances that characterize the travels of theories, and theorists, between places in the 'First' and 'Third' worlds".[24] It is the rejection of linearity and the associated possibility of re-ignition that should be emphasized in any understanding of the Toussaint's "travels" in the light of Said's speculations. Quite how the representations of the revolutionary fit in to such reflection is perhaps initially unclear. At the beginning of "Traveling Theory", Said certainly claims: "Like people and schools of criticism, ideas and theories travel – from person to person, from situation to situation, from one period to another", but there is no further consideration of the parallels suggested here; and besides, as this study has already made clear, to posit the "historical" Toussaint as an albeit necessary point of origin is problematized by the fact that even during his lifetime the revolutionary was in many ways always-already irrecoverable – mythologized, romanticized and demonized ante-mortem in equal measure. Once Toussaint is considered in these terms – that is, as what Roland Barthes dubbed a "myth" as opposed to a "phenomenon" – his posthumous representations may then be understood in Saidian terms as the complex reinterpretation and re-emphasis of a loose set of ideas (historical anecdotes, episodes or statements, themselves freighting a range of political dilemmas and revolutionary solutions), a transfer from Haitian origins to a globalized network of interrelated refigurings.

To suggest how Toussaint might be seen (in these terms) to travel, the conclusion to this chapter will, by way of illustration, sketch out one such interrelated network of twentieth-century affiliations, centred in various ways on Paris (and more specifically on James's *Black Jacobins*), but reverberating according to the more complex routes to which Clifford alludes. The interrelationships of James's work, Aimé Césaire's *Toussaint Louverture* and Édouard Glissant's *Monsieur Toussaint* are complex ones. There is no straightforward process of sedimentation whereby these texts progressively supplement, influence and confirm each other; the three works instead are drawn into dialogue and exchange with one another. The process challenges the apparent restrictions of cumulative chronological appearance for the emergence of James's and Glissant's texts involves the use of paratextual apparatus to indicate their uneven publishing histories.[25] *The Black Jacobins* represents a clear trigger to both Césaire and Glissant, their two texts representing substantial interventions in what was then an ongoing engagement from a French-language perspective with James's historiography.[26] On his arrival in England in 1932, C.L.R James decided to develop his plans for a "project stuck away in the back of [his] head for years",[27] a biographical account of Toussaint Louverture. Dissatisfied with existing accounts of the Haitian Revolution, James initially engaged with key texts of French radical historiography imported from France while he was in Nelson, before travelling to Paris. Here he read the work of radical historians such as Jaurès, Mathieu and Michelet, and immersed himself in documents relating to the Haitian Revolution, held in different official archives and at the Bibliothèque Nationale. At the same time, he met the historian and soldier Auguste Nemours, who talked James through Toussaint's strategies, "using books and coffee cups upon a large table to show how the different campaigns had been fought".[28] For James, General Nemours was "an enthusiastic admirer of Toussaint but exceptionally fair", but this generous acknowledgement of an invaluable source disguises the radical differences between the two men's interpretations.[29]

Nemours continues a Haitian tradition that transforms Toussaint into a messianic figure;[30] James saw in Toussaint a more contemporary and incendiary figure, whose example had implications for current and future anticolonial struggle (as well as for revolutionary struggle more generally). It was only in the 1963 appendix, situating the Haitian Revolution in relation to recent events in Cuba, that James fully explored the pan-Caribbean dimensions of Toussaint. In James's study, the revolutionary might therefore be seen as over-determined, as a vehicle of a series of interconnected concerns, relating primarily in the 1930s to pan-Africanism and the implications for world revolution of post-revolutionary Soviet ideological struggles.[31] Toussaint's emergence in the work of contemporary Soviet artists – especially that of Eisenstein and Vinogradov – has been mentioned above, yet the former's film was never made and the latter's novel, as James makes clear in his bibliography, is peppered with inaccuracies.[32]

It is perhaps James who offers the clearest Marxist reading of the Haitian Revolution, relating Toussaint's decisions and dilemmas directly to those of Lenin, and focussing on the perceived need for selected elements of bourgeois culture to allow post-revolutionary progress; for James, Toussaint's flaw was his inability – unlike Lenin – to communicate this vision to the people, an autocratic (and in Trotsky's terms "Bonapartist") failing that would not only lead to the execution of Moïse (cast by James in a Trotskyite role) but be amplified in Dessalines's own Stalin-like post-independence self-elevation.[33] *The Black Jacobins* is a meticulous study in the internal dynamics of revolution; it is also, however, a reflection on the possibility of revolutionary alliances across ethnic and national boundaries, and an illustration of Trotsky's view in *The Permanent Revolution* that isolated activity in

non-Western countries required the support of workers in the West itself.[34] In a suc-
cinct and often quoted phrase, James claims that "Toussaint's failure was the failure of
enlightenment, not of darkness",[35] suggesting that the Haitian Revolution was undermined not so much by local events as by the failure of the French to carry through
their own revolution to its logical conclusions. It is in this emphasis on the need
for political and material solidarity that world revolution and pan-Africanism meet.
James's concluding paragraphs allude directly to what might be seen as implicit in the
rest of his narrative, "written", he states, "not with the Caribbean but with Africa in
mind".[36] Here he alludes to the "long and difficult road" towards African independence, and to Toussaint's potential as a simultaneous source of pre-independence hope
and marker of post-independence caution.[37] In the 1980 foreword, James recounts
a meeting in Ghana in 1957 with South African pan-Africanists, who described the
circulation of mimeographed extracts of *The Black Jacobins* dealing with inter-ethnic
relations. It was with such "translations" of his book into different contexts, creating
new connections, that the mature James seems fascinated: "revolution," he notes,
"moves in a mysterious way its wonders to perform".[38]

Consequently, in a discussion with Stuart Hall, James clearly recognizes the
interviewer's account of the book's "journey" back to the Caribbean: "I once met
a Haitian intellectual who told me the story about how astonished people were in
Haiti to discover that *Black Jacobins* was written first by a black man, secondly by a
West Indian. Because of course it had come back to them through London, through
Paris."[39] The role of James in the development of a francophone Caribbean consciousness is difficult to gauge, but the impact of *Les Jacobins noirs* on both Césaire and
Glissant is manifest.[40] Simultaneously but separately in the late 1950s, both were
engaged in projects involving the insertion of Toussaint into their contemporary situations. Césaire had drawn on Toussaint as an early indication of upright négritude in
his *Cahier d'un retour au pays natal,* in which he transforms captivity at Joux into an
illustration of black oppression and its potential resistance. He returns to the revolutionary – and engages with James's subsequently published interpretation – in his
1960 political essay, a reflection on the dilemmas of dependency in the contemporary francophone Caribbean. Haiti, he claims, was the first country to expose "dans
toute sa complexité sociale, économique, raciale, le grand problème que le XXe siècle
s'essouffle à résoudre: le problème colonial" [in all its social, economic and racial
complexity, the great problem that the twentieth century is getting breathless in its
attempts to solve: the colonial problem].[41] Whereas, without underplaying issues of

ethnicity, James had insisted on the predominance of class in understandings of the Haitian Revolution, Césaire's aim, suggested already in the *Cahier,* was to join, in his interpretation of Toussaint, both Marxism and négritude. James had treated Haiti in a predominantly allegorical fashion, applying the implications of its revolution to interwar sub-Saharan Africa; Césaire, however, created via négritude a mediation between Africa and the Caribbean that James himself would later celebrate, exploding, in E. San Juan's terms, "the axiom of linear, uniform evolution and introduc[ing] the dialectical leap: 'that salvation for the West Indies lies in Africa, the original home and ancestry of the West Indian people' ".[42]

For Césaire, Toussaint was "le premier grand leader anti-colonialiste que l'histoire ait connu" [the first great anticolonial leader known by history], for he transformed "l'insurrection nègre" [black insurrection] associated with his precursor Boukman into the discipline required for successful revolution.[43] Moreover, Césaire contextualizes this emergence in more general terms, seeing Toussaint's rise in parallel to the "montée d'une classe" [rise of a class], as the transformation of a "race opprimée" [oppressed race] into a "classe conquérante" [conquering class].[44] Césaire differs from James in claiming that Toussaint, from a relatively early stage, had understood the eventual need for a break with France; yet like James he underlines the dilemmas faced by the revolutionary leader attempting to pursue nevertheless a strategy of dialogue with the enemy whilst continuing to carry the masses with him. It is principally on the outcome of this failure to communicate that the two differ, with James seeing Toussaint's arrest as the result of a miscalculation and an implicit acceptance of failure, and with Césaire interpreting it as an enlightened act of political self-sacrifice: "son dernier acte politique et, sans doute, un des plus féconds" [his last political act, and perhaps one of his most fruitful acts].[45] Whereas Toussaint is largely absent from James's final pages, Césaire's study, in quasi-biblical terms ("au commencement est Toussaint Louverture" [in the beginning was Toussaint Louverture]), concludes with a eulogy of the revolutionary's catalytic and unifying role, offering a clear critique of French republican universalism and underlining Toussaint's role as a concrete historical illustration of the necessary inclusiveness of the "rendez-vous de la conquête" [rendezvous of victory] central to the *Cahier.*[46] Césaire's claims that Toussaint's belief in "un Commonwealth français" [a French Commonwealth] is "en avance sur son époque, et d'un bon siècle et demi" [ahead of its time by a good 150 years] may certainly be read in relation to departmentalization of the former French possessions in the

Caribbean;[47] but it is with a poetic – and, for his critics, pragmatic – transcendence of the politico-historical Caribbean context that the text concludes.

In the 1961 preface to the first version of his play on Toussaint, Glissant records his indebtedness to both James and Césaire for providing "l'essentiel de ce qu'il faut savoir sur ce héros" [the bulk of what you need to know about this hero].[48] Claiming that a dialogue already exists between these two source texts (particularly in relation to Toussaint's "surrender" to Brunet), Glissant suggests that his purposes are different, denying political inspiration and casting his drama as "une vision prophétique du passé" [prophetic vision of the past]. As with most authors' comments on their own work, this claim is an ambiguous one: although the *Jeune Afrique* reviewer of the first version of the play claimed that the work was allegorical, relating Toussaint's destiny as a victim of historical circumstance to that of the recently assassinated prime minister of the Democratic Republic of the Congo,[49] the second version of *Monsieur Toussaint* was published in the later 1970s when Glissant was actively questioning his commitment to conventional politics; however, the play's focus on its protagonist's ambiguous relationship to Frenchness must clearly be read in the light of Martinique's progressive departmentalization and the role of Césaire's politics in this process. Whereas James and Césaire (along with many other authors committed to exploring their subject's revolutionary potential) see Joux essentially as a postscript, Glissant foregrounds and prolongs Toussaint's death since such incarceration permits him to focus on an individual experiencing the logical repercussions of the dilemmas and choices that characterized his earlier career. Despite a conclusion that appears to transcend regional specificity, Césaire had posited Toussaint as "le centre de l'histoire haïtienne, le centre sans doute de l'histoire antillaise" [the centre of Haitian history, and perhaps the centre of Caribbean history]; Glissant interprets this comment as a literal dramatic device, placing the imprisoned revolutionary as "le mitan" [the middle], the point around which figures from past and present, from France and the Caribbean circle.[50] "Il n'y a pas de frontière définie," comments Glissant, "entre l'univers de la prison et les terres de l'île antillaise" [there is no definite boundary between the world of the prison and the land of the Caribbean island], and his drama, despite its French location, offers a vision of *antillanité,* of a creolized Caribbean moving beyond the transatlantic axes of neocolonial dependency in order to draw on its own multiple resources.[51] Toussaint is no longer the conventional, Raynal-reading Enlightenment hero, but a contradictory, hybrid character whose conversations with Maman Dio, Mackandal and Macaia reveal associations with *marronage* often eclipsed in other representations. As such, Glissant's Toussaint is a post-négritude figure, dialoguing with an African past, acknowledging latent European influences, but firmly rooting any quest for a Caribbean historical consciousness in the Caribbean itself. Unlike the Toussaint of James and Césaire, Glissant's protagonist is not the vehicle of any clearly identified ideology; he is instead a prototypical embodiment of the openness of intercultural "Relation" [Relating] that would be privileged in the author's later works.

This rapid reading of three key texts by James, Césaire's and Glissant suggests, as does Said himself, that any initially schematic notion of "travelling" ideas and interpretations should be replaced by a more uneven understanding of the processes of transmission – an understanding that moves away from a model of progressively declining revolutionary impact in order to develop a more attenuated understanding of shifts that occur. Moreover, "travelling" depends, as Clifford has stated, on other non-linear patterns such as "feedback loops": the publication of Césaire and Glissant's texts in the early 1960s was complemented by James's 1963 appendix to *The Black Jacobins,* in which James becomes a reader of Césaire, inviting re-reading of his 1930s history in the light of the latter's own work. James underlines the fact that *The Black Jacobins* appeared just a year before the *Cahier d'un retour au pays natal,* and seems to suggest that he was struck more by this poem than by the later 1960 historico-poetic essay (itself "lacking the fire and constant illumination which distinguish most of the other work by Césaire").[52] In the final paragraph of his 1938 text, where James had alluded to the need for a vanguard party to prepare the way for anticolonial struggle, he foregrounds the importance to such an endeavour of "the people heaving in action", and accordingly downplays the importance of "the isolated blacks at . . . the Sorbonne, the dabblers in *surréalisme*".[53] Although Césaire is not directly targeted, as James could not yet have come across his work, the Martinican poet would nevertheless have fitted the description; by 1963, however, it is Césaire's poetic expression of négritude (and the fostering of cultural consciousness with which it is associated) that leads James to acknowledge more fully the pan-Caribbean dimension of the history he had told a quarter of a century before.[54] "The first step to freedom," James writes, for himself, for Césaire, for the West Indian intellectual, "was to go abroad", and again the role of travel in the formation of ideas is privileged.[55]

Any conclusion to this reflection on nineteenth- and twentieth-century translations of Toussaint Louverture is inevitably provisional and projective, for the travels it describes remain unfinished. This volume is published to mark the 2004 bicentenary of independence, in whose celebration Toussaint will inevitably undergo in Haiti itself and elsewhere further reconsideration and memorialization. The word "celebration" is perhaps too positive, and Haiti's current instability reflects the two centuries of post-revolutionary upheaval that followed Toussaint's death. It remains to be seen whether Toussaint will prove central to the achievement of the unfulfilled revolutionary potential inherent in what Glissant dubs his "prophetic vision of the past"; or whether, with the increased emphasis (in the light of the work of historians such as Caroline Fick) on a sense of revolution from below, Toussaint's impact will be challenged along with that of what Maryse Condé dismisses as the "conventional revolutionary bric à brac" dominating Caribbean history.[56] Yet from other recent commemorations – the one hundred and fiftieth anniversary of abolition in 1998, the bicentenary in 2003 of the death of Toussaint himself – what is already very apparent is that the interpretation, mythologization, instrumentalization and exemplification of this travelling revolutionary will continue to evolve.

NOTES

1. See Percy Waxman, *The Black Napoleon* (New York: Harcourt, 1931). Cited by Kara M. Rabbitt, "C.L.R. James's Figuring of Toussaint-Louverture: *The Black Jacobins* and the Literary Hero", in *C.L.R. James: His Intellectual Legacies,* ed. S.R. Cudjoe and W.E. Cain (Amherst: University of Massachusetts Press, 1994), 118.

2. For James's judgement, see C.L.R. James, *The Black Jacobins: Toussaint L'Ouverture and the San Domingo Revolution* (1938; reprint, London: Allison and Busby, 1980), 388.

3. See Gabriel Debien, Jean Fouchard and Marie-Antoinette Menier, "Toussaint Louverture avant 1789, légendes et réalités", *Conjonction: Revue franco-haitienne,* no. 134 (1977): 65–80.

4. For a study of the shifting representations of Toussaint's incarceration at Joux, see Charles Forsdick, "Transatlantic Displacement and the Problematics of Space", in *Ici-Là: Place and Displacement in Caribbean Writing in French,* ed. Mary Gallagher (Amsterdam: Rodopi, 2003), 181–209.

5. See, for example, Jean Métellus, *Toussaint Louverture* (Paris: Hatier International, 2003), 54.

6. See Roland Barthes, "Phénomène ou mythe?", *Lettres nouvelles* 68 (1954): 951–53.

7. See *L'Incendie du Cap, ou le règne de Toussaint-Louverture; Où l'on développe le caractère de ce chef de révoltés, sa conduite atroce depuis qu'il s'est arrogé le pouvoir, la nullité de ses moyens, la bassesse de tous ses agens . . .* (Paris: Marchand, 1802), xiv.

8. Dubroca, *La Vie de Toussaint-Louverture, chef des noirs insurgés de Saint-Domingue* (Paris: [Dubroca], 1802), 52.

9. Anonymous, *Buonaparte in the West Indies or, the History of Toussaint Louverture, the African Hero,* 3 vols. (London: Hatchard, 1803), 1: 5, 1: 2 and 3: 16.

10. A dominant tradition presents Toussaint himself as a direct counterpart of Bonaparte, in Wendell Phillips's terms, his "black shadow" – "Toussaint Louverture", in *Speeches, Lectures and Letters* (Boston: James Redpath, 1863), 482: in addition to Percy Waxman's *The Black Napoleon* cited above, see James J. Hannon, *The Black Napoleon: Toussaint L'Ouverture, Liberator of Haiti* (Yucca Valley, Calif.: Pacific American; Bloomington, Ind.: 1st Books Library, 1992); Karl Otten, *Der schwarze Napoleon; Toussaint Louverture und der Negeraufstand auf San Domingo* (Berlin: Atlantis Verlag, 1931); Nicolas Saint-Cyr, *Toussaint Louverture, le Napoléon noir* (Paris: Hachette; Edi-Monde, 1985); and Raphaël Tardon, *Toussaint-Louverture, le Napoléon noir* (Paris: Bellenand, 1951). The contrast lends itself also to dramatic representation, staging either the two characters' juxtaposition – Bernard Dadié, *Iles de tempête* (Paris: Présence Africaine, 1973) – or even their imagined encounter – Eric Sauray, *Fort de Joux, avril 2003: Toussaint Louverture face à Napoléon Bonaparte* (Paris: L'Harmattan, 2003).

11. See William Wordsworth, "To Toussaint Louverture", in *Poetical Works,* ed. Ernest de Selincourt and Helen Darbishire, 5 vols. (Oxford: Clarendon, 1946), 3: 112–13.

12. See Cora Kaplan, "Black Heroes/White Writers: Toussaint Louverture and the Literary Imagination", *History Workshop Journal* 46 (1998): 33–62.

13. Anténor Firmin, *De l'égalité des races humaines* (Paris: Cotillon, 1885), 545.

14. See, for example, Félix Desroussels, *Sur les traces de Caonabo et de Toussaint-Louverture: Poèmes caraibes* (Port-au-Prince: Imprimerie de l'Etat, 1953), published to mark the one hundred and fiftieth anniversary of independence.

15. C.L.R. James, *Beyond a Boundary* (1963; reprint, London: Serpent's Tail, 1994), 124. On the genesis of *The Black Jacobins,* see Robert Hill, "In England, 1932–38", in *C.L.R. James: His Life and Work,* ed. Paul Buhle (London: Allison and Busby, 1989), 61–80 (66).

16. As Ronald Bergan makes clear in *Sergei Eisenstein: A Life in Conflict* (1997, reprint, London: Warner, 1999), details of Eisenstein's project remain hazy, with commentators disagreeing over essential details such as sources and the role suggested for Robeson (pp. 266–69). See also Oksana Bulgakowa, *Sergej Eisenstein: Eine Biographie* (Berlin: Potemkin Press, 1997), 188.

17. See Karl Otten, *Der schwarze Napoleon,* Erwin Rüsch, *Die Revolution von Saint Domingue* (Hamburg: Friedrichsen De Gruyter, 1930), and Percy Waxman, *The Black Napoleon.*

18. Raphaël Tardon, *Toussaint-Louverture, le Napoléon noir;* Aimé Césaire, *Toussaint Louverture: La Révolution française et le problème colonial* (1960; reprint, Paris: Présence Africaine, 1981); and Édouard Glissant, *Monsieur Toussaint* (1978; reprint, Paris: Gallimard, 1986).

19. See W.M.A. Jones, *Black Emperor: The Story of Toussaint Louverture* (London: Harrap, 1949), and Ralph Korngold, *Citizen Toussaint* (London: Victor Gollancz, 1945).

20. See, for instance, Jean Métellus, *Toussaint Louverture*; Eric Sauray, *Fort de Joux, avril 2003*; and Fabienne Pasquet, *La Deuxième mort de Toussaint Louverture* (Arles: Actes Sud, 2001).

21. See Edward W. Said, "Traveling Theory", in *The World, the Text and the Critic* (1983; reprint, London: Vintage, 1991), 226–47, and "Traveling Theory Reconsidered", in *Critical Reconstructions: The Relationship of Fiction and Life*, ed. R. Polhemus and R. Henke (Stanford, Calif.: Stanford University Press, 1994), 251-65.

22. Said, "Traveling Theory Reconsidered", 255, 265.

23. James Clifford, "Notes on Travel and Theory", *Inscriptions* 5 (1989): 184.

24. Ibid. Caren Kaplan, in *Questions of Travel: Postmodern Discourses of Displacement* (Durham: Duke University Press, 1996), also attempts to extend Said's reflections in her claim that "it is not only theories that can be said to circulate, but the terms, tropes, and subjects of criticism" (p. 5); it is into the third of these categories that Toussaint would seem clearly to fall.

25. *The Black Jacobins* began life as a play of the same name (first performed in 1936), and was published as a historical study in 1938, with a short author's preface (a French translation of the book with Gallimard in 1949); a second edition in 1963 was supplemented by an appendix, "From Toussaint L'Ouverture to Fidel Castro", and an updated bibliography of related sourced (in which Césaire's 1960 *Toussaint Louverture* is included); a third edition in 1980 included a new foreword. In addition, the subsequent editions include footnotes in which the more mature James comments on his earlier work (see, for instance, p. 82n8). It remains unclear how James adjusted his attitude to this aspect of the text's analysis when, in the period following the Second World War, he progressively distanced himself from Leninism. Kara M. Rabbitt, although focussing only on the 1938 and 1963 editions, nevertheless pinpoints the "layered nature of the work" (p. 119). Glissant's *Monsieur Toussaint* was written in the late 1950s, and published with a preface by Seuil in 1961 after initial extracts had appeared in *Les Lettres nouvelles* the previous year; this *version intégrale,* broadcast for the first time on France-Culture in 1971, was turned by Glissant into *version scénique,* staged in Paris in 1977; an *avertissement* was included when this new version was published in Fort-de-France by Acoma in 1978. This *version scénique* was published by Seuil in 1986, and reprinted by the same publisher in 1998 to coincide with French celebrations of the 150th anniversary of the abolition of slavery in 1848.

26. Louis Ménard's review of *Les Jacobins noirs* – *Les Temps modernes* 5 (1949–50): 1527–1529 – for instance, triggered a lengthy response from James himself (2290–2292), who took exception to the reviewer's questioning of his analysis of Haiti's *véritable révolution* [true revolution] as well as to his claim that the book conflated historical situations in transforming the eighteenth-century revolutionary into a "bolchevik avant la lettre" (1528). James also had a long correspondence with Daniel Guérin, author of *Les Antilles décolonisées* (Paris: Présence Africaine, 1956).

27. James, *Beyond a Boundary,* 119.

28. James, *The Black Jacobins,* vi.

29. Ibid., 382.

30. See, for instance, *Histoire de la captivité et de la mort de Toussaint-Louverture: notre pèlerinage au Fort de Joux* (Paris: Berger-Levrault, 1929): "L'enveloppe d'une grande âme meurt douleureusement! Afin de compléter le sinistre trilogie, au rocher de Prométhée, à la Croix du Christ, il fallait ajouter le Cachot de Joux" [The bodily shell of a great soul dies painfully. In order to complete the sinister trilogy, the Cell at Joux must be added to Prometheus's rock and Christ's cross] (p. 110). In his preface to Césaire's *Toussaint Louverture,* Charles-André Julien describes the "tonalité religieuse" [religious tone] of Nemours's writings (p. 7).

31. Michael Foot describes *The Black Jacobins* as "a Marxist masterpiece with constant, reverberating implications for the whole of our own turbulent century" ("C.L.R. James", in *C.L.R. James: His Intellectual Legacies,* 102). For a discussion of the various levels on which the text operates, see Anthony Bogues, *Caliban's Freedom: The Early Political Thought of C.L.R. James* (London: Pluto, 1997), 41–42.

32. James, *The Black Jacobins,* 389.

33. Ibid., 284.

34. See Kent Worcester, *C.L.R James: A Political Biography* (Albany: State University of New York Press, 1996), 39.

35. James, *The Black Jacobins,* 288.

36. Ibid., vi.

37. Ibid., 377.

38. Ibid., vii.

39. Stuart Hall, "A Conversation with C.L.R. James", in *Rethinking C.L.R. James,* ed. Grant Farred (Oxford: Blackwell, 1996), 22.

40. Glissant makes clear his own interaction with James, whereas Césaire's commentary is more implicit, even if it emerges explicitly in places, such as in his divergent interpretation of Toussaint's return of Sonthonax to France (*Toussaint Louverture,* 251).

41. Césaire, *Toussaint Louverture,* 24.

42. E. San Juan, "Beyond Postcolonial Theory: The Mass Line in C.L.R James's Imagination", *Journal of Commonwealth Studies* 31, no. 1 (1996): 30. Here he cites *The Black Jacobins,* 399.

43. Césaire, *Toussaint Louverture,* 205.

44. Ibid., 236, 234.

45. Ibid., 313.

46. Aimé Césaire, *Toussaint Louverture,* 331; *Cahier d'un retour au pays natal* (1939; reprint, Paris: Présence Africaine, 1983), 57–58.

47. Césaire, *Toussaint Louverture,* 283.

48. Glissant, *Monsieur Toussaint,* 7.

49. See J.D., "Pensez à Lumumba", *Jeune Afrique,* 20–26 December 1961, 24–25: "Glissant n'a pas seulement évoqué le destin de Toussaint Louverture. En filigrane, il paraît nous dire: regardez Toussaint et pensez à Lumumba" [Glissant has not only evoked the fate of Toussaint Louverture. If you read between the lines, he seems to be saying: "Look at Toussaint and think of Lumumba"] (25).

50. Césaire, *Toussaint Louverture,* 331; Glissant, *Monsieur Toussaint,* 74.

51. Glissant, *Monsieur Toussaint,* 12. For a discussion of this interpretation, see Charles Forsdick, " 'Chaque île est une ouverture': Representing the Revolutionary in Édouard Glissant's *Monsieur Toussaint*", *International Journal of Francophone Studies* 2, no. 1 (1999): 28–35.

52. James, *The Black Jacobins,* 389.

53. Ibid., 377.

54. For a discussion of James and Césaire, see Aldon Lynn Nielsen, *C.L.R. James: A Critical Introduction* (Jackson: University Press of Mississippi, 1997), 78–79, and Kara M. Rabbitt, "C.L.R. James's Figuring of Toussaint-Louverture", 129–31. James continued to engage with Césaire throughout the 1960s. For example, in undated notes, probably from the late 1960s, James commented on Césaire's critique of modern society, and on the roots of this critique in European thought. See item IV.33 in Anna Grimshaw, *The C.L.R James Archive: A Reader's Guide* (New York: The C.L.R James Institute and Cultural Correspondence, 1991), 25.

55. James, *The Black Jacobins,* 402.

56. See Caroline E. Fick, *The Making of Haiti: the Saint Domingue Revolution from Below* (Knoxville: University of Tennessee Press, 1990), and Maryse Condé, "Order, Disorder, Freedom and the West Indian Writer", *Yale French Studies* 83, no. 2 (1993): 133.

CHAPTER 11

WHAT CAN TOUSSAINT LOUVERTURE DO FOR THE HAITIANS OF 2004?

RENÉ DEPESTRE

To come together in 2003, in an official ceremony at the Châteaux de Joux, in honour of Toussaint Louverture, commemorating the bicentenary of his death, is to acknowledge that the sacrifice of a man of Jurassian stature can grow over time, so much as to allow his descendants to transform a tragedy of decolonization into a supreme form of well-being for their current crossing of the trials of globalization. On this 7 April 2003, what can Toussaint Louverture do for an unprecedented renewal of the solidarity between France and Haiti? What can his lofty ideals of justice and rights still do to help the Haitian people rise as never before towards democracy? As a Franco-Haitian writer I take responsibility for this double question on the very site of Toussaint Louverture's capture and death.

Anyone who spends some time in Haiti discovers very quickly how the devotion of the country to the founder of its national identity can take on mystical, epic tones, at the risk of seeing the anecdotal, the picturesque and the mythological blur the sense of historical reality. We know well the real events of 1791 to 1802, that movement from the dazzling breakthrough of the black governor of the French colony of St Domingue to his demise in 1803 in the solitude of a fortress in the Jura mountains.

Two centuries after the drama, in April 2003, my aims are to speak about it with tenderness and rigour, avoiding at once any sense of resentment and any eulogy for the occasion. What I want to do instead is to attach my homage to the Louverturian idea of the universalization of rights and of democratic civility: this is in effect the essential area which gives Toussaint Louverture his place and his meaning in the history of Africans and Haitians, in the history of the French Revolution, one might as well say in the historical adventure of a planet which today is becoming, chaotically, painfully, an international civil society.

Toussaint Bréda was born on 20 May 1743, on the estate of the same name, the property of the Count of Noé, at the locality of Haut-du-Cap, in St Domingue. According to the oral tradition, he was the descendant of an African prince of the Arada tribe of Dahomey. He was a second-generation slave, the son of an African. He was small in size, unprepossessing, puny, and did not say much. But he had a great force of character. He was one of those men who, from their youth, "teach their body to obey their mind".

Working in the stables of his master Bayon Libertat, he picked up the rudiments of veterinary science and learned about medicinal plants. His French godfather Pierre Baptiste taught him to read and write. The French language gave him access to a small number of works that broadened the consciousness of the colonial plantation coachman. He would have read Julius Caesar's *Commentaries,* the history of the wars of Herodotus, the *Rêveries* of Maréchal Maurice de Saxe, and the *Histoire philosophique des Indes* by the Abbé Raynal. It is not too far-fetched to think that some of the following prophetic words of Denis Diderot, quoted in the work of the famous abbot, must have singularly struck the imagination of the self-taught man of the Bréda estate:

> All that the blacks lack is a leader brave enough to lead them to vengeance and courage. Where is this great man that nature perhaps owes to the honour of the human species? Where is this Spartacus who finds no Crassus? That will be the end of the *Code Noir.* And how terrible the *Code Blanc* will be if the victor consults only the law of reprisal.

This was precisely the extraordinary plan that Toussaint Louverture assigned himself in 1793, just after his fiftieth birthday, and in the middle of the French Revolution. He presented himself at that time to his fellow slaves:

> Brothers and friends, I am Toussaint Louverture, my name has perhaps become known to you. I have set out on the path towards vengeance. I want liberty and equality to reign in Saint-Domingue. I am working towards bringing them into existence. Let us unite, brothers, in our cause!

These words of hope were greeted enthusiastically in the ranks of the Maroons who, since 1791, after a severely repressed uprising, had maintained a climate of insurrection in the mountains. Apart from the blacks, the other sectors of the colonial society – the white planters, the white commercial class, the trade associations and the free mulattos – were also in revolt, interpreting according to their specific interests the great metropolitan revolution of 1789. In Paris, in the successive assemblies – the Constituent, the Legislative, the National Convention – the revolutionary political leaders were also deeply divided over St Domingue and the colonial question. The defenders of colonial interests – the Barnaves, Malouet, Moreau de St-Méry, the Abbé Maury – did all they could to block any vote which would be favourable to the emancipation of the mulattos and blacks. As they saw it, human rights were not exportable privileges.

Opposing the colonialist lobby, there was the group formed by, among others, Robespierre, Marat, the Abbé Grégoire, Mirabeau, Dupont de Nemours, Condorcet, Brissot, Viefville des Essarts, members of the *Société des Amis des Noirs,* which was created on the initiative of the Abbé Grégoire. These men held liberty and equality to be indivisible values, from which must benefit all French citizens, without distinction, and without regard for the colour of their skin and their status in society. Robespierre had gone deeper into the question when he had cried out: "Let the colonies perish if the colonists want to force us by threats to decree whatever best suits their interests." Marat had gone further yet by affirming fully the rights of colonized peoples to free themselves: "The basis of every free government is that no people is subjugated by law to another; that a people must have no law other than those which it has set itself; that it is sovereign in its own land, and sovereign independent of all human power." In spite of these noble and generous principles the assemblies of Paris were unable to advance the democratic cause in St Domingue, so powerful were the forces of colonial commerce, and so foreign were the anticolonial and antislavery causes to the conscience of the time, even after the great leap forward of the French Revolution.

Toussaint Louverture's first great merit is that he understood, before and better than any of his fellow insurgents, that it was necessary to create another revolution within the French Revolution. A revolution of blacks and mulattos, which would have its own specific laws, its own structures, aims and objectives, without necessarily breaking with the rhythm of the new French society. By observing the two historical situations, Toussaint came to believe that St Domingue had the duty of particularizing and universalizing the experience of human rights and equality, something the metropole would be incapable of promoting from the other side of the "ocean sea".

Once he had determined to bring about a Haitian revolution in the wake of the French Revolution, Toussaint Louverture's second great merit was to transform the Maroons and their sporadic revolts into a disciplined and unified army of liberation. "It is not", he said "a piecemeal freedom that we want, but the absolute adoption of the principle that every man born red, black or white, cannot be the property of another man." This was his way of interpreting the spirit of the Declaration of the Rights of Man in the sinister context of slavery.

And yet Toussaint Louverture was moderate and Christian; he tended by temperament towards wise and intelligent compromise, and as soon as his troops were organized, he hastened to put them to the service of the French Republic. He felt proud to be a fully fledged division general, in the armies of republican France. It was thus on his advice that first the commissioner Sonthonax in August 1793, and then the National Convention on 4 February 1794, decided that the abolition of slavery was the surest way of protecting all of France's interests against the offensives of the Spanish and British forces which were active at that time in the Caribbean.

Thanks to the 1794–1801 decree for the liberation of slaves, everything seemed able to proceed smoothly under Toussaint's careful and responsible leadership. The possibility of a French Commonwealth appeared on the horizon. In the special constitution that General Louverture drew up, the first article specifies clearly that Saint-Domingue and its neighbouring islands formed a single territory that was part of the French Empire, but which is subject to special laws. The "preliminary" discourse to the Constitution of 1801 is marked by political wisdom and good sense, and by the recognition that "there are circumstances which present themselves only once every few centuries to determine peoples' destinies; if we let them pass, they are gone forever".

This constitutional ideal, which the black governor, in a letter of 16 July 1801, faithfully submitted for the approval of Bonaparte, was well ahead of its time. If it had been understood and adopted by the first Consul, it would have allowed France to come together with St Domingue in a joint venture towards democratic civility. Alas! The process of the universalization of the rights of man that Louverture's Constitution embodied was passed over by a great man who, as far as the colonial question was concerned, held on brazenly to the policies of the Ancien Régime. "How could we have", he protested, "given freedom to Africans, to people without civilization, who had no idea as to what the colony was, to what France was." It must be said in the defence of Bonaparte that many years later in Saint Helena he confessed the political narrow-mindedness, and the lack of nobility and generosity, that had characterized his military and political careers as a young man with the fresh wind of history blowing in his sails.

For his part, Alphonse de Lamartine, poet supreme, "unacknowledged legislator of the world", and prominent abolitionist, proclaimed in the 1850 preface to the play he devoted to Toussaint Louverture that "this man is a nation". A century later, Aimé Césaire, the great Franco-Martiniquan poet, similarly placed Toussaint Louverture at the vanguard of global political and cultural thinking: "Toussaint Louverture's struggle was the struggle for the transformation of formal law into reality; the fight for the *recognition* of man, and that is why he inscribed himself and the Saint-Domingue slave revolt in the history of universal civilization." In this regard, Toussaint Louverture was a "major contemporary figure".

Today, more than ever, the world community needs his open, impartial and civilized conception of international law. Nations and peoples – with France at the forefront of the search for honour and hope – are determined to do everything to help the United Nations become the home of legality in the world, in order to promote in international relations a legal and political order founded on civility; that is, on a democratically unified way of being, to give the republican and citizenly impetus required to redress and correct the dangerously chaotic course of globalization.

Here, at the Château de Joux, so close to the destiny of Toussaint Louverture, I believe I can feel a *Louverturian* sensibility, as I thank France for its exemplary conduct in the debates that have accompanied the tragedy of the Middle East. By the blood that flows there, President Jacques Chirac and the minister of foreign affairs, Dominique de Villepin, strengthened by the almost unanimous support of the French people, plead with nobility and determination, for a reconfiguration of the planet which will be enriched by the respect for law, peace, happiness and wisdom of humankind.

Honour to Toussaint Louverture!
Honour to the French nation, which is once again his friend!

Translated by Martin Munro

Index

CONTRIBUTORS

Martin Munro is Lecturer in French and Francophone Literatures, University of the West Indies, St Augustine, Trinidad. He works on Caribbean literature written in French, particularly Haitian literature. He has published articles in journals such as *French Studies, Research in African Literatures, Critique* and *Journal of Haitian Studies* and is the author of *Shaping and Reshaping the Caribbean: The Work of Aimé Césaire and René Depestre* (2000). He guest edited (with Elizabeth Walcott-Hackshaw) *Small Axe* (September 2005), "Profondes et nombreuses: Haiti, History, Culture, 1804–2004". He has just completed a manuscript on the theme of exile in Haitian writing.

Elizabeth Walcott-Hackshaw is Lecturer in Francophone Caribbean Literature and Nineteenth-Century French Poetry, University of the West Indies, St Augustine, Trinidad. She is the author of articles on the Caribbean cultural landscape as presented in the works of Gisèle Pineau, Yanick Lahens, Simone Schwarz-Bart and Marie Chauvet. As a fiction writer her short stories have appeared in the journals *Callaloo* and *Small Axe,* and she is presently working on a collection of her short fiction which will be published in 2006. Most recently, she guest edited (with Martin Munro) *Small Axe* (September 2005), "Profondes et nombreuses: Haiti, History, Culture, 1804–2004".

Bridget Brereton is Professor of History, University of the West Indies, St Augustine, Trinidad. Among her publications on the history of Trinidad and Tobago and the Caribbean in the nineteenth and twentieth centuries are *Race Relations in Colonial Trinidad 1870–1900* (1980), *A History of Modern Trinidad* (1982) and *Law, Justice and Empire: The Colonial Career of John Gorrie, 1829–1892* (1997). She is editor of volume 5 of the UNESCO History of the Caribbean series, *The Caribbean in the Twentieth Century* (2004), and co-editor of *Engendering History: Caribbean Women* *in Historical Perspective* (1995) and *The Colonial Caribbean in Transition: Essays on Postemancipation Social and Cultural History* (1999).

Keith Cartwright is Assistant Professor of English, University of North Florida. He has written *Reading Africa into American Literature: Epics, Fables, and Gothic Tales* (2002), as well as two volumes of poetry. His articles have appeared in jornals such as *Callaloo, Southern Quarterly Review, Mississippi Review* and *Yinna: Journal of the Bahamas Association for Cultural Studies.* His chapter in this volume is part of a nearly completed manuscript entitled "Voodoo Hermeneutics/Creole Swng: Ritual Authority and Writing from the Contact Zones".

J. Michael Dash is Professor of French, New York University. He has worked extensively on Haitian literature and French Caribbean writers, especially Edouard Glissant, whose works *The Ripening* (1985), *Caribbean Discourse* (1989) and *Monsieur Toussaint* (2005) he has translated into English. His publications include *Literature and Ideology in Haiti* (1981); *Haiti and the United States* (1988); *Edouard Glissant* (1995); *The Other America: Caribbean Literature in a New World Context* (1998); *Culture and Customs of Haiti* (2001); and with Charles Arthur, *Libète: A Haiti Anthology* (1999). He is at present working on surrealism and ethnography in the francophone Caribbean.

René Depestre was born in 1926 and is one of Haiti's foremost writers. A novelist and essayist as well as a poet, Depestre published his first poetry collection, *Étincelles,* in 1945, and this was quickly followed by the surrealist-influenced *Gerbe de sang* in 1946, the year in which he first left Haiti. His studies at the Sorbonne brought him into contact with the key literary and cultural figures of the metropole, and also with the Négritude group. In 1951, his militant activities led to his expulsion from France, and thereafter he spent short terms in Prague, Havana, Vienna, Chile, Argentina and Brazil, before returning to Paris in 1956. The following year, he returned to Haiti, but was forced to leave after refusing to cooperate with Duvalier. On the invitation of Che Guevara, he went once more to Cuba, and lived there until his growing disillusionment with the revolution forced him to leave in 1978. Eight years working with UNESCO in Paris followed, before finally retiring to live in the Aude region of France. In 1991, he and his family obtained French citizenship. In 2004, Depestre returned to Haiti for the first time since 1957.

Carolyn Fluehr-Lobban is Professor of Anthropology, Rhode Island College. She is the author or editor of eleven books, including *Islamic Societies in Practice* (1994); *Islamic Law and Society in the Sudan* (1987); and *Ethics and the Profession of Anthropology: Dialogue for a New Era* (1990); *Race and Identity in the Nile Valley* (2004, co-edited with Kharyssa Rhodes); *Race and Racism: An Introduction* (2005); and *Female Well-Being: Toward a Global Theory of Social Change* (2005, co-edited with Janet M. Billson). With Haitian collaborator Asselin Charles she published in 2000 the first major work of anthropology by a scholar of African descent, Antenor Firmin's *The Equality of the Human Races,* originally published in French as *De l'égalité des races humaines* in 1885.

Charles Forsdick is Professor and James Barrow Chair of French, University of Liverpool, United Kingdom. He is the author of *Victor Segalen and the Aesthetics of Diversity: Journeys between Cultures* (2000) and *Travel in Twentieth-Century French and Francophone Cultures: The Persistence of Diversity* (2005), and co-editor of *Francophone Postcolonial Studies: A Critical Introduction* (2003). He is currently completing a book entitled *Representing the Revolutionary: The Afterlives of Toussaint Louverture,* and co-editing the volume *Postcolonial Thought in the Francophone World.*

Georges Fouron is Professor of Education and Social Sciences, State University of New York at Stony Brook. He has published many articles on Haitian transnational migration, education, sociolinguistics and bilingualism. His latest book, co-authored with Nina Glick Schiller, is *Georges Woke Up Laughing: Long-Distance Nationalism and the Search for Home* (2001). He is presently working on a manuscript entitled "Globalization and Migration: The Haitian Case".

Mireille Rosello is Professor of Comparative Literary Studies, Universiteit van Amsterdam. Her publications include *L'humour noir selon André Breton* (1987); *L'in-différence chez Michel Tournier* (1990); *Littérature et identité créole aux Antilles* (1992); *Infiltrating Culture: Power and Identity in Contemporary Women's Writing* (1996); *Declining the Stereotype: Representation and Ethnicity in French Cultures* (1998); *Postcolonial Hospitality: The Immigrant as Guest* (2001); and *France and the Maghreb: Performative Encounters* (2005). Her current project seeks to articulate the ongoing "Creolization" of Europe through multilingual encounters, migrant scripts and border constructions.